Barbara Stanwyck

HOLLYWOOD LEGENDS SERIES
CARL ROLLYSON, GENERAL EDITOR

Barbara Stanwyck

THE MIRACLE WOMAN

DAN CALLAHAN

University Press of Mississippi • Jackson

www.upress.state.ms.us

The University Press of Mississippi is a member of the Association of American University Presses.

Unless otherwise noted, photographs are from the author's collection.

First printing 2012

∞

Library of Congress Cataloging-in-Publication Data

Callahan, Dan, 1977–
Barbara Stanwyck : the miracle woman / Dan Callahan.
p. cm. — (Hollywood legends series)
Includes bibliographical references and index.
ISBN 978-1-61703-183-0 (cloth : alk. paper) — ISBN 978-1-61703-184-7
(ebook) 1. Stanwyck, Barbara, 1907–1990. 2. Motion picture actors and
actresses—United States—Biography. I. Title.
PN2287.S67C36 2012
791.43′028092—dc23
[B]   2011021567

British Library Cataloging-in-Publication Data available

To Keith Uhlich

CONTENTS

Barbara Stanwyck

INTRODUCTION

This book is a heartfelt appreciation of Barbara Stanwyck's work in movies. While there have been many studies and biographies on female film stars of equal stature—stars like Bette Davis, Katharine Hepburn, Joan Crawford, Marlene Dietrich, and Greta Garbo—comparatively few books about Stanwyck have appeared. Of these, Al DiOrio's mid-eighties biography is small but serviceable, while Axel Madsen's 1994 biography paints a grim, insensitive picture of Stanwyck's personal life, relies heavily on gossip, and pays only cursory and inexact attention to her films. Back in 1974, Ella Smith brought out *Starring Miss Barbara Stanwyck*, which is stuffed with evocative photos and features an insightful analysis of Stanwyck's acting, along with helpful interviews with many of the people who worked with Stanwyck, most of whom sing her praises. That book was written while Stanwyck was still alive, and it was meant as a tribute that would please her; for all its fine writing and detail, it doesn't have the long-range perspective that is possible now.

This book includes sections about Stanwyck's personal life, and I will sometimes indulge in educated guesses about this shadowy subject. These guesses are by definition speculative and hopefully open enough to allow you to make up your own mind about her off-screen existence. The main event for me, though, is Stanwyck's films and her work in them. You'll find little of the usual filler about Hollywood at the time, who might have said what to whom at the Coconut Grove, or how much money Stanwyck made for each project. I see Stanwyck as a major artist, and I want to show you the nitty-gritty of what she accomplished and how she managed to accomplish it.

Stanwyck collaborated with some of the finest directors of her time: from Frank Capra, William Wellman, William Dieterle, George Stevens, John Ford, King Vidor, and Mitchell Leisen in the thirties; to Preston

Sturges, Howard Hawks, Billy Wilder, André de Toth, and Robert Siodmak in the forties; to Anthony Mann, Fritz Lang, Douglas Sirk, and Sam
Fuller in the fifties; to Jacques Tourneur and Joseph H. Lewis on TV in
the sixties. She was never tied to one studio, which is why she had more
freedom in picking properties, and, unlike many of her contemporaries,
she found herself in ever more adventurous company in the movies as
she got older. There hasn't been enough analysis of her directors and her
films themselves as a whole. For instance, the earlier Stanwyck books
dismiss her two seminal films with Sirk outright. I hope that my book
can help to open up discussion on her best movies and offer you a close,
in-depth reading of her gifts and the varied, inventive ways she put them
to use.

Orphan of the Storm

The Locked Door, Mexicali Rose

$\mathcal{B}$arbara Stanwyck had a hard childhood, that's certain. She didn't linger over it, and I'm not going to, either, but it's worth mulling over some of the available information and considering what it might tell us about her. We'll never be sure just how hard this childhood was and what experiences might have scarred her for life. In his memoir, Robert Wagner writes that he thought she had been "abused" in some way, and maybe she was abused in all ways imaginable. When pressed about this issue late in life, Stanwyck put on her toughest mask and said, "Alright, let's just say I had a terrible childhood. Let's say that 'poor' is something I understand." The distinctive Stanwyck note of fast-talking, "moving right along" blitheness and bitterness is right there in that "Alright," as if she's just going to level with you, and the repetition of "let's just say" as "let's say," which has the same effect as that wonderful little shrug she did in so many of her middle and late period films.

She was born Ruby Stevens on July 16, 1907, in Brooklyn, at 246 Classon Avenue. Stanwyck wouldn't recognize the old neighborhood now. I live in Park Slope, Brooklyn, and Classon Avenue is within walking distance of my house, so I ventured out on a snowy day to see what was left of her past, only to discover that the house wasn't there anymore. In its place is the Pratt Institute, an architectural and design college. Ruby Stevens never even made it to high school, but not many people of her class and generation did in those days, and college was out of the question.

She was the fifth child of Byron and Catherine McGee Stevens of Chelsea, Massachusetts. Byron was English and Catherine was Irish. There's a lot of the Irish about Stanwyck; Hemingway met her on a hunting trip with her second husband, Robert Taylor, and commented on her "good tough Mick intelligence." In 1905, Byron abandoned Catherine and his growing family to do some bricklaying in Brooklyn. Catherine chased after him, and Byron was apparently not happy when she found him. Their first four children all had names beginning with the letter *M*: Maud, Mabel, Mildred, Malcolm—and then little Ruby, the special child, the gem, born in Brooklyn on Classon Avenue. A photo of Ruby at two years old shows a very unhappy-looking toddler; her entire head seems to frown protectively, as if she's saying, "Please don't hurt me."

In the winter of 1909–10, Catherine, pregnant again, was knocked off a streetcar by a drunk and hit her head. A month later, she died. Two weeks after the funeral, Byron went off to help dig the Panama Canal. Little Ruby was left in the care of her sister Millie, who was making her living as a chorus girl ("[S]he didn't pay much attention to me," said Stanwyck), and her brother Malcolm, whom they called Byron, after their absent father. When Millie went on the road, Byron and Ruby were placed in foster care. In later life, Stanwyck strived to remain objective about this eventuality, too, saying that the foster care system wasn't "cruel," just "impersonal." At the beginning of Axel Madsen's unreliable Stanwyck biography, he tells an unattributed story about Ruby repeatedly running away from foster care and always heading back to 246 Classon Avenue, where her brother Byron would find her sitting on the steps, waiting for her mother to come home.

It's a haunting image. Trying to picture it in my head, I'm reminded less of the sort of Hollywood tearjerkers Stanwyck made in the thirties and more of the unloved little girl in Robert Bresson's *Mouchette* (1967), an awkward, rough kid so totally on her own that she freezes any sentimental impulse, any inclination toward tears. If Stanwyck really was that abandoned little girl, mired in poverty, always waiting for her dead mother at 246 Classon Avenue, surely the seasoned pro she became would not want us to cry for her. She had to get tough and stay tough, and she did, but the well of permanent hurt inside her would remain as pure in *The Thorn Birds* in 1983 as it was in her first Frank Capra movie in 1930.

At a certain point, Ruby realized her mother couldn't come back. That was death, and it was official. But maybe her father might come back someday? Surely she daydreamed about that possibility every now and then, and why not? Why wouldn't he feel some responsibility for his children's welfare? But he didn't. Did he ever feel any guilt about leaving his children? Or was he a man who didn't have time for guilt—or love?

Maybe he was an adventurer, and basically solitary, as basically solitary as Ruby had to be and as Barbara Stanwyck chose to be. There are conflicting stories about what happened to Byron. In some of them, he died on the boat going to the Panama Canal. In another, more dramatic tale, it was said that his children lined up on the dock to wait for his return from the canal but were told that he had died on board ship and been buried at sea.

"At least nobody beat me," Stanwyck later said, trying to make the best of things. Then: "Where I grew up, kids lived on the brink of domestic and financial disaster." Ruby had no real friends, and later she claimed that she was "the stupidest little brat in school." An orphan, alone, in the Brooklyn of 1920. Whatever she saw and heard seems to have made her as guarded as possible; in her most touching moments on screen, she's always struggling to keep her poker face on so that the bottomless emotion she's hiding can't burst out like lava flowing over the sets, the camera, even the audience in the theater. "My clearest memory is of the crowds," she remembered, "of spent old women bent over hot tubs and babies crying and men reeling drunk to their homes. Half the time I slept on a mattress on the kitchen floor."

Maud and Mabel were both married and had little contact with Ruby or, later, with Barbara Stanwyck. It was a fractured family, barely a family at all. Yet, loner that she was, all her life Stanwyck was loyal to two people from this blasted childhood: Byron, whom she helped gain work as an extra in films, and sister Millie's boyfriend, "Uncle Buck" Mack, who became a surrogate father figure for Ruby and ran Stanwyck's household throughout her Hollywood years right up to his death in 1959. A vaudevillian of the old school, Uncle Buck taught Ruby the dance steps she would need to go into the chorus line like her sister. Ruby liked the theater, but the movies were more important to her, and they remained important her whole life. "I'd do anything to get money to go to movies," she said, "I tended children, washed dishes, ran errands." Ruby thrilled to Pearl White's serials and acted out some of them in Prospect Park. "I tried to escape by retreating to a dream world of my own," Stanwyck later said.

At thirteen or fourteen, Ruby got a job at the Abraham and Strauss department store, doing "the plain wrapping, not the fancy," of course. There was a stab at clerical work, and then she was fired from *Vogue* when she said she could cut dresses to a pattern but couldn't manage it. "I knew there was no place but show business that I wouldn't hate," she said, and soon found herself hoofing on the roof of the Strand hotel. The dance director, Earl Lindsay, cast her in a couple of his Broadway revues, and he taught the sullen and resentful Ruby to be professional and to always give her all, even in the back row of the chorus. She took this advice too much to heart, so that he soon had to tell her off for kicking too high and not being "a team player," but she was a star in the making, and a star is never really a team player.

Mobsters controlled most of the clubs in this era, and Ruby probably saw and experienced a lot. "Have you had any experience?" asks a naughty-eyed boy in *Baby Face* (1933). Stanwyck gives him a priceless look of sly impatience and cracks, "Plenty"—Ruby's experience barely visible behind her eyes. Surely there were bad and scary moments for her beyond the ones that are known. In later life, people noticed that there were cigarette scars on her chest; these scars she got from her encounters with men were physical and permanent, and the knowledge of such vicious male violence and the meanness it stemmed from was permanent, too.

In Texas Guinan's nightclubs, fifteen-year-old Ruby would shake for the sugar daddies and get bank notes stuffed in her scanties. She got an education in how to inflame a man's interest and then give him the brush-off; her experience ensorcelling and then coldly denying men would later develop into one of her specialties in movies. Maybe Ruby wasn't able to cool down some of the more powerful men, especially the mobsters, but if she had to put out, she learned how to keep her heart and soul out of it. In early 1930s Hollywood, she said, "Say, you gotta live with yourself. How can a girl live with herself if she hasn't any self-respect? And how can she have any self-respect if she pretends to love a man just to get a job?" The mores of the time might have dictated this statement, but it's interesting that Stanwyck chose to stress that it was the pretense of "love" that was odious to her. Sex without love, of course, was another matter.

Stanwyck remembered her chorus years with fondness: "How my memories of those three years sparkle! My chorine days may not have seemed perfect to anyone else, but they did to me." In her interviews, she always tried to brush off the past. It wasn't so bad, she insisted, or, it wasn't so bad for *me*. She would ricochet between being boastful about the hard knocks and being resentful of the people who hadn't suffered them—but she was never resentful about the hard knocks themselves, whatever they were. That attitude would have been too dangerous. If Stanwyck had really reflected on or tried to come to terms with what she had been through, the whole "Barbara Stanwyck" apparatus and image might have collapsed into clinical depression, or drink, or some other kind of escapism. To her immense and lasting credit, she never entirely let that collapse happen, and her attitude allowed her to become perhaps the finest or at least most consistently fine actress of her time in American movies.

In 1922, she was a Ziegfeld Follies girl, dancing at the New Amsterdam Theater. Ruby lived with two other chorus girls, one of whom was Mae Clarke, a similar "hard on the outside, soft on the inside" type who achieved some fame, or notoriety, as the girl who gets a grapefruit in the face from James Cagney in *The Public Enemy* (1931). During a stifling summer, the girls lived over a laundry on 46th Street between Fifth and Sixth Avenues, and it's easy to picture the three of them soaking their tired feet and wisecracking about stage door johnnies as the Sixth Avenue El rattled by all through the night. "I just wanted to survive and eat and have a nice coat," Stanwyck claimed.

At this time, Jeanne Eagels was making a huge impact on stage in *Rain* as the prostitute Sadie Thompson, the prototype for many of Stanwyck's later heroines. Sadie was a good-time girl led astray into virtue by a hypocritical minister who then rapes her and kills himself, leaving her bitterness about the world reinforced. Ruby saw Eagels in *Rain* four times, and this great actress had an effect on the later Stanwyck style. In her one surviving talkie, another W. Somerset Maugham adaptation, *The Letter* (1929), Eagels is a kind of missing link in acting culture, a bizarre, not easily classifiable bridge from the old to the new: from, say, the sheer presence of a Tallulah Bankhead to the Method neurosis of a Kim Stanley. Addicted to drugs, Eagels pours out emotion all over the place; she's an uncommonly messy actress, like a sparkler giving off blinding light before burning out. Stanwyck accessed the same type of seemingly uncontrollable personal emotion, yet somehow managed—through strength, stamina and practice—to build a kind of controlling technique around her displays of feeling, so that she gave us fresh rage and sorrow on command for decades, something the doomed Eagels was only able to do for a few years.

Oddly, Ruby became good friends with that famous neurotic of the piano, Oscar Levant, who wrote that she was "wary of sophisticates and phonies," as if she wanted to both protect what was genuine in her heart and also protect herself from social disqualification, a perilous balance that would define her work in *Stella Dallas* (1937) and many other films. As a chorus girl, she was a "Keep Kool Cutie" (I love the *K* in "Kool"); did a number called "A Room Adjoining a Boudoir" with Johnny Dooley;

and performed a striptease behind a white screen in one of Ziegfeld's "Shadowgraph" tableaux, a discreetly sexy stage convention that survived into some of the Warner Bros. musicals of the early thirties. There are photos of her dating from this period that show her tiny eyes still shiny with the openness of youth; a more hooded look would come later in photographs of her taken during the forties and fifties. But even in the early photos, she holds her body away from the camera, protecting it with her arms or a stiff stance. If she hadn't done this, the men and the mobsters would have grabbed at her until there was nothing left.

Ruby and Mae Clarke moved to the Knickerbocker Hotel on 45th Street with their other roommate, Walda, and in April 1925, Ruby and Mae danced until dawn at Anatole Friedlander's club on 54th Street. Ruby tentatively dated a boy named Edward Kennedy; he wanted to marry her, and she wanted to wait. As a kid, she had written her name in chalk on the sidewalk "to show everybody how it's going to look in electric lights." Her ambition was always spurring her to reach for the top, not settle near the bottom or the middle; it was a drive that never left her. "Of course, I've always had a burning desire to be the best of all, and, though I know most things you dream of pass you by," Stanwyck said, "I'll go on working with that same desire til the last role I play." That ambition is what set her apart from somebody like her roommate Mae Clarke, a pretty girl, a talented girl, but somebody who didn't have the urge to make herself major, to be "the best of all."

Ruby hung around The Tavern, a restaurant on 48th Street run by Billy La Hiff, a man who loved and helped out show biz types of all kinds. It was La Hiff who introduced her to Willard Mack, a man who would play Svengali to the young chorus girl and set her on the road to becoming something more, maybe even "the best of all." Ruby knew this was her big chance, and she grabbed it. "When I'm frightened, even now, I try to act bold," she said, assuming a gambler's attitude that again sets her apart from the cautious, the "maybe" people, the Mae Clarkes. She got herself a job in Mack's new show, *The Noose*, and also got jobs for her roommates (they later dropped out of it on the road).

Ruby still thought of herself more as a dancer than as an actress, but the seeds of something else were always there, even when she was a little girl waiting on those steps at 246 Classon Avenue. In *The Noose*, Rex Cherryman played a condemned man who is loved by a society girl and a chorus girl, played by Ruby. She had just a few lines in the play until Mack started to tinker with it out of town, realizing that the third act needed a lift. He then wrote a scene for Ruby where she pleads with the governor for Cherryman's ashes: a showcase moment.

In the Belasco Theatre, Mack saw an old program, "Jane Stanwyck in *Barbara Frietchie*," and so he christened his protégée with her new name, Barbara Stanwyck. A hard name, an impressive name, a name to keep visitors out—and a far cry from "Ruby Stevens," who sounds like a forlorn girl swatting away male advances and teaching herself not to weep in her room later. Levant called Mack "a Belasco hack," but Mack was successful and he knew his business. He was a man who had been married to the earthy Marjorie Rambeau and the grand Pauline Frederick, obscure names now, but performers who, in their surviving work, might be seen as earlier versions of the Stanwyck image. He was also sensitive enough to draw Stanwyck out of her shell and teach her some reliable techniques. Mack taught her how to make an entrance and, more importantly, he taught her how to assault an audience with emotion and then draw them into the remorseful aftermath of such outbursts.

Elisha Cook, Jr., the future movie character actor, was in *The Noose* at the time, and he claimed that Stanwyck's emotional involvement in her scene hit him on such a gut level that he had to go and vomit after he saw it. Clearly, this was a diamond in the rough who would always somehow stay rough, a Jeanne Eagels who had the discipline to learn how to judge and control uncontrollable emotion to such an extent that the push and pull between her feelings and her technique would lead to astonishing work in her movies in the thirties. Much like her contemporary, James Cagney, she had a freshness mixed with stylization. Some name performers of the twenties and thirties would look utterly lost and foreign to an audience in 1960—let alone our post-Method present—but Cagney and Stanwyck could easily play in the best films of today with only the slightest modification of scale.

In 1927, Stanwyck made her film debut in *Broadway Nights*, a silent movie, now lost. She played the friend of the heroine, having lost out on the heroine role itself when she couldn't cry for her screen test. The press agent Wilbur Morse, Jr. later said that the cameraman for the test "wanted to make her," but she wasn't having that. (How many times would she cry, "Get yer hands offah me!" in movies?) Worse, Ruth Chatterton, an established star, came on the set and started to laugh and carry on with her maid when the test director brought out an onion and had some schmaltzy music played so Stanwyck might access her tears. Trying to cry, Stanwyck finally told Chatterton to shut up, but this was one of the few professional battles that she lost.

A crush on her *Noose* leading man, Cherryman, seems to have led to a tentative relationship which was dashed when he died of septic poisoning. "Everything about him was so vivid," she remembered, "or perhaps it was because he was an actor and knew how to project." She would always gravitate toward actors or performers. She said that she "nearly died" getting over Cherryman. And so the Irish in Stanwyck must have wondered if she was cursed, if she would ever love anyone or anything without seeing it snatched away from her. Cagily, she shifted away from "life"—whatever that is—which seemed to have it in for her, and concentrated on her work as an actress: her other life, her real, imaginative life.

In her second and last Broadway play, *Burlesque*, Stanwyck played a dancer whose comedian husband (Hal Skelly) throws her over for another woman and gets hooked on booze, so that she has to rescue him for a final curtain. She was asked to test for the screen version of *Burlesque*, but she was still busy with the play itself. Also, on the rebound from Cherryman, she had taken up with Frank Fay, the self-proclaimed "King of Vaudeville," a master of ceremonies, an insult comic par excellence, and someone who was sure of himself and fun to be with—up to a point. Fay was ten years older than Stanwyck and had two marriages behind him. He was a carousing Irish Catholic and a virulent right-winger, a "born in a trunk" type with an enormous ego that needed to be fed or else. Stanwyck had known Fay for a while and had disliked him at first, but she was vulnerable after Cherryman died, and so she fell for Fay and his promised protection of her. It was a whirlwind romance, as they used to say. Fay proposed to Stanwyck by telegram from a theater in St. Louis and she accepted. Only four weeks had passed since Cherryman's death. Stanwyck and Fay were married on August 26, 1928, and soon went out to Hollywood, where Fay had been signed to a contract with Warner Bros.

Aside from a few trips here and there, including a disastrous vacation in post-war Europe, Hollywood is where Stanwyck stayed for the rest of her long life. There's a lovely picture of her perched on Fay's shoulders on the beach at Malibu, where they had a house, a picture in which her face is ecstatically open to the warmth and air and freedom of California after the cramped heat and cold of Brooklyn and Broadway. It would take some time to get going in movies, and she would have to let go of some of her resentment and feeling of social inadequacy, but the story of Barbara Stanwyck in Hollywood is a triumphant story, not personally triumphant most of the time, but professionally so in every way.

Her film career didn't begin smoothly. Joe Schenck had signed her to United Artists to do one picture, *The Locked Door* (1929), an adaptation of a play by Channing Pollack called *The Sign on the Door* (Schenck's wife Norma Talmadge had filmed it as a silent). George Fitzmaurice, the director of *The Locked Door*, reportedly screamed on the set that he couldn't make Stanwyck beautiful. "I staggered through it," she said. "It was all one big mystery to me." And later, showing her skill with the telling wisecrack, she added: "They never should have unlocked the damned thing." She just missed being cast in the film of *Burlesque*, which was renamed *The Dance of Life* (1929) and directed by John Cromwell for Paramount. Skelly reprised his role, while the female lead went to Nancy Carroll, another talented Irish girl from New York (and the niece of Billy La Hiff), whose career foundered because of the kind of temperament Stanwyck never allowed herself.

The Locked Door has a bad reputation, mainly deserved, but it's fairly well filmed for such an early talkie, especially the opening scenes on a "drinking boat" filled with whoopee-making extras. Stanwyck is second-billed under Rod La Rocque, under the title, and Fitzmaurice has a pretentious "signed" title card to himself in the credits; he tries to earn that signature with some fancy camera moves, courtesy of cinematographer Ray June, including an impressive crane shot over the party and a tracking shot across a bar, as the revelers shout for gin and more gin.

We first see Stanwyck in a two shot with mustachioed La Rocque; he asks her how she likes the party. Cut to her close-up: "It's like being on a pirate ship!" she says, a forced smile plastered on her face, as if Fitzmaurice has just told her that she isn't pretty enough for him. In this first scene, and some of her others in *The Locked Door*, Stanwyck has the air of someone trying hard to have the correct reaction to things. This early effort allows us some insight into her real life at the time, when her "make the best of it" attitude wasn't invigorating, as it would later become, but instead slightly sad.

The camera catches her in an amateurish, "we're talking, we're talking, and now I'll laugh!" pantomime blunder, as the lecherous La Rocque ushers her into a private room for dinner. When he offers her caviar, she repeats this word with a British or standard American style *a*, which must have been drilled into her by Willard Mack. Stanwyck's British-sounding *a* lasted the rest of her career, defiantly emerging from her Brooklyn purr to prove that she's as much a lady as anybody—even more so, because she's had to earn it.

La Rocque reads his lines in such a sour, affectless way that he'd be right at home in an Ed Wood movie. Stanwyck is forced to draw into herself, but she's not able to do this as deeply as she will in later films. We see her character starting to wonder if she's made a mistake by entering the room with La Rocque. When he starts to attack her, she gets her Irish up, rather sketchily, and he cracks, "I like you in a temper!" (The whole world, of course, would eventually love Stanwyck in a temper.) The boat is raided, and there's a cut back to the private room: Stanwyck's hair is mussed and her dress is disarranged. It's unclear just how far La Rocque's cad has gone with her, but as they exit the boat, dodging a newspaper cameraman and the police, Stanwyck projects a powerful sense of shame. It is the shame of Ruby Stevens after one of her first nights at a mob-run nightclub, when she has gauged just what will be expected of her and what parts of her body and her soul she can manage to keep for herself.

Eighteen months pass: Stanwyck has married her new boss (William "Stage" Boyd) and tells him "I love you" with all sincerity, the reliable mark of a great movie actress (even if this mark means that she might never be able to say those three words quite so sincerely away from the camera). Her line readings can be a bit wooden here; strangely, Stanwyck always kept a vestige of this stilted delivery, which she used as a kind of control or safety valve for her explosions of emotion. For some reason, the word "to" was always her wooden word. When she tries . to divert La Rocque from her sister-in-law (Betty Bronson), she says, "And you promised not *to* see Helen again?" Did Mack scare her when he heard her saying a Flatbush "tah" for "to"? It's as if Stanwyck had some kind of verbal or mental block about the word, but she learned to use this block to her advantage, just as she learned to bring up and then tamp down her Brooklyn accent like she was raising and then lowering a light—or the hem of her dress.

In early talkies like *The Locked Door*, the actors are trying out many different styles. Almost none of these styles are valid now, but they're so alien that they exert a kind of fascination. No one knew yet just how different a talking picture was from a silent picture or a stage play, so actors from the stage, like Stanwyck and Boyd, jostle up against former silent stars, like La Rocque and Bronson, and everybody tries out a little of the others' techniques until you can barely keep track of the weird pauses, ringing declarations, and inward emoting in close-ups. Bronson, who was an incomparable Peter Pan on screen in 1925, is a hopeless case here, a wilted gamine waiting for title cards that never come, and La Rocque sometimes seems like he's trying to be deliberately funny despite his villainous role.

Stanwyck is too young and vulnerable yet wised-up for her noble, oblivious part; the later Stanwyck would have known not to enter that stateroom with La Rocque, but this later Stanwyck also had a knack for attracting grueling filmic ordeals. She survives her first one here when her husband shoots La Rocque in his hotel room, and she finds herself trapped with his body behind the titular locked door. Stanwyck makes a fuss in the dark and pretends that she shot La Rocque, which brings some welcome comedy relief in the form of Mack Swain, the hotel proprietor, and ZaSu Pitts, the lobby receptionist. When Stanwyck tries to pull up the strap of her torn dress, a horny cop yells, "Stop that! The way your dress is now is . . . evidence!" The DA (Harry Mestayer) sneaks a shameless look at her left breast before grilling her in a way that feels more than a little vengeful and sexual. In the middle of this exploitative stuff, Stanwyck tries to convince her husband to be quiet, jumping off a couch and grasping at the air, a graceful, original gesture that signals her still-embryonic talent.

Whatever its failings, *The Locked Door* at least offered Stanwyck a clearly defined role in a clearly defined story. Her second film, *Mexicali Rose* (1929), at Columbia, is a bottom-of-the-barrel programmer of the worst sort, the kind of movie where no one has given much thought to anything. It runs all of sixty minutes and features a scenario by head Columbia writer Dorothy Howell (working under the pseudonym Gladys Lehman) that makes little sense. In a capsule review, Pauline Kael wrote, "Barbara Stanwyck called the film 'an abortion,' and she wasn't being too rough on it"—one wisecracking dame quoting another's wisecrack and then amplifying it, a neat trick. Seen today, *Mexicali Rose* is the kind of picture so primitive and so muddled that it defeats any effort to mock it.

It opens with another barroom scene, this time set south of the border. In a tired running gag, a drunk is always running to the bar whenever a free drink is offered. Stanwyck's first close-up shows her beautifully lit and made-up, decked out in a flowing gold robe that opens strategically at the legs. It swiftly becomes clear that the film is only interested in her as a sex object, and in a limited way, at that. After she sits down on husband Sam Hardy's lap ("Gee, I could go to the devil in your arms!" she cries), the camera comes to a full stop when she gets up so that it can stare at her behind.

Later on, when she's exiting a boat, the camera is placed low and again lingers on her rear end as she walks down a gangplank; it's a "forget your acting, let's see your ass" part that forces Stanwyck to place her hands on her hips a lot and sashay around. Hardy buys her an anklet, a harbinger of double indemnities to come, and she has him tie it on her. You can practically hear the director barking, "We've done her ass, now let's do her legs," behind the camera. But whenever the camera gives her a close-up, Stanwyck is clearly a star already, so that we want to watch any emotion that she cares to show us on her hard little face, with its tiny, mistrustful eyes.

Hardy discovers bruises on her leg and another man's tie in her room, so he sends her packing. Rose has a few lines about how a married lover turned her into a tramp, but Stanwyck can't do either the manipulation or the anger of such a moment yet. Yet green as she is, she's Eleonora Duse compared to Hardy, who has a lot of laugh lines that fall flat, and to the inept William Janney, who plays Hardy's young charge. Stanwyck marries Janney, and it's not made particularly clear, either in the script or in her playing, if Rose does it for revenge or out of genuine love. When we hear Rose has killed herself off-screen, this development feels as be-wildering as the rest of the film; it seems that everybody just wanted to get this turkey finished.

These two bad experiences with movies—the second far worse than the first, which was no prize—thoroughly demoralized Stanwyck and undermined her confidence. Fay was getting a big build-up from War-ners, where he did his emcee act for their revue, *The Show of Shows* (1929). At this point, he was still the star in the family, and he could still afford to be solicitous of his wife because she was having a hard time get-ting started.

There were no more offers after the sleazy *Mexicali Rose*, and Stanwyck was stuck at home for a few months. Finally, she made a color test of her scene from *The Noose* with Alexander Korda, who gave her some encour-agement, even though she knew she was being given the brush-off and might even be washed up. "At twenty-two, they had me on my way to the Old Ladies' Home," she later said. Harry Cohn at Columbia still had an option on her services, and he asked Frank Capra, the studio's wun-derkind director, to meet with Stanwyck and see if she might do for the lead in his film *Ladies of Leisure* (1930). She muffed the interview, and Capra called her "a porcupine," but then Fay got him on the phone and urged him to look at her Korda test. We owe Fay a lot for that phone call.

The Capra Miracle

Ladies of Leisure, The Miracle Woman, Forbidden,
The Bitter Tea of General Yen, Meet John Doe

*J*udging by Joseph McBride's surely definitive biography of the director, Frank Capra lied about a lot of things, appropriating credit whenever he could, but he could also be brutally frank about others and about himself. There's something of Elia Kazan about him—but even messier, less calculating. An Italian immigrant, Capra was filled with hate and resentment, and these served as fuel for his work and as a link to Stanwyck, whose own hatred was the slow burning, quietly bitter kind. Capra was more open about most of his feelings. "Mr. Capra was not afraid to show emotion," she said. "He understood it." And so did she. Together, they made five films that are devoted to the most extreme expression of emotion, which acts as a fire of purification on both threadbare plots and audience expectations.

Ladies of Leisure was based on a play by Milton Herbert Gropper called *Ladies of the Evening,* which had been produced by David Belasco, and Capra himself did a first draft of the film script. Jo Swerling, a newspaperman and committed leftist, nervily told him that his adaptation was bad, and so Capra nervily told Swerling to do his own version of the material. "It's the old Camille story, but it needs a new twist," said Swerling, who polished off his draft quickly. Shooting started eleven days after Swerling turned in this draft, on June 14, 1930.

Stanwyck is still billed under the title, and Capra is billed as "Frank R. Capra" (he thought the initial might give him an aura of respectability). Joseph Walker's camera pans up a tall skyscraper and into the middle of an arty sort of party, where Bill Standish (Lowell Sherman), a soused dauber, is painting a girl's bare back. It's clear that we're a world away from the "whoopee" boat of *The Locked Door.* It's 1930 now, and the

17

Depression is on, seeming to depress most of the revelers, including the party's host, Jerry (Ralph Graves), who complains of a headache. Jerry takes off in his car and gets a flat tire; from across a lake, he sees a girl in a boat hitting the shoreline.

The lady of the lake is Stanwyck's Kay Arnold, a gum-chewing, self-described "party girl," with mascara running down her face. Talking to Jerry, Kay flashes an intensely angry look at him. She's been on a boat filled with men; she's a hooker, but it seems like something happened on this boat that has thrown her for a loop. Kay, like Stanwyck, is a wearer of masks, a person who hides her feelings, so she immediately tries to fall into a practiced wisecracker persona with Jerry in order to blot out that questioning look of rage and contempt she couldn't help but lay on him. A party girl, that's her racket, see? She asks if Jerry "totes a flask," and he says no. But he wants to paint her portrait, and she accepts in a "why not?" sort of spirit.

We then see Kay with her roommate Dot (Marie Prevost), a pleasingly plump fellow prostie in a feather-boaed negligee. Kay has been sitting for Jerry, and she marvels that he hasn't tried to make a pass at her. We dissolve from a shot of Kay pouring coffee to a shot of Jerry's dowager mother (Nance O'Neil) pouring tea. Jerry's father is a railroad magnate, a classic Capra capitalist ogre. Even though the director himself was a right-wing Republican who hated Roosevelt, he allowed screenwriters like Swerling and Robert Riskin to grace his movies with left-wing senti-ment because it was fashionable during the thirties and guaranteed that most critics would take him seriously.

Jerry wants his model Kay to look up at the ceiling and pretend to see stars, but sensible, low-class, uneducated Stanwyck/Kay only sees the ceiling. Capra himself wants to purify his leading actress and present her to us in an unvarnished state, and he includes a close-up of Jerry stripping off Kay's false eyelashes. This act has the effect of making Stan-wyck's small eyes seem even tinier; Capra wants us to look at this girl closely, intently, to see what character she has. "Do you want me to be homely?" asks Kay. No, not that, but Capra wants Stanwyck to be some-thing as unusual for the Hollywood of that time and place. He wants her to be real. He wanted Stanwyck to show the truth about herself so that he could tell the truth about himself, and that transference takes patience, the same patience Jerry exhibits with all of Kay's gaucheries and self-protectiveness. Without some of her make-up, Stanwyck's face is plain, severe, and beseeching, crying out to the man behind the cam-era for help and love.

As if freed by this close-up, Stanwyck lets loose with some off-the-cuff "behavior," little jokey voices and nonsense noises. She's charting her way, instinctively, to the best kind of naturalistic film acting. Capra let it be known that she was a spontaneous performer, a "primitive emotional." He quickly realized that she was at her best on the first take, so he didn't rehearse her with the other actors and used multiple cameras to capture her at her best.

"That first take with Stanwyck was sacred," said Edward Bernds, Capra's sound mixer. Throughout her life, Stanwyck was always best in first takes. "That's the stage training," she explained. "The curtain goes up at 8:30, and you'd better be good. You don't get a retake." It's as if she pressed a kind of button in herself, and there it all was, controlled, pure feeling—but it was only available once. To keep this concentration, Stanwyck always memorized the entire script before shooting so that she would know where she was and keep up a kind of emotional continuity.

"You should shoot for the first time," she said. "And if you have an emotional scene you only have so much water in you to come out! About the third or fourth take, you start drying up, not because you want to, but it's a physical thing that happens." There are a lot of actors who like to rehearse a scene and do a few takes for the camera, and they only get better as they go along. They get more deeply into it, more detailed, more involved. But Stanwyck's involvement was of the instant kind. She had to believe, somehow, that the scene was really happening. Ask her to do it again right away, and that belief would be shattered.

On the stage, presumably Stanwyck could believe in the same scenes night after night, but the movies gave her a way to be "in the moment" to the nth degree. When she got older and more experienced, Stanwyck could sometimes joke with the crew before scenes, but generally, if she could, she would withdraw into herself into a kind of self-hypnosis. A writer on the set of *Clash by Night* (1952) compared her preparation before a scene to that of a prizefighter waiting to enter the ring. That comparison sounds apt; she developed a gallantry that had a distinctly masculine tinge.

In Jerry's studio, his pal Bill stares at Kay a little too long. She snaps, "Take a good look . . . it's free," inaugurating the justly celebrated wisecracking style of the thirties Stanwyck, much more direct in its delivery and implications than the quizzical style of a Jean Arthur, the worldly jabs of a Claudette Colbert, the deadpan mistrust of a Ginger Rogers. Stanwyck's laugh lines hint that there's a vestige of amusement somewhere in her, but her taunts come from a much darker place than that of the other 1930s film heroines, a place of unspecified trauma that has to remain mysterious and well below the surface. If even a bit of her anger somehow emerges, there can be no more jokes—only murder, suicide, or revenge. As Kay holds her own against Jerry's snooty fiancée, Capra gives her a few silent close-ups where Stanwyck registers clear thoughts on her face and even makes gracefully smooth transitions between them. "It's nice to have very nice dialogue, if you can get it," Stanwyck said (that "if you can get it" is classic Stanwyck, the Stanwyck tough girl "note"). "But great movie acting . . . watch the eyes," she continued, a skill she said Capra had taught her.

Sweetly, the little girl emerges from the party girl as Kay takes a bath, staring up at the ceiling and trying to see the stars but still just seeing a ceiling. The camera dollies back, and with some backward camera movement Walker dissolves to Kay getting dressed—a lovely effect, but one as extraneous to Capra's vision as Swerling's often sophisticated and impressive dialogue. Without Capra's overriding and somewhat inchoate need to get to "the truth" about Stanwyck, about himself and about life, Ladies of Leisure would just be a fine early talkie with a star-making performance from its lead actress. With his ambition, it's much more than that: It's an elating and even exhausting experience. Capra has the nerve and the talent and the actress to make exhortations to feel more and feel deeper seem like a call to arms. The film has the air of having been created in total freedom (Columbia head Harry Cohn left his boy genius alone, for the most part) and with full artistic inspiration.

Like Stella Dallas, Kay is low-class in looks and manner but high-class inside, a rich dichotomy that Stanwyck mined throughout her career. Kay tells Dot that she went to the opera, and it transported her. She compares listening to the music to being in the middle of the ocean. In 1930, opera was still the music of the Italian people, not the closed-off specialty act it has become, and it proves the perfect bridge for hardened Kay to cross over into the arena of high art. High art here equates with heightened feeling, a heightening that Stanwyck herself expresses in her own acting style, merging the best kind of theatricality ("this is happening *right now*, in front of you, only once") with a miraculous kind of freshness. This freshness made for a vivid contrast to the kind of artificial and outdated theatricality running rampant through all the film studios during the period Capra and Stanwyck made their first masterpiece together.

Capra loved Stanwyck and he identified with her totally, the key combo when it comes to director-actress artistic collaborations. McBride seems to think that they had an affair. "We were very close," Capra told him. "I wish I could tell you about it, but I can't, I shouldn't and I won't. But she was delightful." This quote is not typical Capra; he usually outright lied or was too frankly honest, but rarely was he really coy like this. Capra wants to insinuate that they had some kind of affair without actually outright saying so, which strikes me as the gambit of a man who did indeed fall madly in love with his leading lady, but who might not have gotten as far with her as he would have liked.

Stanwyck, still married to a not-yet-faltering Frank Fay, surely recognized right away what Capra could do for her as an actress. His films made her a star. She was probably fond of him, and she might have encouraged his romantic attentions to a point so that his creativity would be similarly encouraged. Whatever happened between them, for Stanwyck, the wish to be "the best of all" blended any true affection she might have felt for Capra with careful calculation that kept his interest burning through three more films.

Kay literally finds herself as an artist's model, and *Ladies of Leisure* is itself a metaphor for the partnership between Capra and Stanwyck. It's an intense, almost grueling film, lingering over set pieces as if Capra doesn't want them to end, as if these set pieces are a kind of lovemaking that he wants to prolong. Take the long scene set late at night in Jerry's studio. Done painting her for the day, Jerry looks at Kay warming herself by the fire. Walker frames Stanwyck against the light so that it outlines the curve of her behind. This isn't the crude and unfeeling ass shot we got in *Mexicali Rose*, but rather the kind of outright sexual idolatry that Josef Von Sternberg brought to his seven Paramount films made in worship of Marlene Dietrich. Capra had fallen in love with Stanwyck, and a love like this includes a love of her body.

Jerry tells Kay that she should spend the night, and we see on her hardening face that she thinks he only wants her sexually, like all the rest of them. The suspense of this sequence becomes almost unbearable as we watch Kay undress against a rain-spattered window (in his autobiography, Capra wrote that he always found rain erotic). Walker shines adoring light on Stanwyck's face as Kay waits for the man she loves to come to her and turn her into just one more meaningless lay. We see Jerry's feet entering the room, and we assume along with Kay that he's going to force himself on her. (It's hard to read Jerry a lot of the time. Ralph Graves is stiff in the role, but this quality of his sometimes works to the film's advantage because he starts to seem like a solid object for Stanwyck to work against, a monolith for her to project on.)

When Jerry simply pulls a blanket over Kay, the camera holds on Stanwyck's face as it's transformed by a look of unadulterated joy. Kay's joy is compounded because it feels like Stanwyck herself has found a kind of artistic happiness for the first time—a heartening sight for anyone who loves her, or her work, which are really the same thing in her case. There's something almost pornographic in Capra's focus on Stanwyck's newborn, newly virgin whore—if we can take pornography to mean steadily looking at the foundation of all life. Capra's Italian soul flips out over Stanwyck's "look to the stars" Irish poeticism, so zealously hidden behind a toffee-like front.

When Kay looks at Jerry over the breakfast table the next morning, her face is full of love that's almost indistinguishable from pain. Capra and Stanwyck both understand that when a put-upon, abused woman lowers her defenses and loves someone, this surrender leaves her vulnerable and wide open to attack. Old defenses kick up a fight for dominance and a maelstrom of reasons *not* to feel love. Old, cruel memories that have been buried come back to haunt Kay and Stanwyck, but both actress and character valiantly struggle to keep them at bay.

The sound is a bit muffled in *Ladies of Leisure* (it could certainly use some restoration), and some of its accouterments are unavoidably redolent of 1930 at Columbia, but Stanwyck's work here will always be modern because it will always be "true to life." Stanwyck is emotionally raw here, totally exposed, and this raw exposure is disturbing because real emotion is always a disturbance, a call for change. She makes you realize how often the movies and the people in them try to distance us from life, so that we luxuriate in the cradling, annihilating falseness of "it's only another movie." Stanwyck at her best—and especially when working with Capra—never just acted in another movie. Her films are a matter of life and death to her, nothing less.

In the stock scene where Jerry's mother confronts Kay, asking her to leave him for his own sake, Stanwyck interestingly chooses to play the first part of this encounter coolly and reasonably, as if Kay really doesn't understand what was happening. When she realizes what is being asked of her, Stanwyck gives us our first glimpse of her force-of-nature, hysterical sorrow, the most impressive of all her modes on screen. Understandably, she doesn't quite have full control of this mode here; it makes her head tilt back wildly, and there are moments when she's slightly dried up, as if she needs to try to locate the feeling again.

What makes this scene more than stock is the way Stanwyck establishes a deep rapport with the mother (kudos to O'Neil for neither under- nor overplaying her hand). After the scene is over, Walker films a spent Stanwyck sitting on a couch with her head thrown back from a highly unflattering low angle. I love this particular shot above all the others because it proves that Capra and Stanwyck do not care a damn about how she looks or about the Hollywood posturing of the time. Let Ann Harding or Norma Shearer or Ruth Chatterton decorously pose against fireplaces in profile; with Stanwyck and Capra, we're right in the middle of a real tragedy, and there's no time for artful camera angles or careful make-up. *Ladies of Leisure* is a major film about learning to live without protection and gambling all on one person. It's maybe a little shapeless, a little all-over-the-place, like a John Cassavetes film (Cassavetes revered Capra), but it still casts a spell.

Kay leaves with the likably caddish Bill to get out of town on another "boat of vice." On board ship, the camera dollies in on her face, which glistens with an almost evil-looking passionate sorrow. An image of water dissolves in under this uncanny face. On the deck, Kay looks up at the stars. Where's Ruby Stevens's mother? Where's her father Byron? Up there? Or down below? Kay jumps off the ship, just as Bresson's Mouchette rolled herself gracelessly into the water. The end. But not really: Kay wakes up and Jerry tells her everything is all right. The end.

Well, maybe it will be all right. Maybe Kay will become a kind of Frieda Lawrence in Arizona, where Jerry says he'll take her, and where she might be the formidable wife of a great, or at least good painter. *Ladies of Leisure* isn't a perfect movie; perfection would go against its "let it all hang out" grain. A lot of important moments seem to take place off-screen, and we could do with a little less Prevost and Sherman, fine as they are, and get a sharper picture of Graves's Jerry and what he sees in Kay and what he wants from her. The ending is too truncated, especially in relation to the rest of the film, which positively takes its shoes and girdle off and settles in for a good long soak in the tub.

Capra's ambition swelled for his next collaboration with Stanwyck, *The Miracle Woman* (1931). He was always someone whose reach exceeded his grasp, but his more craven fears flinched from the subject he chose this time. It was based on a commercially unsuccessful play by Robert Riskin and John Meehan called *Bless You, Sister*, which had starred Alice Brady. A parody of Aimee Semple McPherson's lucrative religious revival meetings, with their tasteless, show-bizzy underpinnings, it proved too strong a brew for theater audiences, and Riskin himself told Capra that he was being foolish to adapt it to the movies.

But Capra had it in his mind that the film might prove both a contro-
versy and a success—and provide a juicy part for Stanwyck.

A star now, Stanwyck was starting to have trouble with Frank Fay,
who was floundering in a series of lover boy parts at Warner Bros. that
were unsuited to his talents, such as they were. Capra seems to have
pursued her more avidly on *Miracle Woman*, even planting a line with a
press agent that Stanwyck was "so pleased with her last wedding that she
can hardly wait for her next one." In spite of his hopes (and his confused
claim in his autobiography that he would have married her after she
divorced Fay if he hadn't loved his wife Lu more), Capra and Stanwyck
could never have made a go of it off the set, whatever her feelings for
him. He needed a helpmate, a housewife, and a steady booster—which
is what Fay needed too, of course—and Stanwyck was not at all suited to
that task.

Swerling did the screenplay for *Miracle Woman*, retaining much of
Riskin's structure and some of his dialogue. Capra wrote in his autobiography that he had hedged his bets on this project by placing the blame
too squarely on the shoulders of a heavy played by Sam Hardy, who's
not quite as objectionable here as he is in *Mexicali Rose*—but not by much.
Capra was being hard on himself so that people would say, "He's being
too hard on himself," but there can be no doubt that *The Miracle Woman*
begins strongly enough that anything that comes afterward is bound to
seem flimsy or half-hearted in comparison. There's no caution here, as
in *Ladies of Leisure*, no careful handling of Stanwyck. Capra knows what
she's capable of and he just turns her loose, having her start the film on
a toweringly high note.

The movie begins with two title cards, one of which reads, "Beware
of false prophets which come to you in sheep's clothing." Just so that
there's no mistaking the film's intentions, a second card adds, "*The Miracle Woman* is offered as a rebuke to anyone who, under the cloak of
religion, seeks to sell for gold God's greatest gift to Humanity—FAITH."
The religious faith Capra is dealing with here can be seen as akin to emotional truth in *Ladies of Leisure*, but somehow this religious faith seems of
a lesser order of importance and makes for a lesser film. Capra himself
was a religious man, and Stanwyck had a core of religious faith in her
somewhere. There was no God on Flatbush Avenue in 1915, but she
yearned for Him, all the same. Late in life, she said, "I believe we *must*
believe in God. Without God, there would be nothing. Nothing at all."

A pastor is set to deliver his farewell address. In a brief snatch of gossip, we hear that he has basically been fired from his post. Stanwyck

stiffly enters the church, as if she's entering a cage full of lions. She plays Florence, the pastor's daughter. Florence ascends the pulpit and begins to read her father's last sermon in a cool, dutiful voice that sounds as if it's about to crack under some strain. Then she breaks off. "You can see that he stopped in the middle of a sentence," she says, and pain and rage start to flood into her face and her voice. "My father is dead," she says, with a tinge of hysteria in her delivery that will rise up thrillingly as Stanwyck begins one of her all-time great arias.

Her hysteria is a weapon that she uses as a sword but also to whip herself, and it seems to thicken her voice, to make it throb. Watching Stanwyck in *Burlesque*, her friend Mae Clarke said, "I have never heard one person get as many vibrations into her voice as Barbara got into hers then. It was like a symphony chorus in the Hollywood Bowl instead of just one person speaking." What was the source of Stanwyck's hysteria, and how was she able to channel this quality into her voice? Was it a curse from her childhood that blossomed into a God-given gift for her professional life?

The deacon of the church was instrumental in having Florence's father removed, and the actor who plays him tells Florence to stop, shouting in a stagy, false voice that makes a striking contrast with Stanwyck's natural, air-that-I-breathe acting. "This isn't a house of God, it's a meeting place for hypocrites!" she howls, letting her voice crack into a hundred jagged pieces on the word "hypocrites." Florence (and Capra) is going to tell these phonies "the truth," even if it's something they can't hear, even if it's dangerous. The parishioners begin to file out, slowly, but one woman tells Florence to keep going and tell it like it is.

Stanwyck swaggers down from the pulpit. Now she not only has her symphonic voice but also her body to put her points across. She lets her body literally *propel* her forward, one hand on her hip and another hand on a pew as she lands each and every one of her vengeful words against these people who have exploited, over-worked, and destroyed her father. At the climax of the aria, Stanwyck leans back on her heels and throws her head all the way back as she shouts and basks in the full glory of letting herself go—and in the glory of the technique she has acquired that allows her such control over her feelings, which come right from the gut. After this climax, we see Florence run to the church doors and close them; suddenly she's a small, lonely figure, weeping huskily, quietly, privately, like a balloon with all the air let out.

Where can we go from here? No place much, alas. Hardy's crooked promoter takes her up and makes Florence into an Aimee Semple

McPherson star on the revival circuit, where she meets up with a blind aviator (David Manners) who restores the faith she's lost. I suppose it would have made Florence look too unsympathetic if, in her disillusionment, she bilked the faithful deliberately and cynically, but such a turn of events would have added color to a girl who seems to withdraw from us just when she's opened herself up so fully. Hardy's character is a kind of director, cracking down on the down-on-their-luck vagrants he hires as plants to be "saved" by Sister Florence, and he expresses Capra's ill-concealed distaste for his own audience and for crowds in general.

"I'm crazy about you when you're mad, baby, you look more beautiful," Hardy tells Stanwyck, as she lies down after a performance with a distant look on her face, her hysteria cooled to embers. Against all odds, there is some interest in her interactions with Manners, an attractive, gay, strangely mannered young actor. "On the set, Barbara was tremendously centered in her work," he later said, "much too much so for any social chit chat. . . . I see her sitting alone in a studio chair—almost in meditation." They're charming together, but their scenes go on too long and distract us from what should be the meat of the movie, Florence's crisis of faith.

The Miracle Woman is an unforgettable first scene in search of a movie to follow it. Perhaps that scene might be more effective at the end of a movie: We could see Florence grow up, see her father belittled and bled dry by his parishioners (Walter Huston could have played the part), and then die of heartbreak, so that his daughter finally goes out to tell everyone off, shuts the doors of the church, and then commits the ultimate blasphemy, killing herself in front of the altar. The movie audience of the time wouldn't have had the stomach for that film, but Stanwyck could have played it for all it was worth.

Capra wrote the story for their next picture, *Forbidden* (1932), a messy takeoff on Fannie Hurst's popular novel, *Back Street,* but most of the Columbia writing staff had a hand in writing the film, and it shows. *Forbidden* is filled with inane dialogue and rushed plot points. The movie represented a kind of last chance for Capra to win Stanwyck as his wife, and it has a distinctive "time is running out" quality that does the muddled narrative no favors. The production was plagued by bad luck. Stanwyck held out for more money from Harry Cohn, which delayed shooting and can't have helped the frayed continuity. On October 4, 1931, Stanwyck was shooting a beach scene on horses with her on-screen lover (Adolphe Menjou), when a reflector flared into her horse's eyes. He threw her, then fell on top of her and kicked her spine, dislocating her coccyx.

Already playing the masochistic trouper, Stanwyck insisted they finish the shot before her legs stiffened. For two weeks, she worked during the day on *Forbidden*, then went to the hospital to spend the night in traction. In 1984, her terse comment on this accident was, "It hurt. It still hurts." All for a few seconds in a movie. A few seconds in a movie, though, meant everything to Stanwyck.

At this point, a failed Frank Fay was drinking heavily and batting Stanwyck around in public. She took this abuse as she took her on-set accident and all her other lousy luck, stoically. Her other co-star on the film, Ralph Bellamy, said that Fay was "a very unpopular guy—he worked at it." And Fay's jealousy was misplaced: Stanwyck later told Bellamy that Fay had thought they might be having an affair, when in reality Capra was making his last pitch for her.

Forbidden is a personal movie. Menjou's crippled wife is called Helen, the name of Capra's first, alcoholic wife. Bellamy's character is a news-paperman who pursues Stanwyck throughout the film; rejecting one of his many proposals, she says he's "married to his newspaper." Menjou's character is a cad of the most selfish sort, and it's clear that Menjou is a stand in for Fay, as Bellamy is for Capra. Stanwyck is playing a woman named Lulu, named after the other woman in Capra's life, Lu, who finally issued an ultimatum to the director and became the second and final Mrs. Capra, a role for which she was eminently suited.

Unfortunately, as any non-doctrinaire auteurist can admit, "personal" doesn't always equal "good" when it comes to movies, and *Forbidden* is a case in point. It begins promisingly with a fast montage of town life. We see a plow, trees in bloom, bees pollinating flowers. A dog yawns, and an older man takes up the yawn. The older man is excited because Stanwyck's Lulu is late for work at the public library for the first time in eight years. She never misses weddings, he says, except "her own." Lulu is supposed to be a bespectacled, incipient spinster ("Old lady four eyes!" yell some kids as she enters the library), but Stanwyck still walks like a chorus girl, and spring fever swiftly takes Lulu out of town for a two-week vacation in Havana, funded by all her savings. A gamble, life or death.

She cruises around on yet another "boat of vice," and though Lulu has taken off her glasses and glammed up a bit, she can't seem to snag an escort. In her stateroom, she finds a drunken Menjou and inexplicably takes a liking to him (just as Stanwyck's fondness for the gruesome, abusive Fay looks fairly inexplicable to us now, unless we presume that she felt she deserved trouble). In *The Miracle Woman*, Stanwyck and David

Manners play most of their love scenes with a ventriloquist's dummy called Al, and in *Forbidden*, she and Menjou share their happiest moments on screen when they play around with commedia dell'arte-type masks. It's as if Capra is trying to reassure Stanwyck that she'll be protected and that the exposure of *Ladies of Leisure* needn't be an around-the-clock vocation. And Stanwyck seems uncommonly relaxed in the mask scene. She's always touching when she tries to be lighthearted, because you can see how much effort it takes for her to forget 246 Classon Avenue, where part of her lives permanently, waiting on those steps.

Forbidden becomes a formula illegitimate baby saga for most of the rest of its running time; a complicated plot twist means Stanwyck has to give up her child to Menjou and his wife. She becomes an advice-to-the-lovelorn columnist for Bellamy. Time passes, and we see some grey in her hair (Stanwyck makes her face seem subtly older by holding it more stiffly than she did in the youthful scenes). The musical score goes into overdrive for her big scene with Bellamy, where he threatens to expose her secret and ruin Menjou's career. He punches her in the mouth, leaving a trickle of blood that looks alarmingly *right* on Stanwyck's face.

She shoots him from behind a door, then opens it and shoots some more, jabbing the gun in the air like a knife, just as Jeanne Eagels does at the beginning of *The Letter*. The camera moves close for an iconic shot of her face; there's blood on the left side of her mouth and a jewel-like tear glistening in her right eye. In her last scene with Menjou, he remembers how he called her "the world's best loser," and that's an apt description of Stanwyck's persona here (in the forties, she might have been dubbed the world's worst winner). *Forbidden* ends with Lulu walking alone down a street, her man dead, her life over, but her mood rather tranquil after all her upheavals.

Capra later told his trusted sound man, Edward Bernds, that his next film with Stanwyck, *The Bitter Tea of General Yen* (1933), "didn't make money, but it has more real *movie* in it than any other I did." He had reason to boast, for this is his most fluid, audacious, original work as a director. It's the kind of movie even those who don't like the Capra of *Mr. Deeds* and *Mr. Smith* can embrace, for he takes his often confused, touchy talent and applies it not to politics or social messages, but to sexual longings and fantasies, important subjects that suit his brand of impassioned, mixed-up emotionalism. *The Bitter Tea of General Yen* cost a million dollars to make, and it was the first film to play Radio City Music Hall; scheduled for two weeks, it was pulled after eight days. Capra underestimated the engrained racism of an American 1930s audience, which couldn't handle the thought of a Chinese warlord making love to a white woman—let alone the sight of it on screen—even if General Yen (Nils Asther) was a suave, gay Swedish actor in yellowface.

This is Capra's best film with Stanwyck, the most unusual, and maybe the most personally revealing. "I accepted it, believed in it, loved it," she said later. It begins with a map of China and some dissolves to Chinese natives running for their lives. Joseph Walker's glistening cinematography lets us know that Capra has caught Josef Von Sternberg fever in his visuals, and he seems to want to piggyback on the success of Sternberg's *Shanghai Express* (1932). These two films look alike and share a common background and technical filmic vocabulary, but their effect is as different as Stanwyck is from Marlene Dietrich—which is to say, as different as can be imagined.

We cut to a wedding party with English missionaries, as the Chinese keep running outside the door. The contrast is unsettling. Capra himself could be racist, as shown in McBride's book, but he was an unsettled racist, a "let's say everything I think and work it out later" sort, and this has the effect of pleasingly destabilizing all the racial points in *General Yen*. If a director of today were to cut from Chinese peasants evacuating to an English missionary social event, the film would almost be obligated to hit us over the head with the point about English obliviousness. But because Capra comes to this scene from his less certain 1930s viewpoint, the missionaries are seen as three-dimensional people, misguided in the extreme, but human and interesting.

At the party, Chinese men sing "Onward Christian Soldiers," and a repressed, bespectacled girl says she can't wait to see the betrothed couple kiss. (She gets sternly reprimanded.) An old man missionary who has spent fifty years in China tells a story about teaching the tale of Jesus's crucifixion to Mongolian bandits, who listened to the details avidly. Later, he found out that the bandits crucified their next victims. "That, my friends, is China," he says, and the camera whip pans to an older Chinese man, looking inscrutable. The actor playing this old missionary delivers his lines in the phony, portentous way of the deacon in *The Miracle Woman*, so it's clear that Capra is not at all on his side, even as his crucifixion story makes an uncomfortable impression.

We've been told at the party that Stanwyck's Megan Davis, the bride-to-be, is from an old Puritan family and that her father is a publisher. By this point, Capra knows that Stanwyck's range has widened and that she can play different kinds of women, women from different backgrounds and classes. Stanwyck was able to emphasize her Brooklyn accent if the part called for it, but in *General Yen* she represses it to the point that it's barely noticeable.

Megan is introduced in a rickshaw that gets hit by General Yen's car, killing her driver. When she reprimands the General, he merely smiles and says, "Life, even at its best, is hardly endurable." Bewildered by his heartless sophistication, Megan gets into another rickshaw (the camera frames her behind the wood of this vessel, as if she needs to retreat from what she's just experienced), and she stares at Yen and the beautiful Chinese girl in his car with tender curiosity. Stanwyck's face is open and vulnerable, but it's Megan Davis's vulnerability, not Barbara Stanwyck's, or Ruby Stevens's. Paradoxically, Stanwyck has discovered that the more you hide behind a part that is different from yourself, the more you can reveal of your true self, an irony that might have pleased General Yen.

At the wedding party, Megan is boxed in again behind a wooden frame; she's been cloistered, but she wants to break out. She tries to share her experience with her hostess (Clara Blandick), saying that Yen looked "so civilized," only to be met with a blast of concentrated racism: "They're all tricky, treacherous and immoral," snaps the hostess, "I can't tell one from the other. They're all Chinaman to me." This grossly energetic little outburst conveys exactly the kind of finger-pointing ugliness that Megan wants to escape.

Her fiancée, Dr. Robert Strike, is played by Gavin Gordan, who was the callow minister to Greta Garbo in her 1930 vehicle, *Romance*, and he's cast to type here, a solid do-gooder who wants to rescue some orphans from behind enemy lines, but has to get General Yen's permission first. The General scoffs at Megan's fiancée. Why does he want to save a few orphans? After all, he says, they're nameless. Such expressions make us see that the libertine General is almost as bad as the wedding party hostess, albeit in a radically different way. He's as awful as she is, but his awfulness is dangerously alluring because it's so aligned to sex, which he reveres, whereas her awfulness is a vile substitute for sex.

The firelight glistens on Megan's face as she rushes into the orphanage with Strike. She saves the kids but gets clubbed on the head for her trouble, and she is soon scooped up by the General, who has been hovering around her in his car. A series of dreamy, associative images of her fiancée and the General suggest Megan's confused psychological state as she wakes in a train with a cold cloth on her head. Sexual tension builds as Megan half-realizes her position, takes in Yen's concubine Mah-Li (Toshia Mori), then covers the small bit of her leg showing with her skirt when she catches Yen staring at her.

Capra then cuts to a phallic train hurtling through the night, having established a mood that is sensitive to Megan's fear and desire while also shyly identifying with Yen's viewpoint. Stanwyck is now lost to Capra. He's married another woman and given up hope of marrying his actress, but he wants to glorify her one more time, maybe exorcise her from his system, and he does so by making her play a repressed woman who opens up sexually on screen, just as the sexually abused Kay Arnold learned to open up emotionally.

Boldly, Capra wants to get at the truth of a certain kind of dirty, sexual power dynamic that is not aligned to anything pure or nice or conventionally romantic. From what we see of him, Gordan's fiancée is fine and good and Yen is a cruel, cynical dictator, yet we can tell right away who is the more deeply attractive man. We later learn that Yen had drugged Megan on the train and it's planted in our minds that he might have taken liberties with her, maybe with Mah-Li's enthusiastic help. Only later do we learn that his pride is such that he needs to conquer and destroy a woman's "good person" emotions before he can conquer her body. The General sees everything as conquest. And so Capra makes his film an anatomy of the sexual masochism he either experienced or sensed in Stanwyck.

Race is the dominant spice of this particular erotic dish. "You yellow swine!" Megan snarls the next morning, grabbing a nearby knife when she feels intimidated by her captor. Even Yen's easy-going Caucasian flunky, Jones (Walter Connelly) gets scared about the situation. "This is a white woman," he whines, in the tone of someone who feels he ought to half-heartedly lodge an official protest. But Yen zaps him: "I have no prejudice against the color," he quips in his jaunty way (Asther almost sounds Latino at certain points here, and this effect only emphasizes his bizarre, everything-rolled-into-one sexiness). Megan refuses dinner with the General and goes outside for some air; she looks at the moon, smokes a cigarette, and sits down in a large wicker chair. Across the way, some of Yen's people are frolicking playfully together, in a natural, sexy way, and Megan drowses in her chair.

We see a watery door. A caricatured "Chinese" Yen with long fingernails and feral looks breaks the door down. "Chinese" Yen is then superimposed over the real Yen, an effect that conveys Megan's racially based fear of him and her confusion over her feelings. Capra frames "Chinese" Yen's talon-like fingernails around Megan's horrified face as he creeps up on her to take her. The fingernails settle on her shoulders as she "struggles," voluptuously (we can see that this is not a rape, but a rape fantasy). A masked man comes in the window to save her: Is he her fiancée, or her father? The masked man punishes the Bad Yen, who disappears into a wall. He takes his black mask off . . . and it's the real Yen. There's a close-up of Megan's face, her eyes shining like distant harbor lights as a blurred background whirs behind her. And then she kisses Yen, amazingly enough (I imagine half of the Radio City audience of 1933 walked out at this point).

Megan wakes up and finds herself talking to Yen by the light of the moon. He says that he's banned all missionaries from his territory, and then he says that he'd like to laugh at her yet finds her admirable. The distinction he makes lets us know that Yen is a very intelligent man who too often retreats into adolescent nihilism. Then he puts the screws on: "There's never been a people more purely artist . . . and therefore more purely lover . . . than the Chinese," he drawls, in Asther's cadenced, hypnotic voice, which finally seems to have no specific regionalisms at all.

This does it. Megan bathes, and Capra indulges himself filming Stanwyck's beautiful legs and then her bare back in a freestanding bathtub, with her hair up. He wants to pamper her and wait on her and turn this poverty-bred Brooklyn girl into an international movie goddess, worth idolizing not because she's remote, like Garbo or Dietrich, but because she's real. It's as if a husband suddenly saw his careworn wife in their Flatbush apartment as the sun hit her at just the right angle through the kitchen window, transfiguring her, but revealing her, too.

Megan looks at her made-up face in a mirror. In *The Miracle Woman*, Florence puts on make-up as her crooked promoter fusses around her, and the make-up seems to burn her skin, bringing home her own corruption, her prostitution of her faith. The make-up on Megan makes her look hard, even whorish, and this won't do; she wipes most of it off, just as Capra stripped Kay Arnold of her false eyelashes. Capra made a fetish of Stanwyck's naturalism and her open, yielding face. This stripped-down face is clearly sexy to him, and a large part of why he loved her on screen and in her dressing room, too, when he risked breaking her fabled concentration to murmur a few words of direction.

He sees in *General Yen* that her coolness can have a puritan quality, a kind of "I am above this" that Stanwyck used for protection, but which Megan Davis has been forced into. Perversely (*The Bitter Tea of General Yen*, like sex itself, is nothing if not perverse), Capra makes Stanwyck give up her coolness from a "sheltered young girl" perspective that stands in total opposition to her own background. If *Forbidden* was personal but poor, *General Yen* and Stanwyck's performance in it have the rarefied impersonality of the highest art.

Megan preaches the Christian doctrine of mercy to the faithless Yen. "We're all of one flesh and blood," she argues, as if she's falling back, with relief, on her old life, on things she's heard and believed to be true without ever testing them. "Really?" Yen asks, sniffing out her hypocrisy and taking advantage of it. "Do you mean that?" He puts his hand on hers; she recoils. "Words," sneers Yen, "nothing but words." At this point in her career, Stanwyck's slightly stilted way of talking, with all the emotions burning underneath the words, is due to her anxiety to speak correctly and not give away her lack of education. Capra uses this anxiety to represent Megan Davis's entrapment in learned attitudes that are not her own; inside, she's ready for rapturous, incorrect, liberating sexual enslavement.

Helplessly, Megan sentimentalizes Mah-Li, who actually is as treacherous as the General thinks she is, and he lets his whole empire go just to prove his point to Megan and disillusion her. She thinks she'll have to sleep with Yen because Mah-Li has betrayed him. When he intimates that she'll pay with her life instead, her shuddering reaction makes Yen cry, "You are afraid of death as you are afraid of life!" They embrace, and over the General's shoulder we see a startling close-up of Megan's eyes, glimmering with some recognition of her own nature so profound that it must extend to Stanwyck, too. Megan's recognition might be the polar opposite of what Stanwyck has discovered about herself, but that's the joy and the puzzle of acting on this elevated a level.

Yen goes to kill himself with the bitter tea of the title, while Megan makes herself up as heavily as Mah-Li did and humbly offers her body and her love to this man she cannot escape or explain. The last scene sees Megan on a boat with Connelly's Jones, who drunkenly talks about Yen while she stares off into the distance, her face caught in some frozen yet lively and yearning expression. Jones says, "You can crowd a lifetime into an hour." He wonders if Yen is now a cherry tree, or the wind that is playing in Megan's hair. The film ends on this tantalizing bit of mood-making, as open and suggestive an ending as anyone could wish for this sublime work about the vagaries of desire, one of the most complex love offerings from a director to an actress in film history.

Seven years passed before Capra and Stanwyck made their fifth and final movie together, *Meet John Doe* (1941). In that time a lot had changed in their careers, particularly for Capra, who had won three best directing Oscars and had become acclaimed for bewildering "films of ideas" like *Mr. Deeds Goes to Town* (1936) and *Mr. Smith Goes to Washington* (1939). *Meet John Doe* was the last of this queasy cycle of Capra message movies, and it's something of a nightmare picture, lost in contradictions, second-guessing, and an overall self-hatred that often bleeds, hair-raisingly, into a pitch-dark misanthropy.

Meet John Doe includes some of the worst scenes Capra ever filmed, especially a long drunk interlude with James Gleason's newspaper editor that exhibits the lowest kind of right-wing, flag-waving barroom self-pity, an unpleasantness that is only matched by the left-wing caricature of Edward Arnold's soft-spoken, absurdly villainous capitalist/fascist (with Capra at this point, you get the worst of all political persuasions). At the center of the movie is Gary Cooper, playing one of his mid-career bumpkins in a self-consciously dopey, "oblivious" manner to put over a character of incredible naiveté.

So where is Stanwyck in all this? She's Ann, a newspaper columnist who gets fired in the first scene and pleads for her job. The newborn stiltedness of the early thirties is gone; by 1941, she's a sleek, stylish dynamo in tailored suits and lusciously long hair. When she goes to her typewriter to write a last-ditch gimmick column signed by John Doe, an unemployed man bent on suicide, Capra frames her demonic-looking eyes over the clattering keys. In the movie's first hour, Ann is an unscrupulous go-getter whose sole purpose in life is to make money for her mother and her two cutesy sisters. We are told that Ann's father was a doctor who was always taking on charity cases, and her mother (Spring Byington) gives away any ready cash to needy people, so Ann's rebellious, selfish drive for lucre makes psychological sense, up to a point. When she delivers a lightning-fast spiel to Gleason on how to hire someone to play her made-up forgotten man, Stanwyck delivers her hard-sell lines in such a concentrated, breathless manner that she turns her "no sir" speech into an aria that merits applause for its technical virtuosity alone.

Ann is a jerk and an opportunist, and Stanwyck limns her unstoppable drive to succeed as funny but also alarming. When she first sees Cooper's highly exploitable face, her own face takes on the look of a wolf that has spotted its dinner; this seems to be a woman without any vulnerability. Stanwyck is playing the director-like heavy role that Sam Hardy played in *The Miracle Woman*, while Cooper is playing the Florence figure, a dupe who starts to believe in his own publicity. Identifying with Ann, Capra also seems to side with John's fellow hobo, Colonel (Walter Brennan), a nihilist (like Yen) who never buys the platitudes Ann puts into his friend's mouth. Yet in the end we're supposed to swallow and celebrate the smarmy, demagogic "love thy neighbor" bromides picked up by Doe's sheep-like, idiot audience. Capra obviously hates this audience, yet he feels forced to endorse it in his sell-out happy ending.

This is quite a complicatedly flawed movie. It's almost impossible to say where it goes wrong, because going wrong is all it does—in as many different directions as possible. To her credit, Stanwyck often looks apprehensive, glancing off-screen every now and then with an "is he actually on the level with this stuff?" expression. Capra gave her her start, and he gave her two and a half major films, but he prostitutes her talent in the last half hour of *Meet John Doe*, where he uses the rawness of her hysteria to paper over the holes in his scenario. It's a shame that they ended up mired in *Meet John Doe* instead of on the heights of *General Yen*, and it's a shame that Capra's talent led him to such a self-destructive place.

There's one suspiciously extended scene in *Meet John Doe* where John tells Ann about a dream he had about her and then goes on and on about how he spanked her. Ann looks tickled, but it's a little more than that, for Stanwyck herself seems tickled, too, so that the scene plays like a kind of private joke between former lovers. "He'd been kicked around," she said of Capra, "maybe not as much, but he understood it." That "maybe not as much," says a lot about their basic honesty, their kinship, and the life-or-death connection that still burns bright in *Ladies of Leisure*, some of *The Miracle Woman*, and supremely in *General Yen*, which shimmers more ambiguously and profoundly every time I see it.

The Rough-and-Tumble Wellman Five

*Night Nurse, So Big!, The Purchase Price, The Great Man's Lady,
Lady of Burlesque*

In the same years she was laying the groundwork for her career with
Frank Capra, Stanwyck made several films with another director, William "Wild Bill" Wellman, an adventurous teller of tall tales so rip-snortingly vigorous and "manly" that in interviews he almost comes across as
a parody of a take-no-prisoners brawler. His reputation as a filmmaker
has always been shaky; he made movies fast and furiously and was not
always well suited to the subjects he took on. Though his filmography
is filled with missteps, it also contains neglected, hardboiled classics like
Wild Boys of the Road (1933) and *Safe in Hell* (1931), an eye-openingly
sordid melodrama about a hooker (Dorothy Mackaill) who gets sacrificed
to male lust and corruption. Most intriguingly, his best-known film is
probably the first official version of *A Star is Born* (1937), a property that
was based on the embattled marriage between Stanwyck and Frank Fay,
a union that Wellman was able to witness firsthand during the filming of
the first three movies he made with her.

Their initial film together, *Night Nurse* (1931), is one of his best, a
brutally concentrated dose of grisly working girl melodrama for Warner
Bros., a studio that brought out Stanwyck's street smart, roll-with-the-
punches style. The film opens with an ambulance bringing in a car crash
victim. Inside a hospital, an expectant father says he hopes he has a
boy, and his wife says she'll do her best. Wellman immediately plunges
us into a world where girls are seen as expendable, which means that
they'll have to work harder for a satisfying life and even play dirty if need
be. Stanwyck's Lora Hart wants more than anything to be a nurse, but
she hasn't been able to finish high school, and so the sourpuss matron in

charge of new nurses turns her down and literally coughs her out of the building.

A doctor (Charles Winninger) bumps into Lora outside, knocking her pocketbook to the sidewalk, and Wellman holds his camera low on Stanwyck's ankles as she impatiently taps her foot. The doctor looks up: Lora's face is sullen, closed-off. When she senses what's necessary, her eyes flicker slightly and she smiles at the doctor, and that's all it takes: She's hired. This is the most restrained vamping imaginable, played as if Lora knows that men are such dopes that she doesn't need to put any real effort into attracting them. Sex is an essential tool for the lowborn working girl of 1931 if she expects to get anywhere, and Stanwyck seems very Zen and stoically dignified about that reality.

There's a real flash of desire in her eyes—or at least a recognition of kinship—when Lora meets Maloney (Joan Blondell), a saucy, big-eyed blond who becomes her roommate. Wellman is forever contriving ways for Maloney and Lora to strip down to their lingerie so that horny interns can leer at them, but this gambit never feels exploitative because these girls can clearly look out for themselves and view the more out-of-control male sex urges with detachment (Stanwyck) or amusement (Blondell). Frightened by a skeleton left in her bed by one of the interns, Lora hops into Maloney's bed to cuddle and they keep each other warm; it's as sweetly and suggestively dyke-alicious a bit as any in Stanwyck's career.

More happens in any ten minutes of *Night Nurse* than happens in two hours of most Warner movies of the forties, and Wellman thrives on the studio's patented, jam-packed scrappiness here, as does Stanwyck. There's room for on-the-fly inspirations, but there is also room for mistakes and carelessness, which occasionally mars even Wellman's best work—as if lingering over something to get it right might tend to dissipate the testosterone-fueled energy he valued so highly. The men are all horrors in *Night Nurse*, either treacherous villains or patsies (either Fay or Stanwyck's second husband, Robert Taylor, in fact), and Lora even seems disillusioned with Maloney by the end of the movie, when her pal proves too cynical. As they take their nurse's oath, Lora's eyes shine with happiness, but Maloney repeats the oath by rote; it's just a job to her, a way station until she can get some rich patient to fall for her. Wellman gives Stanwyck several nice silent moments here that let us know how much Lora values her work.

Stanwyck is at her best when she's sizing up a man, as if she's saying, "Alright, what's your angle?" Her natural skepticism is one of the most likable things about her as a performer at this point. When she warms to Mortie (Ben Lyon), a cheerfully murderous bootlegger, Wellman gives her a few wordless "hmm, OK"-type close-ups to make her attachment believable; he knows she often does her best acting without any dialogue. Wellman deeply respected Stanwyck's toughness as a corollary to his own, but even he must have felt that hers was more truly earned. She had a certain knowingness, along with a capacity to be outraged and make that outrage seem like a point of honor.

In the film's freewheeling, casually scary second half, Lora has to deal with a plot to starve two little girls for inheritance money. When one of the girls says a sister of theirs has died, Lora says, "You mustn't think about her anymore," a moment that Stanwyck makes personal by the gravity with which she says it. You have to forget about the mother who won't be coming home anymore to Classon Avenue, and the sooner the better, yet *Night Nurse* posits that having a mother like the proudly dipsomaniacal Mrs. Ritchey (Charlotte Merriam), who does nothing but drink while her children are being starved in the next room, is sometimes much worse than having no mother at all.

When Lora sees that Mrs. Ritchey doesn't want to think about her children's plight, she blows her top: "Why do poor little children have to be born to women like you?" she shouts, with a ferocity that seems to take in not just these two abused girls, but *all* abused children, including Ruby Stevens. This lost girl has an artistic forum now, and she has to speak out for all of her brothers and sisters, all the kids that never made it out of Brooklyn, and the ones who came out of deadbeat homes either physically or spiritually dead.

Lora tries to drag Mrs. Ritchey out of her stupor, but the other woman falls on the floor and passes out. "You . . . *mother*," Lora sneers, making the slight hesitation mean both, "You? A mother?" and "You motherfucker!" Clark Gable's nasty chauffeur Nick socks Lora on the jaw at one point, and she gets her revenge by punching one of Mrs. Ritchey's libidinous men, delivering a heartening, symbolic blow to all the men who have physically accosted Lora in the film, all the men who grabbed at Ruby in the nightclubs of the twenties—and for all the women on earth who have had to fend off male violence with their wits (it's a moment, too, when I can't help but hope that Stanwyck herself landed more than a few punches that counted on the wife-battering, jealous Fay). The ending of *Night Nurse* is rather strange: By doing the right thing and standing up to Nick, Lora gets booted from her beloved profession and falls in with Mortie, who has had Nick rubbed out. This is a woman who needs to work; she'll find a way to continue nursing somehow, just as she shouldn't have much problem rehabilitating her man.

So Big! (1932), Stanwyck's next film with "Wild Bill," was based on Edna Ferber's popular novel, one of her lengthy "through the years" sagas that Wellman gives a bracingly fast treatment. As a young girl, Stanwyck's character, Selina, is played by Dawn O'Day, who later acted under the name Anne Shirley and played the daughter in *Stella Dallas*. Selina has no mother and a charismatic gambler father. Over a fancy dinner, he tells the girl that no matter what happens in life, good or bad, it's "just so much velvet," whatever that means. The film repeats this bromide twice, once in voiceover as Selina remembers him saying it, and once on a title card halfway through.

Selina is in thrall to her father, and when Stanwyck's grown-up Selina finds out that he's been shot, it's a kind of death for her, too. Approaching his dead body, Stanwyck keeps her face frozen and still. She draws back a coat covering the body to look at his face, makes a small movement forward with her hand, as if to comfort him, then withdraws it when she realizes that there can be no more contact between them: the enormity of death and separation, all in one precise physical movement, forward and back.

A girlhood friend secures Selina a job teaching boys on a farm run by Alan Hale, who will also play an important role in *Stella Dallas*. Selina says she thinks the cabbages on the farm are beautiful, and Hale laughs at her for putting on such airs. For this role, Stanwyck labored mightily to keep Brooklyn out of her voice, even when some of her "er's" are just dying to become "ah's," a process that results in some line readings that sound like she's performing an elocution lesson. But such technical problems don't really stop her from creating a woman who couldn't be more different than Lora Hart, who's so close to the real Stanwyck.

In her early scenes, Selina is an innocent, untouched, immaculate sort of person, but when she gets married to a farmer, she seems to age rapidly. Wellman gets this aging across in just a few quick shots of her doing back-breaking work that seems to destroy her from the outside in. In one fleeting instance, Stanwyck looks up from scrubbing a floor with a pitiful, "Why?" expression on her face, another striking plea for justice.

Wellman's shorthand method in *So Big!* is far more powerful than a more studied, leisurely approach would have been. He makes us think about what's happened between scenes, while making each episode land with a jab or an outright punch. In Stanwyck, he has an actress who can convey the fact that Selina is tired of her husband with just one split-second look (the director joins in his leading character's contempt by dispatching this husband with a shock cut, lasting only a few seconds, of a piece of black fabric on a door). When Selina is really old, Stanwyck lets her hair go wispy and grey, and she squints into the light like some old people do (later, she would age to more than one hundred for Wellman in *The Great Man's Lady* [1942]). The sense of time passing, one of the cardinal virtues of the novel, is here replicated by speed, which takes the place of Ferber's literary elaboration.

In the last half hour, Bette Davis enters the movie and gives it an electric jolt, but her energy is all over the place. Both she and Stanwyck were still a little green in 1932, though Stanwyck is far more accomplished at this point and would always be more focused than the flashier Davis. When Selina is being manipulative to get her son back on the right track in the final scenes, Stanwyck doesn't play the manipulation at all; she's too busy, unfortunately, being less of a person and more of an idealized heroine. And there's a big, unintended laugh: Selina is always saying, "How big is my little son, how big is my boy?" and her small son stretches his arms wide and answers, "So big!" When he's a man, Selina asks this question, and her son beams, "So big!" while measuring out the size of the average erect male penis with his hands (you can't tell me Wellman didn't stifle a laugh behind the camera).

The ending of *So Big!* is inconclusive. We're told in dialogue how beautiful and fulfilling Selina's life has been, but what we've mainly seen, and sensed in between vignettes, is that this is a story about ceaseless physical work breaking a woman's spirit. In the last scene, Selina tearfully shrugs and says that she doesn't care about never really seeing the places she wanted to see when she was a girl. But Stanwyck puts a tiny oomph of hurt in her eyes as she says it, and it's details like that that always make her worth watching as closely as possible.

For their follow-up, Warner Bros. found Wellman and Stanwyck another "back to the land" script, *The Purchase Price* (1932). It begins well, in a naughty nightclub, where Stanwyck's torch singer, Joan, decked out in a dress that sits lazily around her shoulders and seems about to fall off, haltingly croons a song called "Take Me Away." Stanwyck could just barely carry a tune, and she looks like she's about to crack up; it's not clear if she's embarrassed to be singing, or if her character is just amused by the song. Joan saunters over to a ringside table where she easily seduces a chump male. Back in her dressing room, she takes off her make-up with cold cream (Stanwyck made a career out of putting on make-up and wiping it off before a mirror) and goes into a well-written speech about how she's been on Broadway since she was fifteen, just like Ruby Stevens had been. "I've heard all the questions and I know all the answers," she says, "and I've kept myself *fairly* respectable through it all." I love the way she says "fairly," as if she's gained enough distance to be good-humored about all those men and their messy advances.

In one early scene, Stanwyck trips slightly when walking through a hotel lobby door, but she keeps on going in order to sustain the Wellman speed of this period. (After a Turner Classic Movies showing of *The Purchase Price*, Wellman's son explained that his dad liked to shoot only one or two takes at most and didn't do a lot of coverage, so that his films were "cut in the camera," and couldn't be tampered with in the editing room). Stanwyck has some amusing moments here, especially when she waves away her married lover (Lyle Talbot) so that the gesture reads as, "Bye . . . bye . . . screw you!" And when her maid Emily (Leila Bennett) talks about getting a husband and confides she'd like to "try the goods" before she buys them, Stanwyck says, "Emily!" in a very funny, mock-shocked manner. She's lighter here in these opening scenes, playing a woman who seems well adjusted.

When Joan becomes a mail-order bride to a farmer (George Brent) in order to get out of town, however, the film sputters and dies, and Joan herself starts to take on a masochistic tinge. Brent plays this man as a bumptious moron, so that when he goes after Joan on their wedding night and she slaps him away, we can't blame her. Then, for the rest of the film, Joan tries to win him back, for reasons that remain mysterious. Her lover shows up on the farm toward the end, and he explains her behavior by calling Joan "a natural mud lark" (the title of Arthur Stringer's original story was *The Mud Lark*), and that explanation will have to do. Joan chasing after this dumb lug farmer for so many reels makes about as much sense as Stanwyck staying loyal to Frank Fay. These things happen in life, alas; they shouldn't have to happen on screen, too. For the final scenes, set during a fire, Stanwyck did her own stunts and got her legs burned as a result. She wore her burns and falls and physical blows on set like medals of her professionalism.

Nine years later, Stanwyck reunited with Wellman for another through-the-years saga, *The Great Man's Lady*, which is at least as episodic as *So Big!*, but far less effective. The film was contrived by Adela Rogers St. John and Seena Owen from a Vina Delmar story, though the screenplay is credited to a man, W.L. River. The basic material is magazine-like, and Wellman does nothing to flesh out the various crises in the life of Stanwyck's "woman behind the man." The film opens with an obnoxious title card about all these little women the world over and how they've helped their men. And then Wellman indulges himself with a crane shot up from a rocking chair, up, up, up over a town until we dissolve to a newspaper office, where an editor bemoans the little old lady of the title, centenarian Hannah Sempler (Stanwyck), who might or might not have been married to the man who founded the town, Ethan Hoyt (Joel McCrea). There's a wipe to a room where a reporter sits surrounded by female wax dummies, suggesting discarded wives, mistresses, daughters, and other women associated with all the world's so-called great men.

The press gathers around for the unveiling of a statue of Hoyt, and a pretty young Hoyt biographer (Katharine Stevens) beams as the figure is revealed; Wellman then cuts to another reporter yawning. The press all convenes on Hannah's house to ask questions, and Stanwyck makes her first entrance in long shot, heavily made-up. "To what do I owe this peculiar honor, may I ask?" she says, making a nice "sh" sound on the word "ask"—as if Hannah were wearing dentures. So far, so good, but that first line of Hannah's is an initial indication that there are going to be problems here: creaky lines, foggy motivations. This type of advanced old age is probably beyond the reach of any actor, even one as resourceful as Stanwyck. Her lines sound dubbed in later, and she has to deal with Stevens's inane cheerfulness in all their scenes together (and the fact that Stevens's name is so close to that of Ruby's dead mother).

"The year was 1848," reminisces Hannah, standing by a window in her bedroom, and Wellman dissolves to a young Hannah in the exact same position by the window. Stanwyck's youthful enthusiasm as this sheltered, girlish version of Hannah is slightly overdone. She giggles at one point, an odd sight—but at least she's willing to try new things out, even if they fail. Back at the window, looking down at her beau Ethan, Hannah asks, "Are you mad?" and he replies, "Stark, staring mad!" There's really nothing any actor can do with lines like that, so Wellman just speeds the pair along into an elopement behind some covered wagons on an obvious soundstage prairie. There's almost no location shooting here, which hurts the film. Wellman takes advantage of the studio setting just once. Sitting in front of a landscape, Hannah and Ethan talk about the city he wants to build, and it magically appears behind them, a charming, F.W. Murnau-like effect.

Wellman's movies are filled with pictorial grace notes, but sometimes these inventions seem extraneous to the film itself. When he stages a confrontation between Ethan, Hannah, and Steely (Brian Donlevy), an inexplicable third romantic wheel, he has the actors play it all in shadowed silhouettes; this just seems like a way of keeping his interest up visually because he's not involved in the story. When Hannah loses her two babies in a flood, Wellman could be expected to give Stanwyck a proper moment to grieve, but as she drags herself out of a river, he keeps her in long shot, and Victor Young's gloppy score kills any genuine emotion we might feel for this woman.

If Wellman is mainly indifferent, Stanwyck is not (she believed in this movie and was disappointed when it wasn't a success). Steely finds Hannah again when she's middle-aged, with white streaks in her hair, stiff-backed in a chair. "I thought you were dead," he says. "I am," she replies, so simply that she wakes the film out of its stupor. Her grief is so intensely centered in this scene that it stands as a prime example of the hypnotic way Stanwyck could draw us into her moods on screen. When Hannah becomes the queen of the roulette table (this story leaves few clichés untried), Stanwyck wears a doozy of a black Edith Head dress with what look like silver seahorses studded all over it (Head said in her memoir they were birds). We return to Hannah as a centenarian, and Stanwyck's performance has deteriorated into little old lady "har-rumphs" and fussy business. Although she's a far more accomplished actress here, her portrayal of age in *So Big!* is superior.

From this prestige production, the team then unexpectedly moved to the lower depths of show business for their last film together, *Lady of Burlesque* (1943). By this point, Stanwyck was one of the highest paid women in movies and an established, distinguished player, so it feels more than a little perverse to have her play a striptease artiste wrapped up in a murder mystery plot courtesy of real-life stripper Gypsy Rose Lee, who wrote the source novel, *The G-String Murders*. Wellman shows us the outside of The Old Opera House, which once presented famous singers but is now exhibiting "50—Fifty—50 Beautiful Girls" and promising "Laffs" by cut-rate comics. "Girls, that's what the public wants," says a manager outside, and inside Wellman plunges us into a world of rump-shaking tawdriness and overall 1940s tackiness (one girl looks bored with her dance routine, then glances at an energetic chorine next to her and swiftly remembers to plaster a fake smile on her face). As a finish, the burlesque girls present their rear ends to the camera, and we cut to an audience of dirty old men enjoying the rock-bottom program.

A crooner comes on, and the girls parade a bit before Stanwyck's Dixie Daisy makes her entrance for her solo number. A lone violin saws away in the pit. Cut to Dixie's bored, "something stinks in here" face, as she cleans her teeth with her tongue. "Beautiful, junior," she snaps, "but it's not fuh me." Then she starts her song, an inspired little ditty called "Take It Off The E-String, Play It On The G-String" (apparently, most of the public at this time didn't know what a G-string was, which is why they changed Gypsy's forthright original title).

"If this gives you a thrill," Dixie sings, huskily, "it's happening much against my will," as succinct a line about Stanwyck's relation to her male audience as we're likely to get. When Dixie warns she sometimes starts "breakin' in bumps," the camera cuts away from her gyrations and stays on the orchestra leader's inflamed reaction. But such censor-pleasing tactics are soon dropped: Stanwyck shakes her upper body so that her breasts jiggle in her scanty Edith Head outfit, and Dixie stops her song for a very funny spoken plea: "For listen, broth-uh, I've got a moth-uh, old and grey . . . I support her this way!" she shouts. "Just by shakin' this way . . . four shows a day!"

Dixie grabs the stage curtain and starts wielding it back and forth like a sword while the music sizzles and heats up to a horn blast, "duh duh duh duh duh," followed by two dirty drum beats. During these beats, the camera moves in for a close-up on Dixie's face as she twice mimes a classic stripper bump. It's a tantalizing shot because, for a few moments, Stanwyck communes with herself and takes a kind of autoerotic pleasure in her own sexuality, just for itself, not for the men in the film audience or the audience watching this movie. It's a glimpse of a kind of sexuality that you rarely see in films. Rita Hayworth displays this private sort of self-enjoyment for a few scalding moments when a man tries to undo her dress at the end of her "Put the Blame on Mame" number in *Gilda* (1946), but with her it's taunting, pissed-off. Strangely enough, in this "bump bump" Stanwyck close-up, we don't feel any anger or resentment coming from her, as we would have had she played this role in say, 1933, instead of 1943. Instead, we see a mature, fully-blossomed woman and performer casting a look back to where she came from, contrasting it with what she is now, and enjoying the contrast, because the past is truly past.

"G-String" is a tasty, memorable number, but the rest of the film doesn't live up to it. The other strippers are a rather dreary, mean lot, and Wellman is totally uninterested in the murder plot, so that the interrogation scenes in the girls' dressing room seem interminable. The film is staged unimaginatively, and there are none of Wellman's usual visual flourishes (though it can be hard to judge this aspect because *Lady of Burlesque* has been floating around in spliced public domain prints for years). In the middle of the low-concept narrative, Stanwyck's Dixie is involved in another stage performance, and it's amazing. She does a full-throttle jitterbug—complete with splits—a Russian dance, and then an expert cartwheel, so that we're left wondering if there's *anything* Stanwyck can't do. As she performs all these unlikely things, there's a look of purely childlike happiness on her face. Wellman understood Stanwyck as a person and as a performer in a more direct way than Capra did, and if this superior insight made for less dreamy idealizing, it also made for a tough-minded consolidation of what she stood for.

Pre-Code Sex

Illicit, Ten Cents a Dance, Shopworn,
Ladies They Talk About, Baby Face

*T*here's been a lot written about movies made before the censorious Production Code cracked down on Hollywood in 1934—probably too much, so that the talkies made from 1930–34 are now endlessly packaged at New York's Film Forum repertory theater and on DVD as "dirty" old movies, quaint novelties that hint about the more relaxed sexual mores of the time, a relaxation that really began in the twenties, with the first flappers, women like Colleen Moore and Clara Bow. In her early years on screen, Stanwyck found herself in several of these so-called pre-Code items, one of which, *Baby Face*, is practically synonymous with this whole quasi-genre.

Right after she filmed *Ladies of Leisure* for Columbia, Stanwyck made *Illicit* (1931) for Warner Bros., testing the waters for the kind of independent hopscotch between studios that let her have more control over her career. Ann, the girl she plays in *Illicit* (which is based on another perilously outspoken play co-written by Robert Riskin), is the independent type. In the first scene, we see her relaxing in a loose robe with her hair down and picking up a love song from rich boy Dick (James Rennie). Ann is in the kitchen preparing what is clearly a post-coital meal; it's nighttime, but she's whipping up some breakfast. Stanwyck works up a nice natural chemistry with Rennie, and then he drops the other shoe: "We really ought to be married," he says, a cue for the 1931 audience to gasp happily. They're living in sin, though they keep separate apartments.

Ann is afraid of marriage. She briefly describes how divorce ruined her mother's life, but this explanation feels like just a sketchy cover, a "reason" that doesn't begin to impinge on this girl's highly sensible ideas about keeping a romance alive. Sprawled on a couch, she playfully runs down her list of lovers for Dick (a technique that Stanwyck will perfect in *The Lady Eve* [1941]), and keeps him alert with some trash talk. A discussion about early morning habits leads Ann to conclude that "we're a riot in our underwear!" and when Dick wanders into a conventional complaint about having to pussyfoot around, Ann takes the bait and cries, "Don't say you don't like the pussyfooting—I love it!" Stanwyck is fresh and open here, and she makes this girl's modern ideas about freedom in love seem right-on, even when the script keeps trying to nudge us about the supposed immaturity of Ann's theories.

When Ann marries Dick, they find out fairly quickly that she was right; they get bored with one another. In one radical scene, Ann deplores her own jealousy after seeing Dick squiring an old flame. She wants to be his playmate again, not a petty spouse. Why shouldn't they see other people, as long as their primary interest is in each other? "I'm not through playing yet," she says, "I don't want to get through." Dick suggests they try to have a child, but Ann immediately vetoes this desperate measure. If only Stanwyck herself had been so pragmatic before deciding to adopt a boy, Dion, in 1932, to try to save her marriage to Fay.

The theme of *Illicit* is unusual, but its pacing is meandering and amorphous. It concludes with a stagy telephone scene where Ann realizes, momentarily at least, that she really wants what everybody supposedly wants, the security of marriage. We've seen enough of her to know, however, that she'll be out playing around again in a few months, maybe on the sly. In 1933, Warner Bros. threw Bette Davis back into this property in *Ex-Lady*, a far more interesting film because Davis plays the role challengingly, like a firebrand. Stanwyck is too tentative and vulnerable in her version to really make a big noise about her bohemian convictions.

Movies from 1931 generally don't have theme songs, but *Ten Cents a Dance* claims that it's "based on the popular song by Lorenz Hart and Richard Rodgers," so we get Ruth Etting's soft, torchy version of the tune under the credits. In our first glimpse of Stanwyck, playing a dime-a-dance drudge named Barbara, she's leaning against a railing, waiting for another customer and pensively staring off into space. "What's a guy got to do to dance with one of you gals?" asks a sailor. "All you need is a ticket and some courage," Barbara snaps—*not* good-humoredly, as Joan Blondell would have done, but in a touchy, "fuck you" manner. She chews her gum as the gob steps on her feet, and you can tell that her feet hurt (if you had asked Stanwyck about dance girl feet in old age, she might have said, "They hurt. They still do," à la her reaction to her back injury on *Forbidden*).

The dancehall matron chastises Barbara for not putting more "rhythm" into her dancing, and she clearly means that this girl should give the guys more of a chance to cop a feel. "I'm here because my brains are in my feet," Barbara says bitterly to her persistent suitor, Bradley (Ricardo Cortez). When the band starts up again, she can't handle it, claiming that the music "follows me home and pounds into my head like a hammer." (Anyone who has had to work at a job where the same music is played over and over again will know exactly how frustrated and even murderous this girl feels about her situation.) Yet when she sits with her boyfriend Eddie (Monroe Owsley) and listens to a park band play "Liebestod," she says she feels transported, just as Kay Arnold did when she fell in love with opera music (the screenwriter on this is Jo Swerling, who did *Ladies of Leisure*, so he can provide Stanwyck with some star continuity).

What small momentum the film has is soon dissipated in long scenes where the director, dreaded ham thespian Lionel Barrymore, seems to have fallen asleep (and indeed, Cortez said Barrymore did in fact fall asleep in his chair during many of the takes). The domestic sections where the now-married Barbara persists in seeing the bright side of everything while Eddie does nothing but complain are painful to sit through. Again, Stanwyck is masochistically loyal to a jerk reminiscent of Frank Fay. On set, Stanwyck took a fall: "Backing away from Monroe Owsley, in my desire to be vehement—overacting, I think people would call it—I fell down the stairs," she said, always ready with the self-deprecating wisecrack.

There are Stanwyck moments here worth searching out, especially one when she has a speech about how all the men from the dancehall seem to her like one large faceless man. As she talks this out, Stanwyck pulls into herself in a very Method fashion, as if she's recalling some specific fragments of her own experience to augment and reinforce what her character is saying. When Barbara waits to ask Bradley for some money, Stanwyck is artfully arranged on a sofa so that her shapely legs are highlighted, but when the camera cuts to a close-up, her face is heavy with sleep, her mouth swollen yet tight, like a miserable little girl having a bad dream (did Stanwyck actually drift off to sleep for this shot?). Awake and asking for the money she needs to save her wastrel husband, Stanwyck flirts with the old-fashioned technique of "looking up in despair," which suggests that Barrymore might have woken up momentarily and given her a piece of bad direction. But she doesn't succumb; some bullshit detector inside of her won't let her fall into anything really false, emotionally or physically.

Shopworn (1932) has a poor reputation, and Stanwyck herself disliked the script, the director, and her leading man, Regis Toomey, who is always hovering close to ineptitude. But the film has dialogue by Swerling and Riskin and cinematography by Joseph Walker, and though it's a standard story, at least it's a full-blooded, unashamed melodrama. A huge explosion at a construction camp leaves Stanwyck's Kitty fatherless, but not before Pop gives her some advice about being tough, like some fantasy of Byron Stevens talking to his daughter Ruby. When the old man dies, Stanwyck makes us feel the shock of his death simply by keeping her face still while letting emotion gently flood into her eyes.

Kitty goes to wait on table for her Aunt Dot (ZaSu Pitts). Dealing with rowdy college boys, she punches the "No Sale" sign on her cash register and socks them a knockout sarcastic look. "You may be hot, but the coffee's cold," says medical student David (Toomey), and his indifference to her charms and his obvious education intrigue Kitty. Smiling happily in his car later on, she tells him, "I could cuss when I was six and say 'no' when I was fourteen," as if her own education was just a grand joke of some kind (if Joan Crawford had said that line in 1932, it would have dripped with thick-voiced self-pity). Kitty wants to educate herself for David, and Walker frames a few beautiful close-ups of Stanwyck as she tries to impress her beau with words from the dictionary. Her father is dead, she tells him, and she doesn't remember her mother. "You're my family now," she says, as Walker's lighting casts a seraphic glow on her profile.

David's lunatic mother (Clara Blandick, the racist missionary from *Bitter Tea*) simply won't have her pampered son consorting with any waitress. She talks of having Kitty committed to an institution, but she has a flunky do her dirty work for her. Kitty is expecting to go off and marry David, and as she prepares for this trip, Stanwyck does the kind of "I'm running all over the room!" joy routine that Garbo does in *Grand Hotel* (1932), but Stanwyck's version is much more down-to-earth and believable, less self-conscious. When the flunky threatens her with reform school and then offers her five thousand bucks to get out of town, Stanwyck takes this information in gradually, then works herself up into as fine and precise an explosion of anger as she would ever give us on screen. "If that's being decent, I'm glad I'm common!" she shrieks, a proletarian thunderbolt, priming the 1930s audience to shout, "You tell 'em, Barbara!"

Kitty gets ninety days, as a pious choir sings outside the judge's window. Forced to scrub floors continuously, she starts to feel sick. When her head hits a pillar, Stanwyck lets her forehead *bounce* all the way down it out of frame, a vivid physical choice to show this girl's "let it all go" despair. Laid up in a hospital bed, Kitty wears a face emptied out by total depression, but when she's released, she gets a job in the chorus and is soon a headliner (this plot development, amusingly, takes about thirty seconds of screen time, if that). Six years have passed in a flash, and now Kitty wants revenge on David, but Stanwyck can't play the grand, icy contempt written into their reunion scene (by the forties, this kind of thing would become almost second nature to her on-screen persona).

Whenever the going gets tough, Kitty prods her chin up with her fist, remembering her father's dying words, and Stanwyck makes a stirring leitmotif out of this simple piece of business. Riskin and Swerling amuse themselves occasionally; there's an extended bit where the place settings at a swank dinner seem to gossip with each other as Walker's camera moves around them. *Shopworn* shows what two fine writers, one fine cameraman, and one great actress can accomplish even with a formula story, but nobody can do anything with the climax, where Blandick's villainous Mother brandishes a gun at Kitty and then accepts her basic fineness just a scene later; it plays like a crazy-quilt version of the rich mother/poor girl confrontation in *Ladies of Leisure*.

There are ladies of leisure, and then there are *Ladies They Talk About* (1933), which is a crackerjack women's prison movie that has all the punchy, vital virtues of a Warner Bros. film of this era. Stanwyck's delicate-looking face fills the screen in the first shot; she's telephoning the police to let them know that "there's a man running around with a butcher knife!" When she hangs up, her distressed mask drops, her mouth settles into a "whatever" smirk, and she takes a drag on a cigarette.

In the next shot, the camera pulls back, and we see that she's swathed in furs and has blond hair. Whenever Stanwyck has blond hair in a movie—from *Baby Face* to *Double Indemnity* (1944) to *The Violent Men* (1955) get out of the way, buster, there's going to be a lot of trouble. Police go to check on her story, so Stany and her criminal associates go to rob a closed bank. Outside the door, she once again puts on a "distressed" mask, and amplifies it by using her British *a* : "I cahn't wait," she claims, and we see the bank guard react to her beauty before he lets her in. Crucially, this is the first movie where Stanwyck's acting ability (and unusually wide range) is used as a weapon for duplicity, with her sex appeal serving as the unbeatable cherry on the sundae.

The gang gets away with the loot, but Stanwyck is caught by a copper who remembers her. This woman has gone by many names, apparently, but now she's known as Nan Taylor. In the DA's office, Nan puts the moves on David Slade (Preston Foster), an evangelical reformer who knew her in her youth. She was the daughter of a deacon, and he remembers that she was sweet: "Too much deaconing took all the sweetness out of me," she says, in a weary, "what else is new?" voice. She does a sob act for him (it's as if Stanwyck is mocking her early "stilted sincere" acting), and Slade falls for it. He's about to get her released when she makes the mistake of leveling with him about the bank job. Stung by her honesty, he makes sure she gets two to five years in San Quentin. Stanwyck looks at him with her full bitterness and self-loathing when she realizes what's happened, like she's thinking, "Tell the truth in this world and you get screwed," something Nan probably found out originally with all that "deaconing" in her youth.

"New fish!" cry the inmates in the women's penitentiary as Nan makes her way through the mess hall, which is filled with all sorts of unsavory characters. Stanwyck looks vulnerable on her first entrance into the prison, an interesting choice. Her arms hang limply by her waist, and her face signals the fact that she hasn't got a hard enough mask together yet for such a snake pit environment. Nan befriends Linda (Lillian Roth, the alcoholic singer that Susan Hayward played in *I'll Cry Tomorrow* [1955]), a chummy gal who gives her the information she needs to survive. "Watch out for her, she likes to wrestle," Linda says, and we see a full-on butch lesbian of the Gertrude Stein school. Cut back to worldly Nan, who sighs, "Hmm," as if she can't believe she still has so much to learn about life.

In spite of—or maybe because of—this butch character, who we see at one point exercising in her cell with a lipstick lesbian girlfriend, Stanwyck takes pains to hold herself apart from the girl-on-girl camaraderie, though her eyes light up with enjoyment when she gets to fight with an enemy, Susie (Dorothy Burgess), a fanatic with a yen for Slade. After being told of this girl's troublemaking, Nan swaggers over to Susie, looking tougher than John Wayne. When Susie punches at her, Nan lets her have it with her fist (later, Nan will whisper something obscene in Susie's ear and shake her small but experienced fist in her face). Scenes like this let us know that there can be a convincing sadistic streak in Stanwyck, especially when she's battling other women, though it never got as thorough a workout on-screen as her tendency towards masochism with men.

Nan is loyal to her crew of crooks, assisting in their attempted jail-break, but the escape is botched and they get shot, which leads her to be-lieve that Slade ratted her out. Stanwyck's eyes glow with malevolence when she shouts, "I'll get even with that dirty yellow stool pigeon if it takes the rest of my life!" Out of prison, wearing a veil that looks like it was peppered with gunshot, Nan has some amused byplay with the cop who first nabbed her, telling him that he's got his racket and she's got hers. We can believe the strength of character that Stanwyck sets up for this girl; to lose her "good humor," even if it has to be put on like a heavy coat, would be to give in to total defeat, which Stanwyck usually can't afford to do in her movies.

When she enters a tabernacle and looks at Slade, Nan's face is malign, but it gets more complicated than that: Stanwyck shades this expression until it looks like a kind of disappointed malignity, a weird mixing of ingredients that makes us feel Nan as a three-dimensional, finally un-knowable person, even in the confines of a movie that can only claim to be a first-class, churn-them-out entertainment. Stanwyck dominates the whole film, and it's a classic case of the star as auteur (this picture had two credited directors and a lot of writers).

The legend of *Baby Face* grows stronger and stranger every year. An even franker preview cut of this uncommonly blunt movie was recently discovered, and the new scenes it reveals only deepen the film's nasty, lingering stench. Stanwyck, of course, never really had a "baby face," even when she was an actual baby, but that's part of the film's anni-hilating cynicism. The various men who use and are then used by her Lily Powers (that name!) never take the time to really look at her be-yond her surface trappings of blond hair, warrior legs, and tip-top figure (Stanwyck often holds her hands on her hips in this movie to emphasize her sleek, lithe body). "You don't have to be beautiful," Stanwyck later claimed, referencing her own sex appeal. Then she joked, "I have the face that sank a thousand ships."

We first see Lily mired in the ugliness of industrial Pittsburgh. She stands up to her father and defends her close black friend, Chico (The-resa Harris), then makes her way through the men in the front of her father's speakeasy, serving beer and swatting away their passes—and suf-fering through an insistent player piano (that hammer-like working girl music again, repeated torturously as in *Ten Cents a Dance*). This is the film that challenges Stanwyck most directly with the worst aspects of her past, and it functions as her platform, another "star as auteur" entry to go with *Ladies They Talk About*. (According to producer Darryl Zanuck,

Stanwyck actually provided some input on this script, especially its early scenes.)

Lily stares out the speakeasy window for a second at the belching coal stacks and tries to brush the coal off her few pitiful flowers. This is the rare Stanwyck woman who feels a soggy sort of self-pity. Her frowning glumness is pierced by her friend Cragg (Alphonse Ethier), a foreigner who tirelessly recommends Nietzsche to her as a kind of philosophical blueprint for escape (an unusual movie plot point, to say the least). Near closing time, Lily sits in the sort of contemplative silence that says "hands off," but a point-of-view shot from a corrupt politician lets us know that the unthinking lust of men refuses to read signals like this.

When the politico puts his hand on her knee, she casually spills hot coffee on him, then sneers, "Oh, excuse me, my hand shakes so when I'm around you," using the kind of tone that gets across her contempt for (and jealousy of) upper-class women who might actually be that nervous. Ever since she was fourteen, Lily has been mauled by men and outright pimped by her father, and at last she's had enough. She tells off the old man, and Stanwyck's fury is all over the place here, for this is a blighted, twisted girl, lost in the worst kind of anger, self-hatred, and what looks like a nearly clinical depression. Lily has been so degraded that she seems almost beyond help, making this an anomalous Stanwyck character: a real lost soul.

A fire takes care of the father and his dirty business, and Lily goes to Cragg, who keeps filling her head with more Nietzsche, telling her that she must be a master, not a slave. Cragg corrupts her with the philosopher's lowest ideas: "All life, no matter how we idealize it, is nothing more nor less than exploitation." To my mind, this is the kind of thought that needs to be firmly rejected, but at least it gets Lily on a train to New York, even if she has to service a railroad man to ride free in a boxcar (this is one of the recently recovered scenes from the preview version, and it enhances the film's sordidness).

In Manhattan with Chico in tow, with no money for food, Lily tells her friend to master her hunger. She's been reading Nietzsche's *Will to Power* and learning its mind-over-matter lessons. When she vamps her first man, a cop on the street, Lily finally uses as a weapon the "I'm sexually available" tag that she was stuck with in her youth. Putting the moves on a chubby Southern boy in personnel at the Gotham Trust Company, where she wants employment (not easy to come by in Depression-era 1933), Lily even seems to get a kick out of her blatant maneuvering. If we feel good for her in such moments, however, it's only a base kind of triumph.

In an ingenious bit, the camera moves up the floors of the Gotham Trust building as Lily rises there man by man, from filing to mortgages, where she sets her blond hair in a permanent wave and starts dressing in suffocating clothes edged in ruffles. She uses and throws away a young John Wayne (his later fame creates a nice "take that, patriarchy" frisson), struggles to say "isn't" instead of "ain't" and becomes an expert at doling out sob stories to likely men whenever she needs to move on to another, higher floor. Lily becomes a kind of actress, just as Ruby Stevens did, but her contempt for life makes her an obvious sort of actress who always puts quotation marks around her tales of woe, as if she knows she doesn't need to expend much effort to be convincing (in direct opposition to Stanwyck the actress, of course, an irony that generates creative tension in all of these scenes).

There are a few laughs scattered around in Lily's manipulative schemes, but *Baby Face* has a reputation for "fun" that isn't borne out by the film itself; it's about as fun as *Heart of Darkness*. Lily is funny when cutesily pulling on the bank vice president's curly hair and calling him "Fuzzy Wuzzy," but there's a telling lapse into bitterness when he asks her if anyone in her family played the piano. "Anybody that had a nickel," she says, her weighted delivery making it seem as if she's *shoving* her distaste at her john—and at us. Cragg continues to send her more Nietzsche. We see her alone on Christmas, glancing at a page that reads, "Crush all sentiment." Looking at scenes like this in *Baby Face*, I'm reminded of Stanwyck's great enthusiasm for Ayn Rand's *The Fountainhead*, and of her fervent, thwarted desire to play Rand's sadomasochistic heroine, Dominique Francon. This is the dark side of Stanwyck, the right-winger who struggled to teach heartless self-reliance to her adopted son Dion.

When a collision of two of her men results in murder and suicide, Lily's old, depressive face breaks through her fancy mistress make-up mask. In the conventional but nearly convincing final third, Lily falls in with her last man, Trenholm (George Brent), a playboy who cock-blocks her attempt to blackmail the Gotham Trust. She sees that he's not a fool like all the other men she's known, and so she makes a calculated play for him. He falls like all the rest, and she makes her new ambition known: "I'd like to have a Mrs. on my tombstone," she says dreamily, as morbid a proposal as any in movie history.

Staring at five hundred thousand dollars worth of loot, Stanwyck puts on her most abstracted mask as Lily says, "Someday, I'll have the other half that goes with it," as if this pursuit of money were a kind of religion for her character. The film hits a patch of bad, overly explanatory writing when Lily is made to detail how she's not like other women (we've seen that already). But Stanwyck saves the film with one reaction shot. Following a montage of all the men she's used, Lily looks up and away, and there's some kind of recognition in her face: BAM! Something has happened to her, but we don't know what exactly, so that even the putative happy ending feels consistent with the mysterious girl that we've been watching. *Baby Face* contains some of Stanwyck's most penetrating, disturbing work, and there are moments in it that stand as unreachable heights—or depths—in her art of leveling with us.

Drama Grab Bag, 1930s

Ever in My Heart, Gambling Lady, A Lost Lady, The Secret Bride,
The Woman in Red, Red Salute, A Message to Garcia, Banjo on My
Knee, Internes Can't Take Money, Always Goodbye

*A*s she worked out her contract at Warner Bros. and then acted at
20th Century Fox, Stanwyck found herself in some bread-and-butter
program pictures and a few bizarre ventures into political intrigue. *Ever
in My Heart* (1933) is a total downer, a bold, somewhat crude but forceful
look at bigotry during wartime. The movie is barely known, though it
gets eulogized in Ella Smith's Stanwyck book. It suffers from uninspired
direction by Archie Mayo and a short running time that doesn't allow
the various outrages of the plot to gather momentum. But in a way these
shortcomings add to the film's sense of unfairness, of life being against us
no matter what we do or how stoic we are.

Ever in My Heart starts in 1909, in America. Stanwyck is Mary, a well-
brought-up young girl and "daughter of the American Revolution." The
first scenes are played for comedy, as Mary deals with her immature
brother (a typecast Frank Albertson) and tries to get things ready for
her childhood sweetheart (Ralph Bellamy). The fast pace slows, quite
effectively, when she catches her first glimpse of Hugo (Otto Kruger), a
German schoolteacher. They fall in love with each other at first sight.

Some soft-focus cinematography, courtesy of Leon Shamroy, ideal-
izes Stanwyck in her period garb, as she listens attentively to her new
sweetheart sing a familiar German lullaby, which he translates as: "You
are ever in my heart, you are ever in my thoughts. You make me many
sorrows. You will never know how much I love you." Ladies of her family gossip about his lightning-fast courtship, and in school, Hugo puts
together two foreign chemicals that "don't mix," but the cross-cultural

couple gets married and she gets pregnant. Before her child is born, Mary goes with Hugo to pick out a dog as a pet, and she zeroes in on a German puppy that looks lonely, putting her love and faith in a literal underdog.

Hugo becomes an American citizen, and at a party afterwards his friends and family play "Dixie," the "Marseillaise," "Britannia," and "Yankee Doodle Dandy," pledging themselves to the idea of America as one large melting pot. Immediately, we cut to a newspaper telling us that Germany has invaded Belgium, and then we see a paper that says the Germans have sunk the *Lusitania*. Mary and Hugo suffer social rejection when no one shows up at a party she's giving. Tired of small talk, Mary finally explodes: "Talk about it! Talk about the *Lusitania*!" Stanwyck pushes here because she's obviously been rushed and doesn't have enough time to prepare for this outburst (she's "gone dry," which she saw as "a physical thing," and she would never have the kind of technique that would allow her to fake an outburst as extreme as this). But she does have two extraordinary moments later on in this film.

Her son is deathly ill, and some stifling hot weather isn't helping matters. Hugo goes in to sing to the boy while Mary lies down. The camera stays on her face as she listens and tries to rest, but then Hugo's singing abruptly stops. In a matter of seconds, she knows her son has died. Mary gets up and looks into the boy's room. She is a wretched, skinny, stark figure with stringy hair hanging down on both sides of her head. "Oh my . . ." she says, as if she's about to say, "Oh my God," but then chokes on the word "my" and puts her hands over her face. This is the first time Stanwyck gives us something of the *panic* of grief, of disbelief—her words land like a stab in the stomach, sharp and aggravated. Just when we think it can't get any worse for this couple, neighborhood kids attack their dog because it's a German dog. At this point, it's hard not to wonder who gave the go-ahead to such an upsetting, downbeat project. It was written by Bertram Milhauser, based on his novel with Beulah Marie Dix, and the material feels personal. The script is so strong, in fact, that Mayo's often thoughtless direction doesn't hurt it in the end.

When Hugo finds the dog, which has been stoned and broken up (at least we aren't made to look at its wounded body), he shoots it to put it out of its misery. He's lost his job at the school, and it is intimated that he and his wife are barely getting enough food to survive when her family finally comes to get her (Stanwyck makes herself look older and realistically worn down in this scene; surely Ruby Stevens knew something about hunger). When Mary gets a letter from Hugo telling her he has to leave her and go back to Germany, Mayo holds a long close-up of Stanwyck until her face looks like it's suspended in time. She could crumple her face in tears, finally, or drop her head to end the shot, but no, Stanwyck avoids these physical clichés common in that era, instead finding this woman's state of mind and staying inside it until you are intimately acquainted with it and can feel compassion and then empathy.

Years later, on the wartime front, Hugo and Mary meet again, and she realizes that he has information that will hurt American soldiers. Loving him as much as ever, she collapses in bed with him after putting some poison in their wine. They settle down to die together, star-crossed lovers, believably destroyed by ignorance and hate. *Ever in My Heart* is an imperfect movie, and Stanwyck's performance is uneven, but it packs a wallop and it deserves to be more widely shown.

Gambling Lady (1934) is Stanwyck's first real post-Code movie, and a chill of compulsory virtue affects her performance right away. Her Lady Lee is a far cry from her pre-Code heroines, a cardsharp who insists on playing straight for her winnings (it's as if the Code has forced Nan Taylor or the bilious Lily Powers into an unflattering corset). Stanwyck had a gambler's wary face, and she made a convincing professional sharpie in later years. But this brief little movie doesn't allow her much leeway to do anything but grieve a dead father (again), fall for Joel McCrea (easy to do, of course), and then wait out an increasingly convoluted plot that involves several unconvincing twists courtesy of a villainous society girl (Claire Dodd). In one of her last scenes here, Stanwyck is asked to carry a "hysterical laughter" scene, and she plays this routine admirably, even stumbling over a word or two to make it more real, just as earlier in the film she does a panicked, klutzy run up some stairs when she finds out that McCrea is in jail. Even in a nothing movie like this, Stanwyck makes sure to give us at least a few moments of recognizable human behavior.

Willa Cather was outraged when she saw what Warner Bros. made of her book *A Lost Lady* in 1934, and anyone who has read Cather's evocative, perfectly structured novel can only share her feelings. Marian Forrester, Cather's lead character, is a naturally bewitching woman, flighty, life loving, unstable. She makes a strong impression on a boy named Niel, who falls in love with her as a youth, becomes disillusioned with her when he discovers her sexual infidelity to her much older husband, and finally comes to terms with her profound impact on his life. Cather writes: "Where Mrs. Forrester was, dullness was impossible, Niel believed. The charm of her conversation was not so much in what she said, though she was often witty, but in the quick recognition of her eyes, in the living quality of her voice itself. One could talk to her about the most trivial things, and go away with a high sense of elation." (p. 70). This isn't a natural part for Stanwyck. It's closer to the Julie Christie of Joseph Losey's *The Go-Between* (1971), based on L.P. Hartley's novel, which contains a more dangerous version of Cather's basic theme (Hartley even calls his enchantress Marian).

It's possible to imagine Stanwyck doing a decent Marian at the more expansive Warner Bros. of the 1940s, with King Vidor or Frank Borzage directing. But this Cather book really needs the Orson Welles of *The Magnificent Ambersons* (1942), and what it gets is "let's finish this fast" hack Alfred E. Green, who was more suited to his job on the sordid *Baby Face*. The first sign of trouble is when the credits inform us—with that Warner Bros. "living headshot" style of this time—that Niel is to be played by sweaty, gangster-ish Lyle Talbot, but nothing can prepare us for what this movie does to the book. It uses Cather's basic story outline in the cheapest possible way, opening on Stanwyck's Marian kissing her fiancée at a swank party, then watching him get shot (she puts her hands in the front of her hair, a mechanical gesture to mime the distress she refuses to feel).

On a sabbatical in the Canadian Rockies, Stanwyck starts to emote a little for her maid (Rafaela Ottiano), but she's sitting on a truly hideous striped chair next to a hideous matching striped couch, and this juxtaposition serves to dampen anything she might want to try. This is a movie that reduces an audience to carping over unfortunate set design, or the succession of ugly, unflattering Orry-Kelly gowns that Stanwyck is made to model (the film was originally intended for clotheshorse Kay Francis, and it shows). Her Marian takes what looks like a pratfall and is saved by nice fuddy-duddy lawyer Dan Forrester (Frank Morgan). Schmaltzy music comes on when he asks her to be his wife, saying that they'll live on "honesty" instead of love, and she half-heartedly accepts his hand. No attempt is made to capture the rural atmosphere of Cather's book; instead, the most specious kind of 1930s glamour is endorsed. This Marian takes up with an unappealing lover (Ricardo Cortez) fast and unconvincingly, and when she tells her husband, he retreats to his room and sulks for a long time.

Talbot's Neil finds Marian drinking. Cather's character is a sherry tippler, but Stanwyck's Marian looks like she's belting back straight whiskey. In her tired, desultory drunk scene she is hilariously far from the sensual, hedonistic woman we find in the novel, more a complaining Flatbush housewife than a special vixen grabbing everything she can get hold of. At sixty-one minutes, the film ends with reconciliation between man and wife, though it's hard not to wonder just what has changed between them. Are they going to attempt a regular sex life now, or will Stanwyck's Marian just have to go without for the rest of her years? The film is a travesty of Cather, and it doesn't even work on its own limited terms.

Stanwyck's post-Code slump continued with *The Secret Bride* (1934), an exposition-loaded mystery for Warners that nonetheless features excellent direction from the underrated William Dieterle and a few challenges for its star. Dieterle liked to employ a restless, probing camera, and he opens the film with a picture of Lincoln and the American flag, then pans to the governor's daughter, Ruth (Stanwyck), who looks amused at the prospect of marrying the ever-seedy Warren William. In these first scenes, Ruth is well dressed, in a pampered kind of way, and Stanwyck makes her face look childlike and undisturbed. She uses her most regal, mid-Atlantic-style voice, because she's playing a rich, cloistered girl who sometimes verges on being outright inane. When Ruth finds out that her father is mixed up in a scandal, Stanwyck finds a credulous mask; this most wised up of actresses is playing a bit of a fool, and doing it well. "It's ridiculous of us to worry," she says to William, managing to sound quite vague and Main Line snooty.

Ruth is a girl who grew up in a gilded cage. When she has a confrontation with her father, Dieterle uses some striking low angles, and there's some fast editing to convey the confusion between them. Then we cut to a full close-up of Stanwyck, as she stares at her father and starts to doubt him. Only here does she falter. The sadness in her eyes is too heavy and deep to belong to this girl, but it's probably too much to ask of the former Ruby Stevens to be able to access the first sadness of a happy, oblivious society type. Ruth is convinced of her father's innocence, and Stanwyck quite impressively keeps the upper-crust voice she's been using, even when she's making her intense pitch to William to keep on fighting to clear her dad's name. Glenda Farrell is given the typical pre-Code Stanwyck part as a working girl caught up in the case, while Stanwyck labors to stay interested in the last half of the film. Understandably, she looks bored in some of her last scenes. "She was not happy at Warners and wanted to get out of her contract as quickly as possible," said Dieterle.

Her unhappiness is visible throughout her last Warners contract dud, *The Woman in Red* (1934), a horsey, mechanical drama that has Stanwyck in jodhpurs and then a red coat, which figures in the film's badly cross-cut courtroom climax. Robert Florey, a Frenchman who began his career with some experimental shorts, tries to enliven the film with a few odd camera angles and visual compositions here and there, but he doesn't have Dieterle's touch. "Mush," says a bored Stanwyck at one point, tossing a book aside (is it the script?). Then she walks through a totally unconvincing romance with Gene Raymond.

It's as if she's saying, "You have my body, but you won't get my soul or my talent, Jack Warner." Asked to explode at wicked society woman Genevieve Tobin and her stuffy set in one of the last scenes, Stanwyck shoots the works, but she doesn't trouble to control her emotion, so that it spills out all over the place and makes a silly mess. (Off the set, Fay was at his drunken, abusive worst, which must have contributed to her cold misery here.) In court, Stanwyck's character has another "eruption," as another character puts it, and this instance is expert, but to little end. Clad in the red coat of the title, Stanwyck's character participates in "a notorious yachting party"—but not aboard the omnipresent "boat of vice" of her early films, alas.

After portraying this dull woman in red, a no-doubt demoralized Stanwyck spent six idle months at home before moving into *Red Salute* (1935), an often jaw-dropping, independently made anti-Communist gewgaw. Though she must have been desperate to get out of the house, it's worth stressing that she chose this controversial movie for herself in the middle of the radical thirties, when it was fashionable and even de rigueur in most artistic circles to be pro-union, pro-proletariat, anti-capitalist, and even a shade or two pink. When the film opened at the Rivoli theater in New York, it was picketed by the National Student's League, a leftist student group, and eighteen people were arrested when fights broke out in the theater.

Stanwyck picked up her right-wing politics from Fay, and she held onto them throughout her life. As late as the seventies, she was complaining about Jimmy Carter and his family to artist Don Bachardy, and she fit right into the Nancy Reagan red eighties. During Vanessa Redgrave's acceptance speech at the 1978 Academy Awards, a canny TV editor cut to a resplendent, glittering Stanwyck just before Redgrave pronounced the offensive words "Zionist hoodlums." It was as if she could serve as a kind of conservative counterpoint to radical Vanessa.

Describing a fake sore throat in *Ball of Fire* (1941), Stanwyck's Sugarpuss O'Shea cracks wise on the left: "It's as red as *The Daily Worker* and just as sore!" Off-screen, in the forties, Stanwyck and second husband Robert Taylor helped to found the Motion Picture Alliance for the Preservation of American Ideals, an organization that aligned itself a few years later with the House Un-American Activities Committee. Taylor himself was the only major movie star to name names. Stanwyck wasn't called, but gung-ho Taylor said that if she were called, "[S]he would be tickled to death to come down and she would come a-running."

Taylor's jingoism sounds close to that of the odious Jeff (Robert Young) in *Red Salute*, a restless, cruel soldier determined to uneducate Stanwyck's Drue Van Allen, a general's daughter who has fallen in love with Arner (Hardie Albright), a radical Communist propagandist. The film begins with a shot of an American flag flying in the breeze. We then see one of Arner's Communist harangues. "What's a proletariat?" asks an onlooker, and a man standing next to him snaps, "I'll take vanilla." Arner is described as a brainy graduate student who might be in the country illegally. A beaming Drue tells the "sez you!" dissenters that Arner's ideas are the way of the future. All the sloganeering in this first sequence goes by in a blur.

"He's a radical!" cries Drue's father. "He's a darling," she rejoins, lovingly, her head in the clouds. This is another oblivious rich girl, like the girl in *The Secret Bride*, but this time the character's credulity is leading her right into the hands of the commies. General Van Allen bundles Drue off to Mexico; south of the border, Drue tries to win some money at a gambling house and runs into Young's Jeff, an enlisted man who says that he's dying to "heave bombs" at people, like an army recruiting poster promised. It takes a while to sink in that he is supposed to be our hero.

Jeff calls Drue "Red," and she calls him "Uncle Sam," and their antagonism is uneasy and unpleasant. The film uses an *It Happened One Night* (1934) template, but it's not romantic or funny. Stanwyck plays the whole stinking courtship with Jeff on one single, heavy note of crabby resentment, and the midsection of the film, where she's stuck in a trailer with her enlisted man, only demonstrates that she still can't handle sophisticated banter. Similarly, an early scene at a bar proves that she's oddly resistant and inexact with drunk scenes.

Jeff's argument in favor of strict divorce laws is as ugly as his longing for a fight of any kind. "I wish somebody'd start another war," sighs Rooney (Cliff Edwards), who serves as a driver to the pair. "We're working on it," says Jeff, in a breathtaking moment of vague, aggressive mean-spiritedness. When Jeff threatens to punch Drue in the nose, Stanwyck gets all S & M excited, just like the Ayn Rand heroine that she so wanted to play. They dance, and when she breaks away, the film moves back towards absurdity. "You're not such a heavy thinker," Jeff tells her. "You know how I know? Because a thinker's a dodo on the dance floor."

It's a laughable line, but it remains ominous that the fringe right wing of today likes to endorse ignorance, outright stupidity, and love of brute force for its own sake in the same manner as the hardline American right wing did in 1935. Jeff tells Drue she needs a cop or a soldier like him—some authority figure to follow. Up in her bedroom, she stares into a mirror in what looks like private shame and arousal, then puts on some more lipstick (in her best films for Capra and Wellman, Stanwyck is always taking off her make-up and coming clean). What did Capra make of *Red Salute*? If he saw it, he might have secretly liked it, I'm afraid, but he'd have been canny enough to keep his feelings to himself.

There's one sensible scene here, thank goodness. When the General talks to an official, this government figure reasonably insists that Arner has a right to his free speech under our Constitution and we have to tolerate him until he does something criminal. But it all ends in a repulsive climax where Arner condemns militarism in front of a crowd of supporters, only to have Jeff get up and manipulate the crowd into endorsing his own war-mongering point of view. At first the crowd boos him (and this is clearly one soldier who should be booed), but then Jeff talks about Americanism and patriotism, and how he's always been nuts about "The Star-Spangled Banner," and how the American flag makes him tingle (at least it doesn't give him a lump in his throat). Unforgivably, the camera then pans over the radicals on stage; they're all foreign-looking and bespectacled, playing to the worst kind of stereotyping and rightwing prejudice.

The yahoos in the audience fell for the leftist junk, and now they fall for the rightist junk, all too quickly. The turnaround comes when Jeff shows them the American flag he has tattooed on his arm (I wish I were making this up). When a fistfight breaks out, Rooney sighs, "Oh, this is wonderful," amid the senseless violence. This leads to a (happy?) marriage for Drue and Jeff.

Red Salute is not excusable on any level. It's as if Bette Davis had starred in *Salt of the Earth* (1954). The following year, fittingly enough, Humphrey Pearson, who wrote the offensive story and screenplay for *Red Salute*, was accidentally killed by his wife. It seems he was in a drunken rage and waving a gun around when she tried and failed to disarm him. *Red Salute* is hard to watch. It has to be Stanwyck's worst movie, and I can only wish that she hadn't made it.

Several questions attach themselves to *A Message to Garcia* (1936). The first concerns why Stanwyck was even considered for the part of a Cuban revolutionary. The second is why she accepted the role. The third is why director George Marshall chose to film this adventure story at such a glacial pace. Thankfully, Stanwyck doesn't attempt any accent, though she is introduced crying, "Padre!" and then "Padre mio!" when she discovers her dead father. She wisely tries to blend into the background as the movie goes on, though Marshall (or Darryl Zanuck, the Fox studio head who always had a thing for Stanwyck) manages to isolate her in plenty of glamorous extreme close-ups, where she always seems to be reclining in the foliage of the jungle, her lipstick heavy, her hair freshly tended-to, her clothes spotless.

Stanwyck, John Boles, and Wallace Beery are stranded for the majority of the film, and they have lots of quiet conversations in that studio jungle, all filmed in a static way without any scoring. These scenes seem designed to lull an audience to sleep. At the end, when Stanwyck shouts, "No, no, no!" and then, "Stop!" she finally breaks the spell of this weirdly mesmeric dud. Her all-too-appropriate words are soon followed by some gunfire, a hammy Beery death scene, and the delivery of the titular message to General Garcia, which apparently signals the liberation of Cuba. Young Rita Cansino, later Rita Hayworth, shot some scenes as Stanwyck's sister, but Zanuck had them cut, perhaps because of Cansino's inexperience, or perhaps because her Latin beauty made Stanwyck look even more miscast.

Director John Cromwell favored florid female performances (see Laura Hope Crews in *The Silver Cord* [1933], Bette Davis in *Of Human Bondage* [1934], Eleanor Parker in *Caged* [1950], and Kim Stanley in *The Goddess* [1958]). In the movie he made with Stanwyck, the folksy, slight *Banjo on My Knee* (1936), Cromwell brings out a kind of neediness in her. When she tells a rival that she can "cook better, love better and fight better," her words carry none of the toughness Stanwyck displays in other roles. Here, she seems defensive and uncertain. Her character, Pearl, is clingy and desperate as she waits out the whole movie to consummate her marriage to Ernie (Joel McCrea), and their union is delayed by so many complications that it all gets a little tiresome after a while.

Cromwell engineers several outbursts of emotion from Stanwyck, and he even has her sing and do a dance with Buddy Ebsen (she stares down at her feet a bit, but looks to be enjoying herself). After washing dishes for eleven days and eight hours to pay back a debt, an exhausted Pearl stops and watches a full-scale production number of "St. Louis Woman," headlined by Theresa Harris, who played Lily Powers's best friend, Chico, in *Baby Face*. Harris was almost always relegated to playing servants, and Lily eventually is made to reject Chico to "redeem" herself. But as Stanwyck watches Harris sing here, it's as if their connection has been re-established, and part of the sadness we feel in this sequence is that they've been separated, post-Code. They don't even get to be in the same frame together.

Dave Kehr has called Stanwyck's next movie, *Internes Can't Take Money* (1937), "Ophulsian." It's odd to think that the first entry in what would become the long-running Dr. Kildare series could seem like a Max Ophuls film, until you see what director Alfred Santell is able to do with this medical drama/crime drama script. He begins *Internes* with a few elaborate tracking shots, which is not reason enough to invoke Ophuls, but as the film goes on, it develops an abstract feeling that allows for maximum involvement in the plot. Santell called his work here "a deliberate blending of silent and talking techniques held together by mood, intensity and sincerity." Stanwyck's character, Janet, is desperately trying to rescue her daughter from a bunch of crooks, and the main villain, Innes (a chronic popcorn eater played with insinuating, soft-spoken nastiness by Stanley Ridges), has put our heroine in a bind: If she doesn't sleep with him, he won't tell her where her daughter is.

When Janet decides to go away with Innes, Santell frames a long shot of her buying a bag of popcorn. This little scene might seem silly in other hands, but Santell has built up such a hushed atmosphere that we only feel Janet's deep resignation. At one point, after Janet tries to steal money she needs, Joel McCrea's Kildare says, "Next time you pick a man's pocket, don't do it in front of a mirror." After he leaves, Santell moves his camera to Janet's kitchen mirror, and we see her image reflected there, crouched over a table in defeat—one more instance where a mirror exposes Stanwyck on screen. The upright Kildare eventually saves this bad-luck damsel in distress, and though the story is trivial, the careful direction and the acting by all the principals are exemplary.

Darryl Zanuck at 20th Century Fox wanted Stanwyck to do another *Stella Dallas*-type picture with mother love as a theme. He enticed her into *Always Goodbye* (1938), a little-seen movie with a nicely melancholy title that doesn't fit its jerky shifts in tone. It's a weepie that sometimes acts like a romantic comedy, or a romantic comedy with mother love issues. The score under the credits certainly makes it sound like it's going to be a comedy, and the first shots show Stanwyck's rather high-voiced Margot Weston all aglow with happiness because she's about to be married. There's some poor rear projection shots of city streets behind her as her fiancée gets killed in a car crash, and then noble surgeon Jim (Herbert Marshall) stops Margot from jumping into the drink and convinces her, in no time flat, to go on living.

She has her fatherless baby, and Jim helps her place the boy with a couple he knows. Giving him up, Stanwyck's eyes slowly fill with tears, and the purity of her emotion is at its most impressive here. I can imagine a later Actors Studio guru like Lee Strasberg genuflecting before her talent. This is the sort of close-up that makes you wonder how one person could carry around so much pain and still be able to use it strategically for often claustrophobically small, contained motion picture scenes.

Margot becomes a famous fashion designer in one of those montages that leave an audience gasping for breath. As our heroine embarks on a trip to Paris, it's hard not to wonder if the screenwriters couldn't resist kidding us with this script, which lurches into shipboard hijinks with Cesar Romero (Stanwyck looks amused to find herself dancing with him, insisting, "I'm a working girl!" as he gives her his full continental lover act).

Back with Jim, Margot charmingly remembers being the youngest of six children and only getting to eat the neck of the family's chicken dinner. But if this sounds self-pitying, she quickly insists, "I like it"—and makes you believe that she does. She tries to get her child back, necessitating a fine confrontation scene with a female rival (slinky Lynn Bari). When she vanquishes this woman, Stanwyck leans in slightly, intoxicated with the thrill of battle, her mouth partly open and her eyes shining. Though *Always Goodbye* has to count as one of the worst scripts Stanwyck ever played, it has a kind of lunatic confidence in itself that makes it a minor pleasure.

Screwball Stanwyck

The Bride Walks Out, Breakfast for Two, The Mad Miss Manton,
You Belong to Me, Christmas in Connecticut, The Bride Wore Boots

$\mathcal{C}$omedy is not something that came easily to Stanwyck, but she stuck
to it and eventually mastered the genre. Early on, she professed that she
found light material "a vacation—I was playing, not working." But later,
being interviewed by John Kobal, she confessed, "I am not really a co-
medienne, per se. I'm not very good. But when they are written as well
as *The Lady Eve* or *You Belong to Me* (1941) . . . both of those films are with
Henry Fonda, who *is* a wonderful comedian . . . or if it is a situation comedy, I'm alright. But—just for me to be funny—I'm not a funny person."

In the mid-thirties, screwball comedy was in vogue, and practically
every actress of note tried it, sometimes with spectacular results (Irene
Dunne, Katharine Hepburn) and sometimes not (Loretta Young). We can
take Stanwyck at her word that she wasn't a naturally funny person, and
certainly good humor is not the first thing we think of when we think
of her. But unlike, say, the always-serious Joan Crawford or Bette Davis,
she successfully extended her technique in some small comedies before
finally grasping the brass ring with Preston Sturges and Howard Hawks.

Her director on the RKO film *The Bride Walks Out* (1936), Leigh Jason,
admired the fact that Stanwyck "was the only one I ever worked with
who would dig to the bitter end for what you really wanted—and then
give it to you." The main thrust of the plot (engineer Gene Raymond
won't let bride Stanwyck work, even though he brings in only thirty-five
dollars a week) is consistently irritating. "Women have always worked,"
says Stanwyck's Carolyn, when she wants to continue modeling clothes
for fifty dollars a week. "Why shouldn't they do it in a shop instead of
in a kitchen?" Raymond's unlikable Michael never has a good answer

whenever she asks about this, and that's because there is no good answer (it might be worse if he tried to define his sexist feelings, of course).

During the film's leisurely eighty-one minutes, there are four separate, would-be humorous references to wife beating. The most disturbing one comes from Stanwyck's mouth: "Hit me, that would be the manly thing to do," Carolyn says to Michael (suddenly it becomes clearer that some of the attitudes of this era were to blame for Stanwyck getting smacked in the face by Frank Fay). In many ways, this movie prefigures a sort of fifties conservatism. The married couple sleeps in separate beds, and in this time of the working girl—the high noon of Jean Arthur and so many other career women of the thirties—it feels absurd, even cruel, to put the mighty Stanwyck in an apron in a tiny kitchen in a small apartment and expect her to pinch pennies on milk, when what she really wants is the trunk full of cash and gems belonging to Baby Face Lily Powers. She can't cook, of course, and why should she have to? Because that's what a "real, bona-fide wife" does, according to Michael.

This lunkhead Michael is another Fay figure, and he isn't remotely worthy of Stanwyck, as usual, but *The Bride Walks Out* has time for all kinds of diversions around its main plot. Hattie McDaniel has one of her better roles. In her first scene, she talks about the many men in her life, then cracks that "one or two of them I jilted!" In a later, even more telling scene, McDaniel wonders why white men don't want their women to work (it's interesting, from a modern perspective, that the black servant McDaniel plays is obviously more liberated and happier than the stymied white woman she works for). Stanwyck has a ball in a short dance scene with Raymond, jumping up on his thighs and thrusting her legs straight out into the air. And she finally pulls off a drunk scene with the help of pro-farceurs Billy Gilbert and Helen Broderick.

Broderick's crack timing is notable. Creditor Gilbert takes away the couple's furniture and finally comes to Broderick, who is sitting in the last chair. "What you're sitting on does not belong to you," he says, whereupon Broderick thinks this over for a second or two (a priceless take), and then slowly rises. Jason said that Stanwyck blew a few takes because she was laughing so hard at Gilbert. That's a treasurable image: the self-denying pro finding that her profession could be fun and not all tears and slaps and gunshots. After she marries Michael, Carolyn starts to cry. Stanwyck makes sure to pull back just enough so that they're clearly comic tears, a small adjustment that I would think brought her a certain amount of relief and maybe a feeling of power—or at least expanding horizons.

In her next comedy, *Breakfast for Two* (1937), Stanwyck is completely out of her mid-thirties transitional period and almost fully developed into her streamlined, titanic 1940s self, an actress of near total flexibility and strength. She had just made *Stella Dallas* and saw this rather rough screwball comedy as a relaxation. She was thirty now, and if something was lost in the passage of time—a certain vulnerability, a certain type of raw exposure—this loss was more than compensated for by gains in confidence and control.

In *Breakfast for Two,* Stanwyck plays a Texas heiress named Valentine, and she's decked out in a white fringe dress and white fur coat in the first scene, recovering after a night on the town with irresponsible playboy Jonathan (Herbert Marshall). Stanwyck has made a huge leap forward in her handling of fast, sophisticated comic dialogue, throwing her mammoth fur over her shoulder as she tosses out repartee as if it came naturally to her. Over breakfast, Jonathan asks if he proposed to her the night before; apparently he does so whenever he picks up women. "Ah, I don't remember," Valentine murmurs, and Stanwyck makes this brief moment of genuine disappointment the linchpin of her fierce performance.

This is another RKO film. It has distinctive art deco set design by Van Nest Polglase, and the direction by Alfred Santell is somewhat static, so that the settings are made to feel oppressive (which might have been the intent). Valentine plots revenge against Jonathan and snaps up his ailing company with the idea of making a real man out of this idle-rich parasite. She compares her plan to training a horse: "Slip a bit in his mouth and make him like it," she purrs. It becomes clear that the victimized chorus girl has it in her now to dish out some full-fledged, dominatrix-style abuse. Valentine puts this guy in his place verbally, and thus brings out the caveman in Jonathan, who sneers, "You're the type of woman who wants to wear the pants—alright, Mister, wear them, trip over them and break your neck!" The male/female hostility between these two breaks into all-out brawling. When Jonathan's effeminate butler (Eric Blore) tries to stop them from putting on boxing gloves to fight, Valentine cries, "Keep out of this, I was raised with six brothers!" She socks Jonathan in the jaw, and there doesn't appear to be any fakery here; Stanwyck really seems to give Marshall a whack.

Valentine takes some expert swings at her prey, but he holds the crown of her head until she knocks into a door. Then she turns, and suddenly, out of nowhere, there's feral little Ruby Stevens, age twelve, learning to fight in the streets. This startling image carries through the whole fight, which Valentine wins, of course (it's a much more satisfying bout than a similar one in *Nothing Sacred* from the same year, where Carole Lombard's character is too ill to really get into the battle of the sexes). Later, we see a doorknob fall out of Valentine's glove. When it hits the floor, I could hear, "Ruby don't fight fair!" in my head, coming from some ghost of a Brooklyn boy from 1919 scared of what a girl's anger can do. *Breakfast for Two* is a screwball comedy about antagonism between a man and a woman in its purest possible state, ending in more violent slapstick and finally a wedding, celebrated by holding those boxing gloves in the air.

Katharine Hepburn turned down *The Mad Miss Manton* (1938), a low-grade mystery about a loopy debutante who keeps finding dead bodies and must solve the murders herself with the aid of her society girlfriends. It's easy to see why RKO offered it to Hepburn and easy to see why she nixed it. Why Stanwyck took it is another matter. She had rejected a lot of scripts from RKO and Fox, and I suppose at a certain point you just have to give in and do something or other. Henry Fonda got stuck playing the male lead, Peter, a newspaperman, and he was so miserable that he rudely ignored Stanwyck on the set. But he and Stanwyck already have sexual chemistry together in this first film they made together; maybe his initial rejection of her peaked Stanwyck's masochistic interest.

There are so many *m*'s in the title that it doesn't have room for the heroine's first name (Melsa). And Stanwyck can't play the farcical obliviousness of this dizzy dame, though she tries and even scores a laugh or two, mainly with physical business. Her Park Avenue friends seem like a *Stage Door* (1937) hangover, and writer Philip G. Epstein keeps slipping in joking references to communism that might have rankled right-wing Stany if she hadn't been so busy running around solving crimes and eying Fonda with interest (it was close to one hundred degrees the summer this movie was shot, and the girls were in fur coats, so getting the project done quickly was a priority). It's a film where people keep throwing water at each other, and the biggest laugh comes when Stanwyck jabs a fork in Fonda's rear. The only grace note is the ending, where Peter insists that he'll happily live on Melsa's money, a refreshing reversal from Michael's pig-headedness on this subject in *The Bride Walks Out*.

The perils of being a working woman come into play again in *You Belong to Me*, Stanwyck's third pairing with Fonda after their triumph in *The Lady Eve*, and this issue is resolved most satisfactorily, for once. The action starts out with some Hal Roach slapstick on skis, as Fonda's Peter tries to impress Stanwyck's Helen by yodeling and making hairpin turns until he lands headfirst in the snow. Helen pulls Peter out, and they ride together back to their hotel (Fonda looks very happy to be snuggling up to Stanwyck, while she looks a bit embarrassed—or forbearing).

When Peter finds out Helen is a physician, he asks, "Are there many women doctors?" and Stanwyck answers, "A few," in her huskiest, most melancholy voice (she's bleached all the Brooklyn out of it here, whereas Melsa Manton sounds more like Prospect than Central Park). Stanwyck is a knockout in her tight white sweater and long hair, and she has great fun using nonsense medical terms while she cares for Fonda, nattering on about the posterior and the tibia and the fibia. The whole movie has that creamy Columbia look of the forties, with lots of satin bedcovers and silky robes. Wesley Ruggles, the film's underrated director, realizes that his picture is basically Stanwyck and Fonda and their chemistry with each other, so he keeps them in lingering two shots so that they can create the kind of give-and-take you might see at a good live theater performance. Fonda's "little boy" act can get a bit grating, but he eventually offers a fine portrayal of a rich brat who has nothing but time on his hands to be suspicious of his wife and her male patients.

Stanwyck seems like a doctor, and when she talks about how much her work means to her, it's easy to believe her. She does some inventive physical bits. After a fight leaves some of her hair over her eyes, she takes a moment to see the hair, actually crosses her eyes slightly, then blows the hair back with one big puff (proof that if Stanwyck wasn't a naturally funny person, she could certainly find "humor" if she looked hard enough for it). The plot seems to be turning in an unwelcome direction as Helen decides to give up her practice to be a "good wife," but it quickly gets back on track for a final scene that lets us see that Peter understands how important his wife's work is to her.

Christmas in Connecticut (1945) is the sort of holiday movie that seems to have been made as bland as possible so that audiences can watch it after stuffing themselves with turkey and cranberry sauce. The movie revolves around a single, entirely predictable situation: Stanwyck's city girl writes a popular newspaper column where she poses as a country wife and mother, and when her publisher (Sydney Greenstreet) insists on spending Christmas with her, she has to acquire a husband, a baby, and an antique-stuffed farm in short order. It's the kind of script that might come alive with any halfway-competent comedy director, but Peter Godfrey directs in a plodding, totally uninterested manner.

"Nice firm rump," says soldier Dennis Morgan, staring at a cow, and Stanwyck straightens up for a second, as if she's afraid he's talking about her, but the timing is way off. Stanwyck isn't even at her second best here. In one of her last scenes, she rattles off a list of things she's tired of and finishes with, "In short, I'm tired!" giving this last "tired" a too-cutesy upwards inflection. She begins the film as another craven journalist, but soon the script asks her to be unaccountably ditzy when she falls for Morgan. Surely it would have been more intriguing to see Stanwyck go head-to-head with Greenstreet in a melodrama, à la *Flamingo Road* (1949).

Only Stanwyck's love of horses can possibly explain why she chose to do *The Bride Wore Boots* (1946), a woeful comedy in which she plays the horse-loving wife of horse-hating Robert Cummings (maybe her worst leading man). This is a fifth-rate script, and Stanwyck speeds us through most of it. But what's odd here is that she seems to be giving a performance made up of spare parts borrowed from other comediennes. She tries out some Jean Arthur dithering when she has to be dizzy in a divorce court, scatters practically every other moment with Irene Dunne "ums" and "ahs," and often falls into a Katharine Hepburn "a-ha-ha" laugh. Indeed, this movie asks her to laugh through her scenes so often that the strain really shows. Stanwyck isn't a laugher, and she looks put out by her two obnoxiously bratty on-screen children, one of whom is a blond little Natalie Wood.

In one particularly distasteful plot twist, the mother of the Stanwyck character has the kiddies eat too much, so that they'll throw up and reunite their warring parents over their sickbed. This lapse in taste was reflected off-set when director Irving Pichel ordered Cummings to do a perilous stunt ride over and over again, only to be stopped by a coolly disgusted Stanwyck, who told Pichel in no uncertain terms that if he ordered a further take, he wouldn't direct her in another scene. I wish Pichel hadn't directed her in *any* scenes, and I sorely wish that Stanwyck could have done something less actively unfunny for what turned out to be her last film comedy.

Private Lives

Fay's End, Robert Taylor (*His Brother's Wife, This Is My Affair, The Night Walker*), Robert Wagner

$\mathcal{O}$scar Levant described Frank Fay's influence over Stanwyck during their marriage as "suffocating and total." In a drunken rage, he once threw their adopted baby, Dion, into their pool. When he knocked Stanwyck down in front of a screaming Dion (after she had admitted going to a burlesque show), she finally felt that enough was enough and asked for a divorce in 1935. There was a custody battle for Dion, and when Stanwyck won it, Fay seems to have lost interest in the boy. Fay would sometimes drunkenly call and plead with Stanwyck to come back to him; she finally stopped accepting his calls. As an old woman, Stanwyck admitted to a reporter that if she had one thing to do over again in her life, she wouldn't have married Frank Fay. Early in their marriage, she had said, "Gee, it's swell to have somebody to talk to, somebody who can stand between you and the world," but the protectiveness she liked in him all too soon became smothering and abusive.

In the forties, Fay pulled himself together and made a comeback on stage in Mary Chase's *Harvey,* as a man who has an imaginary rabbit as a friend. Tallulah Bankhead said that it was "one of the greatest performances I've seen," and raved about the way Fay did "a long speech in the last act which just made me cry." So let's give this devil his due. He probably did accomplish one really fine thing in the theater, though James Stewart got to do the movie version of the play. Well into Fay's successful run of *Harvey,* columnist Earl Wilson asked Stanwyck if she had seen it. She said no. He asked if she was going to see it, and her reply was withering—and funny: "A long time ago I saw all the rabbits Frank Fay had to offer."

Her agent, Zeppo Marx, and his wife Marion played matchmaker after her divorce from Fay and set her up with a young up-and-coming actor from MGM, Robert Taylor. Four years younger than Stanwyck, Taylor was totally dominated by his mother, a *Silver Cord* type of manipulator who complained of her health in order to keep him under her control. Stanwyck called Taylor "Junior," and he called her "Queen," and they went out on social dates for a while. Jean Harlow was meant to star opposite Taylor in *His Brother's Wife* (1936), a convoluted melodrama, but MGM paired him instead with Stanwyck to capitalize on their courtship publicity.

Taylor enters the film in a tuxedo, and he's supposed to be drunk. He isn't as bad as he is during his extended drunk scene in John Stahl's *Magnificent Obsession* (1935), which made him a star—but he isn't much better. This is the brief period when Taylor is at least technically good-looking, but there's already something wolfish and downright nasty about his manner—in close-up, there's a creepy and even Dracula-esque quality about his face, as if his hooded eyes were wearing eye shadow. Stanwyck plays a mannequin who's good at gambling, and she looks at Taylor with interest at times—wonderingly, speculatively—while he barely seems to notice her. That's part of what makes him such an obnoxiously poor actor; he always delivers his lines in a hearty, bluff fashion that often deteriorates into discordant displays of ill-temper, which never seem merited by the situations in his movies.

Taylor spent more than twenty years at MGM, and he suited that studio's inattention to nuance and its glossy, respectable surfaces, whereas Stanwyck was too honest and exploratory to fit into the house style. When she gets upset in the early sections of *His Brother's Wife*, her truthful acting disrupts the whole apparatus of the film. "Too bad she had no dignity," she says when she realizes Taylor is casting her aside. She pulls back and sees herself in the third person, distancing herself from the scene and the movie itself to give us a demonstration of how people deal with extreme trauma. In a moment like this, Stanwyck's inventiveness can be awe-inspiring, but there isn't much she can do to save the rest of the fast-paced film.

This is MGM, so a key plot turn whereby her heroine gets revenge takes place mostly off-screen (to preserve audience sympathy for her character, presumably), and when she suffers in the tropics and then becomes a human guinea pig to test a serum to cure spotted fever . . . well, as Taylor's father (Jean Hersholt) says, "Love! It puzzles me more than science." More revealing is an earlier scene where gambling house owner Fish Eye (Joseph Calleia) looks at Stanwyck and says, "What surprises me is why a swell-looking girl like you always falls for a piker." She has no answer for that one, and it would take an expert psychoanalyst to get to the bottom of Stanwyck's own consistently bad taste in men.

At one point in their second team effort, Taylor actually says the title, *This Is My Affair* (1937), and he gets top billing and most of the plot of the movie, a tale of espionage supposedly based on a true story and set during the McKinley administration. More assured and less objectionable here, Taylor even pulls off an intimate love scene with Stanwyck, lying on his back and opening his mouth when she kisses him. As a fancy dance hall singer, Stanwyck has little to do but look pretty, albeit in a softer way than usual. The whole film presents her face carefully, "beautifully," in just the way Capra righteously rejected when he went for the truth of her being in *Ladies of Leisure*.

She sings a song, "I Hear a Waltz," in her own husky voice, and it sounds a little strange—she wanders off pitch sometimes, which might be part of the reason she barred Taylor from watching her do this scene. His vaunted male beauty made her self-conscious in the worst possible way, which is probably why she seems concerned with her physical appearance in this picture to the exclusion of all else. Director William Seiter was more at home with romantic comedy, and he lets Sidney Blackmer make Teddy Roosevelt into a thin caricature while observing the uneasy romance between his stars.

Sheilah Graham wrote an exposé in January 1939 for *Photoplay* called "Hollywood's Unmarried Husbands and Wives," which included Clark Gable and Carole Lombard, as well as Stanwyck and Taylor. If Graham hadn't written this article, Stanwyck and Taylor most likely wouldn't have gotten married, but her piece enraged MGM head Louis B. Mayer, and he insisted that Taylor marry Stanwyck at once. They tied the knot, and Taylor spent his wedding night with his hysterical mother and her heart palpitations. On their brief honeymoon, they stayed with Moss and Kitty Carlisle Hart in Bucks County, Pennsylvania. Once back in Hollywood, they had separate bedrooms.

In 1941, when he was making *Johnny Eager*, Taylor told his nubile young co-star, Lana Turner, that he respected Stanwyck but didn't love her, and Taylor and Turner had some kind of romance. Taylor told Stanwyck about it. She fled their home for a few days and stayed with her maid Harriet Corey, then came back. On October 7, 1941, Stanwyck was rushed to the hospital with wounds on her wrists. The story was that she had accidentally shoved her hands through a window, but it sounds like a suicide attempt.

Nineteen forty-one was the year of *The Lady Eve* and *Ball of Fire*, Stanwyck's two best comedies. Both films revolved around her sexual attractiveness and mastery over men. Yet at home, she was caught up in a marriage that was at least partly a sham. She was hurt when her younger husband chased a more obvious young sexpot to prove himself as a man, for he saw Stanwyck as another mother figure to rebel against. But if this marriage was more an arrangement than a love match, why was Stanwyck disturbed enough to attempt suicide? Could it be that she had fallen a bit in love with Taylor—or in love, at least, with the idea of them as a couple? Or was his infidelity with Turner just a convenient breaking point that allowed her to act on something that had always been inside of her?

To our knowledge, she never attempted suicide again, and indeed, her whole image goes against such an action, so the fact that she once went so far to try to escape from living is bewildering. This marriage to Taylor is tricky to read, but it does seem to have been humiliating in a different fashion from her tormented union with the dominating Fay. She could assert herself over Taylor as she couldn't with Fay; Taylor was weak-willed. And maybe that suicide attempt wasn't truly serious; maybe she did it to make Taylor feel guilty so that he would stay with her. That's an ugly interpretation, but her actions had some effect. He did stay.

Taylor and Stanwyck's main problem was that he liked to go off on hunting trips with his male friends, and she didn't like to go along— he loved flying his plane, too, and she was scared of flying. World War II gave him an out. He was away for years fighting and enjoying macho camaraderie, while she stayed at home. There have always been rumors that Taylor was gay. My guess is that he was so repressed on this score it never impinged on his consciousness. When he was presented with the sexiest women in the world, women like Turner and later Ava Gardner, he had affairs with them, but it sounds like on some level he was forcing himself.

When Taylor got back from the service, the couple went on a trip to Europe in 1947 that worked out very badly. It was only a matter of time before they split, and they did so for good in 1951. My grandmother, who was divorced from her husband, would always ruefully repeat to me, "Barbara Stanwyck was too bossy. That's why she lost Robert Taylor. I read that somewhere, once." The Taylor-Stanwyck divorce in 1951 and the reasons for it had penetrated my grandmother's consciousness as a kind of object lesson.

Taylor had taken up with starlets on the set of *Quo Vadis?* (1951), but most of them were just seeking publicity, and publicity, finally, is what his marriage to Stanwyck was all about. Whatever their arrangement, it seemed to work for Stanwyck, and she never really got over losing it. She liked that she had a movie star husband so many women found attractive. Her marriage reflected well on her, even if their personal relationship was barely functional. When you work as much as she did, you just need someone who can squire you to social events and do interviews with reporters. Stanwyck wanted to hold onto their united front, and Taylor wanted to escape. He was tired of being used and manipulated, and on this score, at least, he deserves some sympathy.

Later on, thirty or so years after the fact, Stanwyck explained their divorce this way: "He wanted it and I'm not the kind of person who wants somebody if he doesn't want me. I just say, 'There's the door, you can open it. You've got a good right hand, just turn the knob, that's all you have to do. If you can't open it, I'll do it for you.'" Bitterness creeps into that statement, but it's in the hardboiled Stanwyck manner; she could have played that scene in one of her movies. Yet at the time Taylor pressed her for a divorce, she was broken up about it, and she stayed broken up, on some level, for the rest of her life. To stick it to him, she vengefully demanded alimony and kept collecting it until he died in 1969.

Strangely, years after the divorce, Taylor was again top billed but entirely subjugated to Stanwyck in her last feature film, the William Castle "shocker," *The Night Walker* (1964). The amiably naïve Castle no doubt saw the exploitation value in having the divorced Taylor and Stanwyck star together in one of his movies. As ever, they don't have any particular chemistry as an on-screen pair (even when she slaps him, the act has practically no impact), but the film is involving in its modest way. It starts with some bargain basement Salvador Dali images and a silly/scary voiceover about dreams (they bring out our secret desires for sex and murder, apparently). At first, Stanwyck looks tired, spreading her arms for Taylor in their first scene and saying, "Isn't this romantic?" when it's anything but. Yet in the following scenes, it becomes clear that Stanwyck has made tiredness a choice for her character, a passive, delirious type who's easy to manipulate. This choice is one final proof of Stanwyck's range.

An elegantly creepy score by Vic Mizzy keeps things moving, and Stanwyck has fun with her juicy role, especially when she gets to scream in horror. Her first set of screams sound succulent, even orchestral, a Phil Spector wall of sound (she ends the last one on a smoker's hacking cough). Later on she does another set of basso yowls, this time putting her whole body into it and throwing her head back to punctuate one of her screams. Best of all, when her tormented dreamer realizes what a jam she's in, Stanwyck decides to amuse herself and us by going all-out hambone. "I can't wake up," she says, breathlessly, letting it sink in. "I can't wake up!" she cries, making the realization louder and more uncontrolled. And then, "I CAN'T WAKE U-h-h-h-h-h-a-HUP!" she howls, putting both arms over her face like some bygone great lady of the stage.

The last half hour gets a little too drowsy, so that the audience might fall asleep with Stany. It's nothing to win a prize on, but *The Night Walker* is not at all embarrassing, unlike the horror features of the time that annihilated Davis, Crawford, Olivia de Havilland, Tallulah Bankhead, Miriam Hopkins, and a score of others. Stanwyck came out of her 1960s horror experience unscathed partly because she didn't have the kind of strong, one-note star persona that could be easily trashed. Even in this genre, she's fresh, alert, and inventive, whereas the peevish Taylor has entered into Bela Lugosi territory—at the end, he takes off a ghoulish mask, but his overly made-up, lined face underneath is far more disturbing. When asked about working with his ex-wife, Taylor said, "It's as if we were never married," and it certainly seems that way on screen.

"I'm supposed to be a hermit," Stanwyck laughed, in the 1960s, "a loner nursing a broken heart because I lost Robert Taylor . . . . I don't think anybody's hilariously happy living alone, but you learn to adjust." Again, this is tricky to read. She's able to step outside of the supposed narrative of her life and comment on it, as if it's a script she's thinking about accepting, but where does real feeling come in? Stanwyck probably couldn't separate that out herself, so there's no way that we can, either. When she attended Taylor's memorial, she wore a yellow dress, because he had once told her that he didn't want her in black at his funeral. She cried openly and loudly during the service, which wasn't her usual stoic style. Stanwyck was crying for a real man who had died, of course, a man that she had known and maybe even loved, in her way. But I think it's fair to say that she always loved the idea of them together more than the reality—which was perfectly pleasant after the nightmare of Frank Fay, but never more than a movie-type deal, at least on his side.

It's clear, however, that Stanwyck really loved her brother Byron, and she made sure that as an older man he had work. Leslie Caron remembers:

Stanwyck's brother Byron was an extra on my film *The Glass Slipper* (1954). We worked on a scene where I'm introduced to the princely court in the great ballroom—I had to step down this long staircase wearing a huge ball dress and the court was massed at the foot of the stairs. Byron stood a little forward from the rest, in a prominent position. He immediately struck me as a hopeless alcoholic, his face very red and his features deformed by alcohol. Strangely, it was evident to me that the assistants were favoring him so it would be impossible to complete the scene without calling him the next day. I asked why this man was getting this treatment of favor. I was told in a discrete way that he was Barbara Stanwyck's brother and that he needed any help he could get. My shock and pain at hearing this were immense. In Hollywood the sense of hierarchy was very strong, it was measured by your success and the salary you earned, the car you drove, the neighborhood you lived in. An extra was way down on the lower rung of the ladder, lower than the craftsmen and the crew while the stars stood at the very top. Democracy didn't exist on a movie set. The huge gulf that separated brother and sister was all the more shocking.

It's a measure of how much Stanwyck was loved by her crew that they made special allowances for the one person from her childhood who had made her feel secure, even though he seemed to be in bad shape by the early 1950s.

Robert Wagner's recent memoir, *Pieces of My Heart*, has opened a new door on Stanwyck's personal life during the period immediately following her divorce from Taylor. After the making of *Titanic* (1953), Wagner says that he took Stanwyck home from a party, and at the door he was met with "a magical look of interest . . . and appreciation . . . and desire." They danced, they drank champagne; he left at dawn. Eventually, she gave Wagner his own keys to her home, and they spent weekends together when they were both in town. Their four-year relationship had to be kept secret owing to the difference in their ages (he was in his early twenties and she was in her mid-forties).

"She cooked for me," Wagner remembers. "She was good in the kitchen, but then she was good everywhere." He says that she was highly sexed and had a lot on her mind. She made regular visits to a psychiatrist who prescribed her sodium pentothal to calm her down (she was a coffee addict and rarely able to get the sleep she needed). "Like so many people in show business, she was a prisoner of her career," he writes.

That assessment sounds about right, though I would probably change his characterization of Stanwyck to "willing prisoner." Now, there is a small chance that Wagner is gilding the lily about what they had together. In his own recent memoir, Farley Granger related a self-serving story about a one-night stand with Stanwyck in the early fifties. The story doesn't sound particularly believable as Granger tells it, but there are a lot of helpful, pertinent details in Wagner's Stanwyck chapter. He thinks that because of his youth and good looks, he brought her a confidence that she had lost being married to Taylor. I can only hope that this was the case.

Wagner says that she owned some of her own movies, and so they would sometimes watch these films together. She screened *Union Pacific* (1939) for him, and *Ball of Fire*, and even *Baby Face*, during which she let him know what it had been like to work for that movie's producer, Darryl Zanuck. "Barbara told me that Darryl had chased her around his office . . . and I got the distinct impression that she hadn't appreciated the exercise." Zanuck just wanted a piece of her, of course, yet his unwanted passes put her in exactly the right state of mind to play Lily Powers; maybe Zanuck sensed as much on some level. Stanwyck told Wagner about how mean Al Jolson was to her when she was starting out, and Wagner thinks that it might have been Jolson who gave her those cigarette burns on her chest.

The relationship with Wagner, whatever it was, couldn't really go anywhere because of their age difference, so finally Stanwyck called it off. Of her later years, Wagner says, "I don't know who the men in her life were, although I'm sure they existed. I know she had escorts, although I assumed most of them were gay." Stanwyck said in her later years, "Oh, yes, sometimes I have to go to something or other. When I do, I just call good ol' Butch [Cesar] Romero and he says rather reluctantly, 'Well, if you HAVE to go, I'll take you.' He does that for all of us old broads."

Wagner wanted to see Stanwyck in the hospital when she was dying, but she advised him to remember her in her prime. As she died, he says, Stanwyck was wearing a four-leaf clover necklace he had given her. On-screen, Wagner looks to me nearly as shifty and unpleasant as Robert Taylor, but off-screen, he seems to have shored up a lot of Stanwyck's broken pride.

The Scratch and the Itch

Stella Dallas

$\mathcal{O}$live Higgins Prouty wrote her bestseller, *Stella Dallas*, after her three-year-old daughter died of encephalitis. Known today mainly through this novel and a story about another misfit that would become the Bette Davis vehicle, *Now, Voyager* (1942), Prouty was also the model for "Philomena Guinea," the famed author of syrupy tales skewered by Sylvia Plath in *The Bell Jar*. By 1961, Prouty had fallen so far out of favor that she couldn't find a publisher for her memoirs and had to have them printed herself. The novel *Stella Dallas* doesn't circulate much; I had to read the one non-lending copy at the New York Public Library during one long afternoon.

The novel has a claim as the prototypical soap opera. For eighteen years, over Prouty's objections, Stella Dallas was a character on a radio soap. Since then she's suffered many indignities, not least the mistaken 1990 movie *Stella*, starring Bette Midler. Nothing I can remember of that movie can top this description in the essential book, *Bad Movies We Love*, which says that Midler is the only one "to interpret this Olive Higgins Prouty chestnut as an occasion to do a bump 'n' grind atop a bar, imitate Carmen Miranda, stage a food fight, and refer constantly to her breasts while insisting that other characters rave over her sex appeal." The book also highlights Midler's "terrifying propensity for transforming herself into Betty Hutton, Ruth Gordon and Jerry Lewis all rolled into one."

Prouty's original novel begins by describing thirteen-year-old Laurel, a girl with perfect taste who looks like an Isadora Duncan pupil. At thirty-nine, her mother Stella Dallas is "a fat, shapeless little ball of a woman" who has atrocious taste in clothes. Prouty tells us that Stella was ashamed of her own poverty-stricken mother, who aged fast and dressed drably, and she has always over-compensated by piling on furs and ruffles and jewelry. Separated from her husband, the patrician Stephen Dallas, Stella runs into her old riding instructor, Ed Munn: "She didn't like Ed Munn. Stephen had been right. He *was* cheap." But Ed's eyes flatter her, and Stella has a weakness for male flattery. Some upright women in town see Ed Munn entering Stella's vacation quarters, and gossip ensues, even though Stella doesn't sleep with Ed. She only wants his attention.

Prouty's Stella, in her youth, had been a beauty: "Her lips were cherry-red, her cheeks peach-blossom pink, and without paint and powder in those days." Stephen, who has buried himself in a mill town after his embezzler father's suicide, gets taken in by her for a time and marries her. He soon discovers that she's a hopeless vulgarian who rearranges his beloved books by color and can't help but flirt archly with every man she meets. We identify with Stephen and Laurel and their antipathy towards Stella in the first third of the novel; no heroine of a book who outright rejects books is ever going to have much of our sympathy. Prouty's style can be saccharine, but the crux of her novel is far from soapy. The main tension here is between necessary and enriching good taste that can turn stuffy and intolerant, versus Stella's low-class energy, "pep" and need for fun, which can turn barbarous and destructive. Beneath this push-pull is a much more upsetting issue, the explosion of primal emotions when a son or daughter is embarrassed in some way by a parent.

In all of the *Stella Dallas* iterations, the most disturbing character by far is Ed Munn, a glad-hander who falls fast into hopeless alcoholism and dereliction. He's the ugly side of Stella herself, the stubborn coarseness she can't shake off that ruins her life. Occasionally, Stephen has found Munn "fondling" the baby Laurel, and when she reaches adolescence, Laurel is violently opposed to Munn as a kind of sexual threat. It's hard not to wonder, from a modern perspective, just what Munn has done to earn Laurel's anger and fear. Each version of *Stella Dallas* carries a queasy feeling that Munn has molested Laurel or is going to give in to his Neanderthal drunken urges and molest her, and that threat lies heavily over the narrative.

Prouty's Stella obviously doesn't care a thing about the sex act itself. She just likes male attention: "Life wouldn't be worth living, Stella felt, if she had no admirers." The famous party scene, where no one comes to Laurel's birthday because of her mother's reputation, is handled in two terse, very effective pages in the Prouty source material. It ends with a desperate piece of emotional blackmail on Stella's part, begging Laurel never to leave her.

At her best here, Prouty has no illusions about her heroine's basic character; she even writes that Stella's famed maternal instinct had to work its way up "through her vanities and self-interests." When Stella hears people making fun of her appearance on a train and realizes that she's holding Laurel back from social acceptance, Prouty's internal monologue for her is admirably pragmatic. This is a woman who has had her entire sense of herself destroyed brutally and quickly, yet she bounces right back and becomes "hard and practical" for the sake of her daughter's future.

Bracing as Stella's practicality is, this is the point where Prouty's novel deteriorates into far too much self-sacrifice; Stella is even forced to disillusion Laurel by marrying the odious Munn. Then comes the famous last scene, where the understanding new Mrs. Dallas (a character so all-knowing and compassionate that she gives me the creeps) leaves her sitting room shades open so that down-and-out Stella can watch Laurel experience her first tea and reconnect with the society boy she loves.

In 1924, there was a stage version of *Stella Dallas* with Mrs. Leslie Carter. A silent film followed in 1925, directed by Henry King, adapted by Frances Marion, and starring Belle Bennett as Stella and the elegant, stiff Ronald Colman as Stephen. The film begins with a ludicrous prologue where Stephen's father kills himself (a newspaper reads, in huge letters, "Stephen Dallas, Embezzler!" and a smoking gun falls directly onto the headline). In her youthful scenes, Bennett is already a blowzy, Helen Morgan-esque figure with large, forlorn eyes. Since we can't hear Bennett, the onus is on her to be visually embarrassing, and she manages to be, most of the time—especially when she's waddling around a fancy resort while Laurel (Lois Moran) recoils in horror.

This Stella is both sloppy and pretentious, a lethal combination. Amidst the detritus of her messy home, Stella extends her hand to be kissed by Laurel's teacher, Miss Philloburn (Miss Phillobrown in the book, and in the Stanwyck version). The town gossips see Bennett's Stella cavorting with Ed Munn (Jean Hersholt) and mistakenly think the two are sleeping together, just as in the book, but Bennett gives you no sense of Stella's need for male attention. She plays a few of her scenes too comedically, and when the big moments come, she throws her head back and bugs her eyes to indicate grief, even if she does let herself go straight to flabby, straw-haired hell physically.

King doesn't shape the major scenes, so everything feels sketchy—especially the birthday party sequence, where Moran ineptly looks like she's going to laugh rather than cry, and Bennett does a sort of puffy self-pity. And King stages the scene where Munn ruins Stella's chance to get back with Stephen so poorly that it seems to have no weight at all. There's an amusing moment when Stella throws aside the text of Shaw's *Man and Superman* that Laurel gave her and pines instead for the new Elinor Glyn trash bestseller. But Bennett plays the train scene all wrong; she looks mildly annoyed, then mistily self-pitying again. For the climax in the rain, where this Stella is watching Laurel's marriage to her young man, Bennett is seen as a small figure behind a large prison-like fence, her arms stretched up to hang onto the bars. When she moves away, she looks deliriously happy—another odd, misguided choice.

This King version was so financially successful for its producer, Samuel Goldwyn, that he decided to do a remake in 1937, and he chased after Stanwyck's old screen test nemesis, Ruth Chatterton, who turned him down, thankfully. While they were making *Banjo on My Knee*, Stanwyck told Joel McCrea, a Goldwyn contract player, that she desperately wanted to play Stella Dallas. McCrea went to bat for her ("Joel McCrea practically clubbed Sam Goldwyn into getting me into *Stella Dallas*," Stanwyck later said), and he got her a chance to make a screen test for director King Vidor, who wanted Stanwyck for the role.

Established stars like Stanwyck didn't make tests, generally, and McCrea had to talk her into doing so. She must have remembered the humiliations of all the useless tests she did when she first came to Hollywood, but Stanwyck wanted the part of Stella so badly that she was willing, finally, to do anything for it. Later, she said that "everybody was testing for it," and even compared the situation to the search for Scarlett O'Hara, an absurd comparison, of course. No other actress of her stature really wanted this difficult and frankly unflattering role, but landing the part meant so much to Stanwyck that she built the casting process up afterwards in her own mind. She was one of the few major female stars never seriously considered for Scarlett. She never made one of the popular "moonlight and magnolia" pictures of the time, like *Jezebel* (1938). Versatile she was, but a Southern belle she was not.

Goldwyn told Stanwyck that she was too young for the role, didn't think she could act it, didn't have the necessary sex appeal, and didn't have enough experience with children, which was really a low blow. Stanwyck and her son Dion never worked as mother and son on any level. She was too solitary, too much the lone wolf, and likely too hung up on her own vanished mother to ever know what it would take to be one herself. This is not to minimize Dion's suffering, or the unhappy, close to destitute life he led (he died on May 16th, 2006). She should never have adopted him. It just didn't work out, and by 1937 she may have already known that she had few feelings for this boy who was becoming something of a problem child. Robert Taylor said that Dion "wasn't a bad kid," but he got bad grades; he definitely got in the way of her insecure marriage to Taylor.

When he was arrested for selling dirty books to teenagers in 1960, Dion was straightforward about his lack of a relationship with Stanwyck:

> I never saw her—except for a lunch date in 1952 that was arranged by an uncle—since she sent me away to military school in Indiana. My first year of high school. I was a bad student. I guess that bothered her. She didn't expect me to be a genius or anything, but she wanted me to take advantage of the education she was buying for me. I didn't. I didn't do anything real wrong. I just wasn't interested. I was told that she would have sent me to any college I wanted to go to. I'm sorry now that I didn't take advantage of the offer. I guess it was more my fault than it was hers. How we each went our separate ways.

I find it admirable that Dion takes some responsibility for their rift, even if he would become more candid and embittered as the years went on and she still refused to see him. She didn't go to his wedding. "I invited her but she didn't make it," he said. "She bought us a bathroom set, though. And when the baby was born, she bought furniture for him and sent us $100. It still bothers me that she's never come to see her only grandson, my son." *Confidential* magazine ran a story with Dion in 1959 with the plaintive title, "Does My Mother, Barbara Stanwyck, Hate Me?"

If she had hated him, of course, she might have come around to loving him. The truth, sadly, was that she seemed to feel almost nothing where he was concerned. Stanwyck sent him a little furniture, a little money, but her heart was closed. She kept a photo of him in her closet in later years. When he was mentioned in her presence, she would simply say, "Oh, he's long gone," and change the subject. Dion remembered the last time they met: "As politely as a stranger I asked about her career. As politely and distantly as the movie queen she was she answered and inquired how I had been."

This is "star's adopted offspring as fan," à la Christina Crawford—a much more serious and scary case, of course, but characterized by the same sort of disconnection. As someone who loves Stanwyck as much as anyone can love an artist, I can't really wrap my head around the fact that she could say, "You can shoot outlaw horses but not kids. The only thing you can do when you have tried everything, and nothing has worked, is to save yourself." This, from the woman who played Stella Dallas!

Judging by most accounts, the "everything" she tried doesn't seem to have been all that extensive. "Uncle Buck" Mack is the only one who cared at all about Dion in the Stanwyck household. At twelve, Dion was hospitalized when a fishing spear went through his leg at summer camp. "The doctors phoned my mother," he said. "I waited and waited for her to come. She never so much as called." At fifteen, he was something of a delinquent (anything to get some attention), and Stanwyck sat him down, with Taylor, to lecture him about his future.

Then, according to Dion, Mack drove him to Hollywood for a specific purpose: "Uncle Buck explained that Mother had paid for the high-priced call girl to teach me the facts of life." If this actually happened, it opens an extremely dark window into Stanwyck's psyche. I have a good friend, the writer Bruce Benderson, an outrageous, unflappable, force-of-nature fellow, and when I told him about Dion's call girl story, even he was flummoxed. But after a pause, he burst out with, "Well, then that proves she loved him!" It was a funny line, but it contains some twisted sort of truth, I think.

Whatever led Stanwyck to do this, if she did indeed do this, it perhaps had some meaning to her that was based in her own concept of "tough love." If we are to understand her and even some of her work, we have to come to terms with this concept, this impulse to both disillusion and enlighten. Underneath, there was probably some contempt for men and for the sex act itself, but the overarching sentiment seems to have been something like, "He needs to learn the ropes"—just as she had needed to as a girl. Nonetheless, her contempt ultimately rose to the top afterwards and stayed there. "Soon after this incident," Dion recalled, "I got a call from Uncle Buck, and asked him if I could come home. He told me to forget it, to forget that Barbara Stanwyck was my mother. He said, 'She wants nothing to do with you.'"

What appears to be at work here is a kind of Darwinian "fend for yourself" non-mothering mothering, mixed with a kind of desire for vengeance on the male sex and its urges, the urges that cost her those cigarette scars on her chest. And so Dion was cast out of her domain, never to return, even though he remained ever hopeful that she might reconcile with him, even on her deathbed. On that deathbed, she left instructions that he was not under any circumstances to be admitted to her room. Some of this directive might have stemmed from financial anxiety. She had forced Robert Taylor to pay her alimony until his own death as compensation for how he had embarrassed her before their divorce. Now, she didn't want this "they shoot horses, don't they?" old child to get a penny of her money.

So how does Dion relate to *Stella Dallas*, one of her key movies and the role that meant the most to her? Stella goes to great lengths to cut herself off from her daughter so that the daughter will have a chance. In life, Stanwyck went to great and on some deep level inexplicable lengths to sever all ties with her adopted son. And Ruby Stevens's pregnant mother was hit on a streetcar by a drunk, who knocked into her so hard that she fell and hit her head and eventually died. There Ruby is, still on the steps, waiting for her dead mother to come home. So, on screen at least, Stanwyck would incarnate a mother who does everything for her child and then goes into self-imposed exile, thereby working a catharsis for Ruby and for the star's audience. At the end, Stella is on the outside looking in at her daughter's life, just as Dion was left looking in on Stanwyck's real life, her career, and hoping in vain to be noticed.

Stella Dallas was a difficult shoot. Aptly enough, it was made during a make-up and hairdressing strike, so the actors had to cross a picket line every morning. Union scabs made them up and did their hair. At one point, Goldwyn came on the set and bawled everybody out; he said the rushes were terrible and that he was thinking of shutting them down. Then he looked at the footage again and phoned Vidor to say that they were doing a fine job. Vidor was and still is one of the giants of American filmmaking, but he only fitfully felt a personal connection to this material. He was probably busiest trying to fend off the stuffy unreality of Goldwyn's production taste, the same kind of "good taste" that murders Stella herself.

As Stella's daughter, Anne Shirley is over-eager, like a puppy bursting to do its tricks. Rehearsing the train scene, where Stella hears the truth about herself—or at least learns what the world thinks of her—Stanwyck said to Shirley, "All these years I spend in movies and I have a scene in bed with someone, and who do I end up with? YOU! *Not* Clark Gable, *not* Gary Cooper!" Her beloved crew roared at that, but this anecdote strikes me as odd. Making a joke before such an important scene is uncharacteristic of Stanwyck. Maybe the scene was so close to home that she had to somehow distance herself from it before actually doing it.

Stanwyck's Stella is a hybrid person, a freak and a figure of fun, always tormented by her dim consciousness of failure before her ultimate failure is thrown in her face. The uneasy question of Vidor's film is whether or not a certain type of ignorance can be so ingrained in some people that they can never really overcome it—a very un-American idea, and one at odds with the dominant mood of the 1930s. Stella's ambition is the same ambition as those of immigrants who first came to this country chasing dreams for themselves, but mainly chasing dreams for their children. Viewed in this way, Stella is like an immigrant parent who refuses to learn English or adapt to a new environment until it's too late.

The screenplay, written by Sarah Y. Mason and Victor Heerman, deepens and enriches Prouty's original in many ways. In this version, Stella isn't a compulsive flirt and doesn't really care about male attention after her daughter is born. The more unpleasant, vain aspects of Prouty's heroine are removed, but this removal has the effect of making Stella's tragedy more ambiguous and more upsetting.

The film begins with a fanfare under Sam Goldwyn's production credit, then segues into Alfred Newman's yearning theme music. Vidor starts us in Millhampton, Massachusetts, in 1919, and he does the whole prologue with period clothes and sets, unusual for a movie of this time. Throughout the film, but especially in the early and middle sections, Vidor uses a lot of woozy dissolves between scenes rather than hard cuts, and this technique is appropriate both for the mood of the movie and the inner life of its heroine.

We first see Stanwyck's Stella leaving her house, carrying some books. Her hair is dyed blond for this role, so that she isn't wearing the "evil" blond wig that always signaled she was playing murderous women. Stanwyck didn't want to wear a wig here, she explained, because, "I couldn't do anything with my hands, like running them through my hair. Furthermore, in her home Stella's hair was neglected, unkempt—and that just can't be done realistically except with one's own hair." Thus, *Stella Dallas* heralds a return to her Capra roots and to the kind of realism that powered her best work with him.

Outside of her house, Stella shyly poses and fusses to make herself look good for the men coming home from the mill, particularly Stephen Dallas (John Boles). She reads from "India's Love Lyrics" as he passes. Her brother Charlie (George Walcott) mocks her for trying to get Dallas's attention, then tries to kiss her himself: "Take yer dirty hands offah me!" Stella explodes, shattering the storybook visual we've had of her. And then we see Marjorie Main as her mother, tottling out from behind the front door and announcing, "Supper," in a voice devoid of energy. Stella wants to get away from this life; she's been taking business courses at night (in Prouty, and probably here, too, she turns to education to meet eligible men).

Inside the house, Stella reads about Stephen's blighted past in the newspaper, and she reacts in a day-dreamy fashion; one of the smartest things Vidor does all through this version is to make Stella into the sort of fan that most movie audiences of the time could readily identify with. Putting down the paper, she sucks in her lower lip and thinks things over; to keep whole and untouched in her sordid environment, Stella retreats into herself and her private fantasy plans whenever she can. Stanwyck was like this in her own youth, but in her best work she was able to meld reality and daydreams, whereas the way Stella is able to totally shut out reality as a girl is one of the first strong clues to her eventual severe problems with self-deception as a woman.

As Ma Kettle Main schleps around the house, Stanwyck's Stella looks admiringly into a mirror, fiddling idly with her hair, living in her own world. She knows that she's pretty, and she's something of a narcissist. When she goes to Stephen's office to capture his interest, Stanwyck seduces him in a way completely alien to her usual style, with a simple, open smile. This is a poor girl, none too bright, but a girl with possibilities. Sitting down while Stephen is in another room, Stella lovingly feels the material of his coat, foreshadowing one of the key components of her downfall: her attraction to clothes and her stubborn lack of taste in this regard. Coco Chanel once said that a woman should get dressed and then, right before she goes out, take something off—one piece of jewelry, or one accessory. Stella Dallas will always make the mistake of stopping and putting something else on top of her outfit, a sign of her lust, the kind of lower-class lust ripe for ridicule among the polite, bourgeois society of 1919, of 1937, and today.

In the office, Stella talks to Stephen as quietly as possible. She's almost whispery. This is the same tactic that Stanwyck tried when she wanted to bleach the Brooklyn from her voice, a parallel that shows us how perilously close she is to this role she so loved. Stanwyck makes it clear that Stella is passing in this scene, as a light-skinned black person would try to pass for white, or a lesbian would closet herself to pass for straight. Like an actress, Stella is playing a role. "I hate glasses that don't shine, don't you?" she asks Stephen. In most of her other movies, Stanwyck would have delivered a line like that as if she wanted us to enjoy how expertly she could con a sucker. The difference here is that Stella so desperately and sweetly wants to become the part she is playing, just as Stanwyck herself wanted to work as often as possible so that she could always be acting. She didn't like reality and neither does Stella, but Stanwyck had an outlet and Stella does not.

Stephen and Stella go to see a silent movie, a society melodrama. As she watches the movie, Vidor films Stella's rapt expression so that we can see just how intensely and damagingly involved she is in this early Hollywood la-la land. Her clothes aren't too loud yet, even if there are telltale signs of fashion outrages to come: some ruffles that are slightly too large, a pattern on a robe that seems a bit too busy. As Stephen and Stella leave the theater, two girls gossip about them, and Stella snaps at them to mind their own business; so much of her later trouble will stem from prying, unsympathetic eyes. This is the fighting Stella, and it's an open question here, sometimes, whether this need to fight has coarsened what could have been fine, or if this coarseness is rooted in her personality. Right away, she reverts to her pretensions, asking Stephen if she can take his arm: "Is that all right . . . is that considered . . . ," she asks, all in a charming rush. She stimulates the Henry Higgins in Stephen, but Boles also emphasizes how horny his character is for Stella.

"I want to be like all the people you've been around . . . educated, and speaking nice," she says, breathlessly, as they take a nighttime walk. Cinematographer Rudolph Maté uses soft lighting here to make Stanwyck's face appear as childlike and plain as possible, and in a scene like this, where Stella is at her most hopeful, there's almost a feel of a Kenji Mizoguchi drama like *The Story of the Late Chrysanthemums* (1939), a calm and inevitable tragedy. Stella chatters about how she wants to be "like the people in the movie, all well-bred and refined." Like so many audiences of the 1930s and after, Stella would like to live in a movie, but such a wish is as impossible as living in Stephen's polite society, with its rules and form and regulation of emotion. Stella most wants the thing that is going to kill her (Stanwyck is heartbreaking already). And Stephen marries Stella that night because he wants to sleep with her, an unfortunate trend in this era and a convention that led to much unhappiness for men, women, and the children they bore.

Vidor jumps ahead a year. Stella has had a baby and is returning home from the hospital. Even before we see her, we can hear in her voice that something is wrong. The soft Stella that bewitched Stephen after that movie date is gone and in her place is a complacent frump-in-waiting who wants to make a splash, not because she desires male attention, as in the novel, but out of a more general kind of exuberance. Stella's voice sounds more certain and more low-class as she climbs the stairs. When we see her, she is dressed in a bulky coat and a deforming black hat that sits on her head like a papier-mâché anvil. She talks about "kindiegarten," and insists that she's had plenty of experience, and she didn't get it outta readin' books! Vidor makes it tacitly understood that she can still hold Stephen with her sex appeal. She hasn't quite noticed her daughter yet. Before going out, she looks at the cradle as if to say, "Ah, I like the kid, but I wanta have my fun!"

This is a new Stella, and sometimes the change in her manner is as bewildering to us as it is to Stephen, but broken, neither-here-nor-there people like Stella are always a little mysterious, especially to themselves. When she whirls around with Ed Munn (Alan Hale) at a dance, Stella is dressed in feathers and netting, and her hair is in tight blond curls. She keeps letting out the sort of high-pitched, nasal, backslapping laugh that seems designed solely to embarrass everyone in sight, but she can't help it. This is just her nature, and Ed Munn brings this side of her out and keeps it there.

The demon Ed! Hale gives the performance of his life as this trashy galoot. Stella thinks he's fun, which is what she's after. And he is fun, but it's the kind of fun that's suited to a barroom and not a country club dance. When she wants to meet a rich man named Chandler, Stella wriggles over to his table (we see that the seat of her dress is far too tight) and gets herself introduced, employing the same softness that intrigued Stephen. At this point in her life, Stella can tone down her effects when she needs to. As she ages, unfortunately, she loses this ability, and this loss is one of the saddest and one of the truest insights of Vidor's movie.

"Gosh, I have to think every time I open my mouth!" Stella cries afterwards, when Stephen is giving her his "usual lecture." She's tired of playing Eliza Doolittle. Her spirit and her pride won't let her be molded into the uptight lady Stephen wants for his wife, and you can't blame her too much. When he tries to criticize her vulgar way of dressing, she won't hear of it. Why, in Millhampton the girls always said she had "stacks of style," she insists. It's only later that we wonder if those Millhampton girls might not have said such a thing maliciously, or if they, like Stella, just didn't know any better.

This matter of clothes isn't a trivial issue; it can be argued that clothes alone wreck Stella Dallas's life, even more than the id-like presence of Ed Munn. Irritated with Stephen, Stanwyck's Stella defends herself and while she does, she scratches her head. It's worth asking just how many actors in 1937 were scratching itches on screen, and the gesture adds a welcome touch of Brando-like realism. But it also says a lot about the character—and about Stanwyck's preparation, for she wouldn't have been able to scratch a wig with such abandon.

Stephen goes to New York, and Stella stays put, a development that never seems to make solid sense in any version of this story (but again, Stella so often does things out of sheer obstinacy). Some years pass and daughter Laurel is now a toddler. Stella has gotten a tad sloppy with time, but not overly so. She's only on the first rung of her descent to the bottom, and Vidor charts this degeneration carefully. Ed Munn barges in and turns Stella's living room into a speakeasy in about a minute flat, lighting a cigar, pouring out drinks for himself and a friend, and then scaring Laurel to death by picking her up and putting her on his lap. Stephen walks in on this scene, and Vidor gives you a shot from his point of view; we can tell that he has come in at the worst possible time. There's no way we can blame him for wanting to keep his daughter away from Munn, but when he tells his wife that he might have to take Laurel away from her, something profound happens in Stella, and in Stanwyck's performance. A fury rises up, crests, then falls as she pulls Laurel away from her father.

"Watch out, you're hurting her!" she brays, even though Ed was the one who upset the girl. "Get out," she says to her husband, making it sound like a choked afterthought. Laurel is crying hard, and Stella takes her child on her lap and tries to comfort her. The little girl keeps on crying, and Stanwyck's face takes on a distant blankness as she says that Mummy is right here. "You're here with Mummy and nobody in the whole world is going to take you away," she says. "Nobody," she says again, then repeats, slightly more quietly, "Nobody."

It's a killer scene, one of the best Stanwyck ever played, and it has the deepest connection to her own life and history. She is thirty years old now and a movie star, and she's playing one of her best roles, a role about a mother's love for her child. And this role must have been her favorite because in some sense she was able to use it to alleviate Ruby Stevens's suffering on those stairs and be the mother that would be alive and come home. Stanwyck could do that as an actress, for all time, but she couldn't do that for the boy she adopted. Alas, as Stella finds out the hard way, life just isn't the movies.

Stephen meets up with his old flame, the widow Morrison (Barbara O'Neil) and her three obnoxiously perfect boys. And then we see an older Stella, her hair a real mess now, her figure dumpy; she still has her dreams, but at this point they're exclusively for her daughter. She isn't so far gone that she can't tidy up in a flash when Laurel's teacher,

Miss Phillobrown (Ann Shoemaker), comes to visit. But one thing she can't tidy up is her Marjorie Main background. She talks loud and makes grammatical mistakes. And every now and then Stanwyck lets off a little flare of panic behind Stella's eyes, as if she knows she might be doing something wrong but isn't sure what.

Some of Stella's problems stem from laziness. Part of her knows that Stephen was right about the surface flaws in her manners, but she doesn't want to put in the work to change them, thinking that she can just slide through. Hey, why not? The teacher leaves, and Laurel, now played by Anne Shirley, finds the birthday dress that Stella has been making for her. This discovery makes Stella yell at Laurel insincerely and then forgive her quickly, a bit of behavior so psychologically accurate to parent/child relations and so outside Stanwyck's own experience that it only serves as proof of the scope of her imagination.

Her performance still gathers in bits of naturalistic detail: "Let me fit it on you instead of the . . . thing . . . dummy," Stanwyck says, stumbling over her words, exposing and using her own verbal awkwardness for Stella's sake. When Laurel objects to an unnecessary bow on her dress, Stella cries, "You're just like your father, you want everything as plain as an old shoe!" (Do frills and furbelows function as protection for Stella, as well as something to catch the eye?) A tipsy Ed Munn comes in and grabs at Laurel in her slip, then howls about getting a kick out of "the young ones being so finicky!" Stella seems agitated by his behavior, but not nearly enough. This is the destructive side of her dazed slowness of mind; she never seems to realize just how close Ed is to abusing Laurel— neither does he, probably, but that's what drinking is for. Alas.

Following this low point, Vidor stages the high point of Ed and Stella's adventures as a platonic couple, a screwball comedy scene where Ed mischievously puts itch powder on his thumb and then shakes hands with a bunch of people on a train. As the people start to itch, Ed begins a running commentary, and Stella reacts just as he wants her to. "I can't stand it!" she cries, choked up with laughter. This is the kind of thing that's difficult for an actor to do, this kind of stifled laughter, but Stanwyck not only does it, she builds on it steadily so that we *have* to laugh along with Stella at Ed's joke.

When two spinsters start scratching, Ed whispers, "They're doin' a sister act . . . they must have rehearsed!" and Stella gets more hysterical with pleasure. "Stop, you're killing me," she whines. Then Vidor cuts to a man lifting his toupee to scratch his itch, which acts as a capper and leads Stella and Ed laughing uproariously into the next car. Vidor made three marvelous comedies with Marion Davies in the late twenties, and he had a talent for scenes like this, even though he rarely used it in his most personal work.

In the 1925 version of *Stella Dallas*, Ed Munn shoots some spitballs at people's heads on the train, but it isn't remotely funny; director Henry King is too much of a prude to ever let us identify with Stella. We all have itches that need to be scratched, but there are some high-minded people who like to pretend that this isn't the case—or at least they seek to rise above such basic needs. When Stella has an itch, she scratches it, regardless of what people think, and of course she finds it hilarious when her friend Ed gets a whole trainful of people scratching away, even those two dignified, dried-up looking old ladies. Ed and Stella collapse in laughter in another car, where a bunch of silent people look up at them. Laurel's teacher, Miss Phillobrown, is in the car. From her point of view, we see Stella with her skirt slightly hiked above the knee, and she does seem drunk with Ed, even though it's only high spirits. "Such women don't deserve to have children," says Miss Phillobrown's companion. It is a line that comes as an ironic conclusion in Prouty's novel; here, it seems completely heartless and unfair.

Vidor cuts back to Ed, who offers his love to Stella, shyly, and she smiles at him and says, "I don't think there's a man livin' that could get me goin' anymore." Then, more to the point: "I guess Lolly just uses up all the feelings I got. I don't seem to have any left for anybody else." Having quieted down, she looks affectionately at Ed and says, "You're such a good sport," in a low, very serious voice. "Such a lot of fun." Vidor, who is always on the side of vitality, makes a case for Ed Munn in these two scenes—at least as Hale plays him—and this approval complicates Prouty's material.

In the next scene, we see Stella all dressed up for Laurel's birthday party. She wears huge flowers on one shoulder and a filmy flower print dress with large white fur cuffs around her arms. Laurel tells her mother that she looks beautiful, and Vidor gives Stanwyck a close-up in which she seems radiantly happy, but doubtful, too, as if she feels somehow that Laurel isn't right about this. "Do I?" she asks, using the exact tone of a parent wondering whether she can fully accept a compliment from her own child. By this point, so many of Stella's dreams have been extinguished by the sloppy, indolent life she lives in her apartment. She can't allow herself to believe she's still attractive; everything now is for her daughter.

Miss Phillobrown sends word that she can't make it, and Stella quickly comes in with, "I guess they see enough of her at school, I know I did my teachers!" Laurel pitifully says that everyone loves Miss Phillobrown, even if what we've seen of her makes her look like a woman unworthy of such love. There's something so sickening about a planned birthday party that no one attends, especially when it's for a child, and no one comes to Laurel's party. They need to punish her mother for laughing too hard with a male friend on a train. That's all it comes down to, really, which is why this midsection of the film works up a fine steam of anger.

Laurel soon falls under the spell of her father's devoted Mrs. Morrison and can't stop talking about her when she gets home. Laurel goes on and on about Mrs. Morrison's complexion, which only needs soap and water, while her mother applies copious amounts of cold cream to her face. "All I can say is there's different kinds of skin," Stella says, in a dry, deadpan tone. It's a potential laugh line, but Stanwyck keeps us steady with what we know is about to happen. She sits in front of a three-way mirror, but Vidor only shows us two images of Stella, and it often feels like that's what this movie is about: the two faces of Stella, the loud woman who's as vulgar as Gladys George, and the moonbeam girl buried underneath, as sensitive as Katharine Hepburn.

Stella has her chin down and she looks up into the mirror, so that her face seems crushed and moldy, the sorry remains of the pretty girl who preened herself in Millhampton. She spots a part of her hair that needs more hair dye, and then Laurel comes into the frame. "I'll do it," says her daughter, trying to fix her mother's hair. Stella's eyes look down, and she touches a finger to her mouth; she knows now what's happening, and she knows that she can't stop it. She can't be dignified and cool and matronly, which is what her daughter wants. She's left there by Vidor, her finger to her mouth, suspended in time, pulled in several anguished directions, yet entirely still in herself, as if such stillness might work some miraculous transformation. There are Stanwyck scenes you don't forget, and then there's this scene.

At Christmas, Ed Munn barges in drunk, carrying an unwieldy turkey and holding some mistletoe so he can get a kiss from Laurel (he's always so close to doing something unforgivable to her). When she hears that Stephen is coming, Stella hustles Ed out the back door and goes upstairs to change. She rejects several gaudy outfits and takes out a black dress, making it plainer for her husband by cutting off some lace and ruffles with a pair of scissors. At last, Stella wants to see if she can be what Stephen wants her to be and if they can all be a family. She looks in the mirror and puts on some lip-gloss, then, after a moment's consideration, she takes it off. This action is a link to Stanwyck's films with Capra and to their idea about truth, which Stella has hidden under a boatload of material junk for some deep-seated, unthinking reason.

Stella wants to "pass" again, but in the right way, without the insecurities of her youth, and she seems to pull it off. Stephen is impressed by her appearance, and he asks her to spend Christmas with him and their daughter as a family. Then, inevitably, Ed Munn comes back in through the front door, and the kicker in this Vidor version is that Ed realizes—all in a flash—that he's spoiled everything for Stella. It's Hale's best scene and a last glimpse of Ed's human side.

Through a lawyer, Stephen asks her for a divorce. A definitively disappointed Stella is at her absolute worst with this lawyer, wearing her clunky clothes like armor, waving her hands around, acting hard-driving and crafty—straightforward and honest, yes—but also 100 percent common and cheap, in the old senses of those words (her worst, though, is far better than Miss Phillobrown's best). Quite disturbed now, not thinking at all clearly, Stella's determined to make a last-ditch effort to be the kind of mother Laurel wants, and so she makes Stephen pay for a fancy resort vacation.

Stella submits to facials and hair treatments, but gets sick (or has a breakdown?) before she can meet anyone at their hotel. Laurel meets rich boy Richard (Tim Holt) on her own while her mother convalesces. We see Stella reduced to a tacky mountain of make-up and hair dye sitting up reading *True Confessions* and eating bon-bons in bed, but when Laurel comes in and bends down to hug her, Stella grabs a strand of her daughter's hair and caresses it gently. The best part of her hasn't been entirely lost.

Outside, Laurel's life becomes, and seemingly *is*, in Vidor's now-uninterested direction, one of those society movies that Stella always wanted to be a part of. But then the Gorgon in Stella rises to the surface, Vidor re-engages, and Stanwyck presents you with the full horror of a middle-aged person who feels the need to act out a grotesque parody of themselves. On top of her Harpo Marx curls, Stella has placed a hat that comes to a big black bow at the top and covers her face with a large spotted veil in front. Her flowered dress clings to every bump and lump in her figure, and her wrists are covered in bracelets that jangle when she moves. About to go outside, she stops, gets a white mink stole, then piles that on top of everything else. She embodies a kind of fashion nightmare, so garish that it feels like someone might arrest her, or at least lead her to the nearest psychiatrist. What is Stella doing here? This is much worse than her usual mistakes with dress. In fact, it seems like some subconscious but deliberate attempt to sabotage everything, a cry for help, an attempt to bury Stella Martin's stupid dreams once and for all through total self-annihilation.

The outfit is shocking, but Stella's manners are worse. When she insists on tipping a reluctant porter, she brandishes her money at him and cries, "Don't be sill!" Combining society pretensions with Ed Munn slang, she charges around the resort and makes a spectacle of herself in front of the guests, who laugh at her and make mean remarks. This is the key sequence in the film. We know Stella intimately at this point and we know what her problems are. We also know that if we saw someone like Stella wandering around and acting the way she does, we too would most likely laugh at her, as we do at anyone who is different—or anyone who is cursed.

Vidor narrows the scene to social class observation when Laurel's friends jeer at her mother, sotto voce. Tellingly, they call Stella "it," as in, "Does it talk?" One guy wonders if her hat is going to light up with some kind of advertisement, a line that brings the whole dicey dynamic of Prouty's material to a head. It's partly the materialistic society she lives in that has made Stella what she is. Humiliated, Laurel tells her mother that they have to leave, and Stanwyck plays her dithering, vague reaction perfectly, as if Stella knows what's wrong, but she can't bring herself to face it. In their train berths that night, Stella and Laurel both hear some young girls mocking Stella; they say right out that Laurel will never marry Richard with such a mother. Vidor's camera moves in on Stella's face slowly as she listens, and Stanwyck shows you that Stella already somehow knew how things stand—and knows that now she is going to have to face it.

Stella, still badly dressed, but at her 1919 hopeful best, goes to see Mrs. Morrison. She knows it's too late to change herself, but she doesn't want to destroy her daughter's life like she's destroyed her own. The character of Mrs. Morrison, once again, doesn't make much sense. Her "I understand!" reaction to Stella's plan to send Laurel away feels false. The reality here is the cattiness of those society girls on the train. Whatever her faults, Stella would never be as mean as they are, or as self-righteous and punishing as Miss Phillobrown.

Laurel realizes why her mother is giving her up and so she comes back to her, but Stella uses Ed Munn to drive her daughter out again. After rousing Ed from a drunken flophouse stupor, Stanwyck goes to his door and then shoots him a look, one of those looks of recognition she gave to Lily Powers and Megan Davis, a kind of artistic signature. As always, it's a recognition of *something*, not something specific, but something about Stella's life in general and how it relates to this old drunk sleeping one off. It's like she's thinking, "This? That's me? That's what I was meant for?" And she answers herself: Yes. Yes, it is. (Stanwyck's nearly Japanese stoicism asserts itself). Kicking Laurel out, Stella now uses her vulgar side, just as she used her sensitive side to nab Stephen. These are just roles she plays, and she'll never be able to reconcile the divided halves of her character. In a nod to her pre-Code past, Stanwyck even puts on a jazz record of "St. Louis Woman," and this music gets rid of her virtuous daughter once and for all.

Then there's the last scene, so corny that your first, correct impulse is to laugh. Mrs. Morrison makes sure that the curtains are drawn for Laurel's wedding to her society man. Stella is outside, of course, and any laugh dies in your throat when you see her Depression-ravaged, wiped-out face, her coat with its ratty fur on the shoulders, her man's hat. As she watches her daughter's wedding from behind a fence in the rain, Stella's face is serene, like it was when she watched that movie on her first date with Stephen. It's her fate to be a fan, to be literally outside looking in, and she has accepted it. A policeman tells her to move along, I'm afraid, but she convinces him to wait until the groom has lifted Laurel's veil and kissed her. We see that and then cut back to Stella, who's chewing on a handkerchief. A tear slides gently down her face and right into her open mouth, a sensual detail that lets us see her instinct for pleasure is still alive.

The show over, Stella turns and dips slightly to the side, like a happy child, then starts to stride toward the camera as the music swells. Stanwyck leaves us on a high of goose-pimply exaltation. In the book, Stella has married the now-helpless Ed, her one friend, and she works in a shirtwaist factory, sewing clothes. She was never good with clothes, God knows, but they can't hurt her anymore, and she doesn't need them to protect her, either. (Poetically enough, a cop at the premiere of *Stella Dallas* briefly and violently detained Stanwyck because she was so plainly dressed that he didn't recognize her). Stanwyck felt that Stella had managed to "cheat failure," at least for her daughter. For such a mixed-up person, a small victory like that counts as a large achievement.

Stage Stanwyck

The Plough and the Stars, Golden Boy, Clash by Night

$\mathscr{K}$enneth Tynan wrote that Greta Garbo couldn't be considered a great actress, finally, because she had never put herself to the test in major theater roles; she had never given us her Hedda Gabler, her Masha in *Three Sisters*, her Mrs. Alving in *Ghosts*. This idea that an actor can only truly prove her talent by scaling the heights of classical theater roles is perhaps an old-fashioned one, tied more to British than American tradition, but stage success is certainly helpful, if not infallible, as a gauge of acting ability. Bette Davis is every bit the equal of Katharine Hepburn as a screen actress, yet Davis never played any Shakespeare leads, as Hepburn did on stage. In late middle age, Hepburn offered a definitive Mary Tyrone in a film adaptation of Eugene O'Neill's *Long Day's Journey Into Night* (1962), and she went on to tackle Tennessee Williams, Edward Albee, and even Greek tragedy in *The Trojan Women* (1970)—albeit with uneven results. The closest Davis came to a testing theater part like this was her Regina Giddens in *The Little Foxes* (1941), and that's a sterling credit. But it's hard not to wish that Davis had attempted a few more of these "prove your mettle" roles, and that Hepburn had been a bit more discriminating about what parts suited her (i.e., no Amanda Wingfield in Williams's *The Glass Menagerie* [1973]).

"I'd drop dead if I had to recite a single line of Shakespeare," Stanwyck joked to a reporter in the 1940s. Classical drama was out for her, but she had three notable tries at parts written originally for the theater. The first of these was the difficult role of Nora Clitheroe in John Ford's abbreviated RKO adaptation of Sean O'Casey's *The Plough and the Stars* (1936), a disenchanted account of the Irish Easter rebellion of 1916.

When the play premiered at the Abbey Theatre in 1926, there was a riot during the fourth performance, led mainly by some of the women associated with the fallen men of 1916. These women objected to the play's satire on the kind of nationalism that destroys Nora Clitheroe's middle-class family and dreams (Barry Fitzgerald had to punch a male protestor on stage to defend the actors). In O'Casey's play, Nora is pregnant, and she eventually loses her mind. She is the heroine of the piece, which employs a large company to play people on the margins of a dramatic event. Though she is often sympathetic, Nora is also a nag and a hysteric, so that the actress playing her has to commit fully to all of her flaws and take the risk of not being liked, at times, in order to be true to the life of this three-dimensional, righteous, sometimes exasperating woman.

For his film of the play, Ford uses the dark, expressionist look he favored in this period, and his introduction of his star is striking. We see a woman's head turn toward the camera, wearing a Virgin Mary–like head-cloak: Stanwyck's face is creased in doubt, almost folded in half, in fact. *The Plough and the Stars* can be most fruitfully seen as one artist, Ford, looking at another, Stanwyck, in purely visual terms, observing her in different moods and at different angles. In many ways, he films Stanwyck here in a similar fashion to the self-denying, rapt, intense way that he shot Katharine Hepburn's shadowed close-ups in *Mary of Scotland*, made that same year, but with a key difference. Whereas with Hepburn, Ford's photographic attention is discreetly romantic, with Stanwyck he elevates her as a kind of maternal figure.

Away from the city, in a contrasting luminescent sequence at a park where Nora wanders with her husband, Jack (Preston Foster), Ford has Stanwyck wear a stiff white lace hat that he lights like it's a halo. Though Ford takes care with the illuminated and then darkened frames he puts around Stanwyck's face, there is no attempt to glamorize or idealize her face itself. Throughout this film, she looks like a real, extremely worried person. Her features are doughy here, as if they were made of lumpy clay, and her swollen Nora looks like a person who sweats and who breathes heavily.

Stanwyck uses only a hint of an Irish accent, allowing her to focus on Nora's feelings without worrying about overly correct phrasings. When she tells her husband Jack that she burned his notification from the Irish Citizen Army, Stanwyck puts her full orchestral force behind the word "burned," so that it seems to explode outward like a shower of sparks. But this is only a preview of her big moment, when she shouts for her husband outside and is told to hush up by the women of the army.

"They're all cowards!" her Nora cries. "Fools, do you think they want to die!" she howls, in a decidedly ferocious, deeply disgusted manner.

It's a risk. When she tried this deeper, more full-blooded hysteria in *The Woman in Red*, Stanwyck just looked silly, because the flimsy film couldn't handle it. Here, she has the material and the director to make such forceful expression land and resonate. Aside from *Ever in My Heart*, she never made another movie that dealt directly with war, for Stanwyck is an urban American creature; she made her own battlegrounds. In this scene in *The Plough and the Stars*, Stanwyck is able to address one of the greatest of outrages, just as she addressed the outrage of suffering, defenseless children in *Night Nurse*, and she has the epic size for the role, so that you wonder if she couldn't have played Hecuba, or Clytemnestra, or a modern Medea slaughtering her children on Flatbush Avenue to avenge herself on a faithless husband. The full arc of her role, however, is sidestepped; Stanwyck's Nora doesn't lose her mind, as she does in the play (she never portrayed outright mental illness on screen, preferring less clinical disturbances of the mind and heart).

The Abbey Theatre players in Ford's *Plough* "project" their roles to the camera. Arthur Shields, brother of Barry Fitzgerald, has a credit as an assistant to the director and seems to have been in charge of these actors. Ford generally preferred more natural performers, but he indulges Fitzgerald and the impish Una O'Connor without really harming the texture of his movie. Ford is the ideal interpreter of O'Casey's ambiguous material, and this little-seen film is admirable on several levels. He does not shy away from the looting that goes on during the Easter uprising, or from arguments about the merits of socialism, which get batted around by some of the characters. In one especially vivid scene, an Irish boy is trapped on a slatted roof, trying to get into a window for shelter. British soldiers shoot him, and his body sticks to the roof for a moment and then slides down—a sickening image, held for just the right amount of time.

RKO tampered with the film when Ford left for Honolulu on vacation. Pandro Berman, who had taken over as production head from Samuel J. Briskin, thought that the movie would be more commercial if Nora and Jack were lovers instead of spouses, and he insisted that Stanwyck and Foster come back and re-shoot some scenes, to Stanwyck's dismay. "I've always felt that John should not have left the sinking ship," she told *Film Comment* in 1981. "God knows I had no power at that time, nor did Preston. Only John could have saved it, and he should have." This re-cut and re-shot version was supposed to be released in America, while Ford's version was shown in England and Ireland (the non-Ford version has all but disappeared at this point, and most of the reviewers in America saw the Ford version). Tag Gallagher, one of the pre-eminent scholars of Ford's work, told me that there is also a second US version of this film that is much longer, with "substantial newsreels in between some sequences—not by Ford." Presumably such a cut was put together in order to pad the film out to reach the length of a prestige picture.

Introducing his heroine, Lorna Moon, in his play *Golden Boy*, Clifford Odets writes: "There is a certain quiet glitter about this girl, and if she's sometimes hard, it is more from necessity than choice." He also writes that her eyes "often hold a soft, sad glance." When *Golden Boy* was first produced for the stage in 1937, Lorna was played by Frances Farmer, a promising young actress who was romantically involved with Odets at that time. Afterwards, he dropped her, and she fell into mental instability. It was the part of a lifetime for Farmer, a serious role in a serious play where she was surrounded by Group Theatre stalwarts like Morris Carnofsky, Luther Adler, Robert Lewis, a young John Garfield, and, as the obsessed gay gangster Fuseli, Elia Kazan. *Golden Boy* was one of the Group Theatre's major productions, but it isn't revived much. In Paul Mazursky's *Next Stop, Greenwich Village* (1976), two young actors complain about Odets's stilted language, but their teacher tells them that the playwright was writing poetically, that he "heightened the thing," and that it takes a special kind of belief—and the right delivery—to make *Golden Boy* work.

Lorna Moon is one of the best and most apposite roles Stanwyck was ever given, and the film of *Golden Boy* (1939) should have been one of her biggies, but it doesn't really work on any level. There are several probable reasons for this failure. Lorna is a self-described "tramp from Newark," but for this post-Code movie, she's a "dame from Newark," and the four credited screenwriters have subtly removed a lot of the guts from the part. In this film, Lorna doesn't talk about how her father beat her mother, or how her mother killed herself, and she doesn't get to say, "If I let myself go, I'd be a drunkard in a year."

As Odets wrote her, this is a self-destructive woman, and all of her interactions with Joe Bonaparte, a self-loathing young violinist turned boxer, should reflect their tense longing for each other, as well as their need for oblivion. Odets sets up his dichotomy of boxing (selling out to Hollywood) versus music (the theater) as a personal indictment of himself, but also of the commercialism of the modern world, and his play still shoots the sort of bullets he intended—even if some are blanks owing to some overly gaudy writing in the last scenes.

Lorna is involved with Tom Moody, a broken-down, married fight promoter who once pulled her out of the gutter. She feels loyalty to him for having saving her and sticks by him because he's a little boy at heart and needs her help. In the film, Adolphe Menjou is cast as Moody, and he's hopeless from the first moments of the first scene, too suave and too hollow to make Lorna's feeling for him make sense. When he mentions the money he made back in 1928, Lorna says that her mother died that year, and it's clear from the outset that Stanwyck just isn't feeling this role. She's disconnected from the fussy Menjou and totally divorced from the emotions of an embittered girl who should be right up her alley.

Rouben Mamoulian directs uncertainly; his camera is always jerkily moving to the right or left to catch up with the characters, and this makes everything feel like a rehearsal rather than a take. He had a habit of telling his actors that the camera was running when it wasn't, for some reason, and when he tried this on Stanwyck, she told him off in no uncertain terms. It's hard to imagine a directorial technique that could have alienated her more, and her inspiration dried up for the actual scenes. Probably some of the best of her Lorna Moon was performed when Mamoulian's camera wasn't running.

Aside from this, Stanwyck was also concerned about her inexperienced young leading man, William Holden, who had been cast as Bonaparte over a large field of likely contenders. He too had trouble with Mamoulian's methods, and Columbia head Harry Cohn was going to have Holden fired until Stanwyck interceded on his behalf, promising to work with him off the set. "I told him much of what Willard Mack had taught me," she said. Holden comes off just fine in the film, but it's likely that Stanwyck's own performance suffered because she was busy making sure his work was as good as it needed to be.

To top all this off, she married Robert Taylor midway through shooting, on May 13th, 1939, and this was another distraction that must have caused her mind to be anywhere but on the job at hand. When he heard the news, Holden sent her a sweet telegram that read, "GOSH, What a Blow!—The Golden Boy." It's been intimated that Stanwyck and Holden might have been more than friends during this trial by fire, but it's more likely that he had a lifetime crush on her owing to the help she gave him. For the rest of his life, every April 1st, the date they started shooting, Holden would send Stanwyck two dozen roses and a white gardenia. Surely Holden was one of the few people that Stanwyck really loved, perhaps a bit romantically, perhaps not. She always enjoyed helping younger, pretty boy actors like Taylor, Holden, and later Robert Wagner.

"See you in 1960, maybe you'll be somebody by then!" Lorna tells Joe. It's a line that isn't in the play, and of course Holden would be one of the biggest movie stars in the world in 1960. By then, Stanwyck's film career was largely over.

In her scenes with Joe, when Lorna is attempting to seduce him into boxing full-time, Stanwyck plays at half-energy, except for a rather too disgusted, enraged reaction after he kisses her. When she's supposed to be charmed by Joe's family, Stanwyck "smiles" a bit, but she isn't a smiler; simple happiness and pleasure are well outside her ken. Lorna is supposed to be torn between Moody and Joe, but Stanwyck is just going through the motions in these later scenes. In the *Meet John Doe*–like happy ending, when she has to sell us another false bill of goods, she can hardly be bothered. Unfortunately, Stanwyck's whole performance is a wash, except for one spine-tinglingly definitive moment that suggests how good she might have been as Lorna Moon. Joseph Calleia's Fuseli looks at her legs (as does the camera) and asks Moody, "This your girl?" Stanwyck is sitting on Moody's desk, impassive, a cigarette smoldering in her right hand. She shoots back, "I'm my mother's girl," in a no-fuss way that suggests that this isn't a woman who's afraid of gangsters, or of anything much—except for the slow-burning anger that's eventually going to eat away her insides.

Stanwyck had another go at an Odets heroine in *Clash by Night*, directed by Fritz Lang for RKO. With this theater role, she still sometimes seems like she's just going through the motions, especially in some of her early scenes (Manny Farber in his review said that she was given to "impersonating a mentholated icicle"). But she does some of her finest work here, too, in some scenes opposite Robert Ryan—this has to count as one of her most uneven performances. The play was first produced in 1941, with Tallulah Bankhead, Lee J. Cobb, and Joseph Schildkraut in the roles that would be played in the film by Stanwyck, Paul Douglas, and Robert Ryan. Odets set his play on Staten Island, and he resolved the eternal triangle between his characters with murder.

In the Lang movie, the setting has been moved to a California fishing village, and this change allows the director to start things off with waves crashing under the credits, followed by some evocative shots of seagulls and seals. We see Peggy (Marilyn Monroe) waking up to go to work in the fish cannery nearby. This scene is staged very realistically; it's a bit of a shock to see the legendary Monroe as a plain girl in jeans. We watch the factory routine (which suggests Lang's futuristic factory in his *Metropolis* [1926]) and all the little silver fish moving along on an assembly line. Lang doesn't make this scene particularly symbolic; you're allowed to draw your own conclusions.

Mae Doyle (Stanwyck) gets off a train with a suitcase and goes into a bar to order a coffee with a brandy to go with it. Douglas's Jerry comes in to get his drunken father (Silvio Minciotti) out of the bar. He tells his dad to go home, and the father whines, "Is nothing, home." We see Mae react, as if to say, "You said it." She's been away for ten years. "Home is where you come when you run out of places," Mae croaks, wearily, tossing her cigarette into a coffee cup. Later on, she tells us about a married man she loved, a politician who died and left her money his relatives wouldn't let her have. Stanwyck delivers all this back-story professionally, competently, but in a way that lets us see that she's not all that interested in this woman or where she's been.

Stanwyck shares a warm look of sympathy with Monroe, who blew take after take and was always late to the set. "She couldn't get out of her own way," Stanwyck later said of Monroe. "She wasn't disciplined . . . but she didn't do it viciously, and there was a sort of magic about her which we all recognized at once." This is generous of Stanwyck, paying tribute to a different kind of movie performer after that performer's untimely death. On the set, though, Stanwyck was heard to say, "With a figure like that, you don't have to know how to act," and she was right. Monroe is stilted in the film, awkward, but in certain moments she does have that movie "magic" that Stanwyck recognized and respected.

Still and all, this is Robert Ryan's movie, and he takes it by force from the moment he first appears as Earl, a savagely disappointed, woman hating romantic (and movie projectionist). Earl excites Monroe's innocent Peggy and Stanwyck's wary Mae, who discreetly looks him up and down while out on a polite date with Douglas's bellowy widower. "Didn't you ever want to cut up a beautiful dame?" asks Earl, talking about film cutting, but meaning something else, a fact that Mae takes in. She can see that he's sexy, but in the worst possible way.

Mae is seduced by Jerry's innocence, which ties her to earlier Stanwyck characters, but Jerry is a tubby, none-too-bright innocent, not Henry Fonda or Gary Cooper, but a last resort for a forty-five-year-old woman who just wants to rest. Mae is burnt-out, and Stanwyck's performance in the early scenes is also regrettably burnt-out, though she sometimes manages to come alive, in isolated moments. When Jerry says that everyone is afraid of getting old and lonely, Stanwyck looks up at him from a ladder she's climbing down, stopping herself, physically and emotionally. She takes in what he's just said as fully as possible and then replies, "I suppose," in that shivery way of hers, as if this statement is coming from disparate sources of knowledge meeting and clashing together.

After this moment, however, Stanwyck plays the role with a generic sort of "charged intensity," which feels a bit forced and all on one level. Lang switches to some cheesecake—Marilyn's Peggy jiggling in a swimsuit on the beach—which gets Earl's attention and then goads his sadism, which is much in evidence. He's cruel to an elderly waiter, calling him "a good boy." When Jerry asks Earl for his "Chinese imitation," Mae considers Earl's racist nonsense coolly (Stanwyck does her mouth shrug and even lifts an eyebrow, but this gesture seems like a choice borne out of either uncertainty or boredom). When Earl gets her a whiskey shot, Mae tosses it back and then stares at him challengingly. This doesn't feel like the "Stanwyck is a stoic" routine from some of her lesser films of this time, but a jolt of real anger. There's nothing ambiguous about this emotion, for it all but broadcasts, "I hate men."

Stanwyck had been the rejected party in her divorce from Taylor, and this status gnawed at her pride. At one point during shooting, she complained to Lang that she couldn't play a scene because it was badly written. "I knew the scene," Lang remembered, "which I thought was very well-written, and said, 'Barbara, may I speak frankly and openly with you?' She said, 'Naturally,' and I continued: 'I think the scene reminds you of a rather recent event in your private life, and that is why you think it is badly written and you cannot play it.' Barbara looked at me for a second and then said slowly, 'You son-of-a-bitch,'—went out and played the two-and-a-half-page scene so wonderfully that we had to shoot it only once."

This is an interesting story, but it's hard to tell just what scene in *Clash by Night* could have reminded Stanwyck of her divorce from Taylor and how she was cuckolded, in the public eye at least, by his flagrant dalliances with *Quo Vadis?* starlets. It's Mae who cuckolds Jerry after she marries him by giving in to Earl and his protestations of loneliness. It sounds like Lang boxed Stanwyck into a corner here; she prided herself on her image as a straight shooter, so she couldn't very well decline when he asked her if he could level with her. I can only imagine her embarrassment when Lang said what he did. She had to take "a second," before building herself back up and calling him out as a bastard, as if she admired him for it—and maybe she did, but maybe she was offended, too. Her performance is all over the place, indifferent sometimes, and at other times engaged in a remarkably fiery way.

It seems to be Ryan, finally, who wakes her up decisively. "If I ever loved a man again, I'd bear anything," says Mae, outside a dive with Earl. "He could have my teeth for watch fobs," she claims. Unmoved by such Odetsian dialogue, Stanwyck satisfies herself with physical business, such as unceremoniously throwing a cigarette away when Ryan's Earl offers her another one. "Don't kid me, baby, I know a bottle by the label," sneers Earl, moving in for a kiss, and getting met with a vicious slap from Mae that looks very real (it's the beginning of *Baby Face* all over again, but this time with a much older, much tireder woman). "Peace on earth," Earl cracks, ironically, getting his hate on, which was Ryan's specialty.

Stanwyck seems unwilling, in this scene, to really meet Ryan's hate, but she gradually lets herself go with him, as if she's saying, "Alright, you son-of-a-bitch, you want hate, I'll give you hate." And she's capable of intermittent inspiration in her scenes with Douglas's Jerry after their baby is born. During a heat wave, Jerry reports that the papers say they're due for some cool weather, and Mae replies, "Well, the papers oughtta know," in a light, enigmatic voice that signals Stanwyck working at her reverberating best.

A drunken Earl stops by, then stays overnight. The next morning, after a restless sleep, Mae bends over some coffee in the kitchen and is attacked by tears. This attack is the kind of crying-having-its-way-with-you that rarely shows up in movies, where an actor is so often trying to cry instead of trying to fight off tears, as many people do in life. Earl stumbles into the kitchen to wash his neck. Both actors vividly get across both the literal and figurative heat of the environment in this scene. Ryan, wearing an undershirt, with his wide back to the camera, goes into some Irish "I should never have been born" keening, the kind of morbidness that the Irish Stanwyck is also susceptible to.

When Ryan grabs Stanwyck from behind and begs her for love, suddenly both actors seem to leap out of the frame, as if you were watching them in a stage performance right in front of you instead of on a screen. This is the closest we'll come to seeing what Stanwyck might have been like in live theater, and she was never more stimulated by an acting partner. So many actresses crumpled up and slunk away when confronted by Ryan at full throttle on screen. Only Stanwyck has the talent and the sheer nerve to stand up to him and meet him more than halfway. He almost eats her over the sink with a DeNiro-like kiss. She struggles a bit, but then she looks right at him and unleashes her own passion, shoving a hand into the back of his undershirt and rifling around hungrily, as raw a slice of sexual desperation as has ever been shown in movies.

That hand in Ryan's undershirt is an indelible image, one of the things you think about when you think about Stanwyck—that daring, that need for flesh. It is a kind of exposure, even if a lot of her other scenes here look dedicated to keeping her safe from our prying eyes. The ending, where Mae goes back to Jerry and her child, is not convincing, but Stanwyck sums up her performance when she talks to Ryan about their sordid affair and levels with herself about their "love," which she sees as "love because we're lonely, love because we're frightened," and then, quieter, "love because we're bored." This is as full an accounting of her own hit-or-miss work here as any I could offer. Seeing Stanwyck live in a role that suited her surely would have been an event, but most theater actors have only word-of-mouth and faded press clippings to suggest their specialness now, whereas Stanwyck will be reaching into Robert Ryan's undershirt in perpetuity—on screen and in our mind's eye.

Sturges/Stanwyck

Remember the Night, The Lady Eve

As we get farther and farther away from the classic Hollywood period of the old studio system, where so many disparate talents flourished, the case of Preston Sturges as writer and director only seems more exotic and unexplained. According to Sturges, he didn't do much up to the age of thirty, though he helped run the cosmetics business belonging to his mother, Mary Desti. The estimable, bohemian Desti (whose real last name was Dempsey) was best friend and confidante to the flamboyant modern dancer, Isadora Duncan. The prototypical culture vulture, Desti merrily led young Preston around to every museum in Europe and was certain he would one day be an important artist. She seems to have realized that she herself had the artist's vocation and temperament, but not the talent. He rebelled against her influence, at first, longing for the business mind and stability of his favorite stepfather, Soloman Sturges, and the unresolved tension he felt between Desti's arty exhortations and Sturges's financial example resulted in the rich, unsettling voice he displayed as a writer of Broadway plays and then screenplays in Hollywood.

The Sturges voice is so distinctive that it comes through in nearly all of his scripts directed by others in the 1930s, and it comes through strongest in two movies directed by the under-valued Mitchell Leisen, *Easy Living* (1937) and *Remember the Night* (1940), which starred Stanwyck (it was originally set for Carole Lombard). On the set of that movie, Sturges told Stanwyck that he would write her "a great comedy"; probably there was a "yeah, sure" twinkle in her little eyes after he said this. "I told him I never get great comedies, and he said, 'Well, you're going to get one,'" she later remembered. She couldn't have known that this cheerful egoist and closet pessimist would give her *The Lady Eve*, which stands, with Leo

McCarey's *The Awful Truth* (1937) and Howard Hawks's *Bringing Up Baby* (1938), as the very best and most representative of this era's romantic comedies.

Stanwyck was mistrustful of Sturges. He wasn't her type of man, and though she reveled in the two scripts he wrote for her, there was something about him that she found phony. Robert Wagner and others have said that she thought he talked too much. William Wyler's wife, Tami, called Sturges "a terrible listener, he would talk and other people would listen." But Sturges had a read on Stanwyck; he told the press that she had such inner beauty that she would be "radiant in old age," and he was right about that. He was right about a lot of things, Stanwyck-wise, and in the two scripts he gave her, he brought her to new maturity as an actress and a sensibility, adding touches of worldliness and optimism until she was able to play the highest of high comedy for him.

Leisen tended to soften some of Sturges's hard edges with his preference for visual luxury in his settings. He also clipped some of Sturges's dialogue when it got too long-winded, which was not entirely a bad thing ("Preston had thirty ideas a minute and no way of evaluating them," said Mel Epstein, the assistant director on *The Lady Eve*, and so Sturges depended on his collaborators to help him make decisions and trim the fat). Leisen begins *Remember the Night* in one of those decadent Paramount jewelry stores that he loves so much. We see a lulu of a bracelet being clasped on a woman's wrist. "Glorious," says the manager, and it is. But we hear the woman's voice say, "Um, *yes*," as if she isn't sure, or as if she has a certain contempt for such expensive glory. The manager moves away for just a moment, and in a flash the woman is gone, his bracelet still on her wrist. It's the kind of smooth scene making that Leisen does so well (when Sturges directed his own scripts, simple things like this scene tended to get over-packed and jittery).

We see Stanwyck's jewel thief, Lee Leander, walking down the street in her fur coat, her head covered in a 1940s-style black turban affair (this was Stanwyck's first movie with Edith Head doing her clothes). The Christmas music on the soundtrack alternates with what sounds like the opening bars of Wagner's "Ride of the Valkyries" as Lee is apprehended in another jewelry store. In court, Lee is defended by "an old windbag" named Francis X. O'Leary (Willard Robertson), a ham lawyer who used to be on the stage, and as O'Leary makes his blustering case to the jury, the whole action stops for quite a time so that we can take in his shamelessness. This highlighting of what would in most movies be a minor character was Sturges's specialty at his best, but it often led him into self-indulgence when he was less sure of himself.

What saves this scene is that Sturges has written in smart-aleck asides for John, the prosecutor (Fred MacMurray). He also gives Stanwyck a few priceless reaction shots. At first, her face registers a kind of bewilderment to her lawyer's exhibitionism, but then she chooses to be amused by him, in an aloof, amiably flustered way, as if she's thinking, "What did he just say? Oh, well, OK, I'm just along for the ride!" It's the lightness of her effects here that lets us know Stanwyck is responding to Sturges's inventions. She might not have trusted him personally, but creatively she gets what he's doing, and so she's willing to try something new for him.

"Fear turned her legs to lead!" thunders O'Leary, telling the jury that the bracelet had hypnotized Lee. Stanwyck looks down at her own artfully displayed gams and looks slightly apologetic, as if to say, "Don't blame me for this, huh?" John knows that he'll never get Lee behind bars until after Christmas, so he works to get a continuance and then feels guilty about sending her to jail over the holidays. He gets his pal Fat Mike (Tom Kennedy) to post bail for her, and Fat Mike brings her to his apartment, where Lee thinks she knows what he's after. "One of these days, one of you boys is going to start one of these scenes differently," Lee says, "and one of us girls is going to drop dead from surprise."

The wonderful thing here is that Stanwyck is taking a situation that she has always played for heavy drama before and turning it on its head. She does have a sense of humor, but it's a very dry one—bone dry, in fact—so that when she gets a big laugh, which is well within her power at this point, it is always based in sorrowful experience. One thing Stanwyck could never be is silly; when Sturges has Lee act a little cute as she realizes that John doesn't want her sexually, Stanwyck plays it as a wholly unnatural ploy. Her manipulation of John is all on the surface and sweetly tired-out, because Lee, like so many other Stanwyck women, is sick of playing games.

They go out to eat and talk about their situation. "Sounds like a play, doesn't it?" asks Lee, which is Sturges acknowledging the whole "movie pitch idea" of his basic screenplay, then mocking it when John replies, "Sounds like a flop." This meta strain in Sturges's work is only in its infancy here; later on, he sometimes went too far with his "you're watching a movie!" stunts. In *Remember the Night*, this exchange leads us directly into the most important scene in the film, where Lee tries to explain her concept of right and wrong to John.

Lee asks John if he would steal a loaf of bread if he was starving, and he says yes. She smiles knowingly and then says that she wouldn't do that; instead, she would go out and have an expensive dinner and then tell the maître d' that she'd lost her purse. He would only steal out of desperation, but she's a career chiseler. For a moment John gets lost in this distinction, then he tells her that her way is smarter. "That's it," Lee says, some deep recognition lighting up her face. "We're smart."

This is one of the most multi-leveled and disturbing of Stanwyck's "realization" moments, probably because for Sturges everything has to be verbal. Stanwyck can't just act here with her face, as she does in *The Bitter Tea of General Yen* or *Stella Dallas*. Stanwyck often claimed that she was not an articulate woman, and people who knew her tended to agree with that assessment, even though she seemed articulate enough in her few filmed interviews. Though she called herself inarticulate, or uneducated, maybe what Stanwyck really meant was that she was afraid of words and what they might reveal about her, and about people in general. And if she was afraid of words, then her collaboration with Sturges becomes even more suggestive. He led her out of her established comfort zones and into the kind of brilliant, yearning talk that could bring her to both new levels of understanding and new levels of desolation, all mingled together in her voice and her eyes when she says, "That's it. We're smart." Lee leads John into an ethical trap, but then his response traps her in the kind of recognition that Sturges can put into words and Stanwyck can convey like a vibrating tuning fork.

While John and Lee dance, he asks if her mother is still alive. "I hope so," Lee says, still a little confused about her feelings for him, and by the band playing "My Old Indiana Home." They're both Hoosiers, it turns out, and John offers to drive her home for Christmas. "Oh, gee," she says, a very un-Stanwyck exclamation, and it's as if Lee wants to try out being the kind of girl who can say, "Oh, gee" and mean it. Lee and Jean in *The Lady Eve* are two crooks who are seduced by innocence, and in Sturges's world, the crooked people who start to long for vanished purity or respectability—or, in Lee's case, a conscience—are usually destroyed for their trouble. They would have been much better off just staying corrupt, a conclusion born of Sturges's deep cynicism. It's this cynicism that feels true, not the squirming toward a happy ending that he tried to pass off as the unlikely reward for American striving.

That cynicism rears its head when an increasingly affectionate John and Lee, on the way to meet her mother, are confronted by a mean Indiana farmer, a gun-toting militia type who has built a detour onto his property just so he can capture and punish anyone unlucky enough to drive through. When this man takes them to a local judge, Sturges mercilessly dissects the narrow-minded prejudice of these two men.

"Weren't even *married*!" says the farmer; tellingly, John picks up on the tone of his words and wanders into a bewildered little digression about how the farmer has just made the word "married" sound, well, dirty. Sturges celebrates the discerning sophistication of John's open sensibility, just as he rightly condemns the crummy ignorance of the small-minded small town men. He also makes us feel that we would need to act like the corrupt Lee when confronted with men like these. John's sensitive deliberations only makes things worse, but she's street smart enough to light a fire in a wastebasket and get them the hell out of there.

In his car, Lee jeers a bit at John's naïveté, and Leisen takes one of Stanwyck's few faults as a performer, her inability to play direct sarcasm, and makes it seem like Lee's confusion about her own feelings. This is the emotional muddle that leads her right into the lion's den, the place where she came from. Lee tries to fool herself along the way that her mother will be glad to see her ("Yeah, I guess she will alright," she chirps), but when she's in front of her mother's house, a bit of instinctual panic sets in: "I'm getting scared," she says finally, her eyes blank and staring.

Lee's emotions trip her up, and she's isn't as smart as John is, but her instincts are 100 percent trustworthy. When she walks up to the door of her former home with John, Lee deteriorates into a frightened little girl talking all in a rush about being a tomboy and climbing trees and how she would have run away to sea if she had been born a man. She knocks on the door and hears a loud dog. Could it be the same dog that . . . . Oh, no, it can't be, she says; he would be too old (at this point, the once glossy *Remember the Night* has become as foreboding as a horror film). A man answers her knock, and Lee asks for her mother by name. "I guess you mean my wife," he says, in a manner that couldn't be less friendly.

Then, suddenly, a forbidding female face rushes out of the dark, and it's obviously Lee's mother (Georgia Caine). This is the sort of moment that's entirely dependent on casting (Caine is chillingly perfect) and lighting, and the scene that follows is Leisen's moment to shine. "Merry Christmas, Mama," Lee says, in a pure, girlish voice. But once Lee and John are inside, Lee's mother bluntly asks, "What you come here for? What do you want?" Lee tries to tell her that she just wanted to see her, but her mother cuts her off: "Good riddance to bad rubbish I said the day she left." Her mother says that Lee is just like her father, who laughed at serious things. Though he doesn't specify exactly what she means, Sturges suggests that the things a woman like this thinks are serious are anything but. Lee laughing at these "serious" things is analogous to

John wondering over the mean tone the farmer uses when he says the word "married," a more open intelligence rejecting the junk that closed-minded people accept without thinking.

Years ago, Lee borrowed some money, but her mother said Lee stole it and then told the whole town that her daughter was a thief. We weren't good enough for her, Lee's mother says. At this point, Sturges's command of psychological nuance is at its most piercing; in just a few moments, we see exactly what kind of woman this is. She's not a villain. She has problems of her own, and a tiny part of her wants to forgive her daughter (we can see that in Caine's face), but she can't. Mother and daughter are at cross-purposes, and it is these cross-purposes that lead to all the trouble between people, especially family members, and most especially parents and children.

Lee and John leave, and Lee's mother returns to the dark from whence she came. But Leisen frames her silhouette peering out the window at her daughter, who is standing on the porch and crying. Lee tells John that she had forgotten how much her mother hated her, and how much she hated her mother, and then she stops herself. Lee doesn't want to say such an awful thing. She can feel this hatred for her mother, but she doesn't want to say it out loud—because once she's said it out loud, it's official (a very Sturges concept). Now that it's official, there's no room for dreaming of a better life or future. Lee wishes that she had fallen out of that tree in front of her mother's house and died, proof that when you can't evade, put-off, or ignore something as bad as hating your mother, among other unmentionables, you might find yourself in a suicidal state of mind, a progression that Stanwyck always understood. It is Sturges, though, who gets her to actually verbalize this concept, out loud, in all its danger.

When John takes Lee home to his picture-perfect family, Sturges can't quite make these family members as believable as he made Lee's mother or those terrible Hoosiers at the courthouse. He tries to add realistic, knotty detail to John's spinster Aunt Emma (Elizabeth Patterson), but he has trouble with John's widowed mother, Mrs. Sargent (Beulah Bondi), who is small-minded but not narrow-minded—a type that exists in life, I suppose, but not a type that is all that fruitful or interesting to observe in action. When Mrs. Sargent mentions that John once borrowed some money and then was given the chance to pay it back, there is too neat a correlation between his past and Lee's. But Stanwyck keeps us focused; when she leans over a bed holding a warm nightgown from John's mother, her face gleams the way it did in the stateroom scene in *Ladies of Leisure*, and this time there is a modicum of hope in her expression. But Sturges can't make this hope feel earned because he has so vividly shown us in the earlier scenes that such feeling is a mirage that might kill you

Mrs. Sargent, who knows the truth about her, gently warns Lee that she might spoil John's career if they were to get married. Lee is standing in front of a mirror, and when Mrs. Sargent puts her hands on Lee's shoulders, Stanwyck freezes, with her mouth wide open, one arm up holding a comb, a vision of complete Mouchette-style awkwardness. Mirrors always bring out Stanwyck's deepest feelings. They seem to tell her that she can't hide and that she needs to show us everything she has in her, even if it isn't flattering or pretty to look at. Since this is a post-Code movie, Lee must pay for her crimes, whereas before 1934 Ernst Lubitsch would have certainly left her free to make up her own mind about what she wants to do next. Leisen films the hushed parting between John and Lee with real tenderness, but the complexities of the early scenes get politely swept under the rug.

"The special tone of *The Lady Eve* is a kind of energetic cruelty, a malicious exuberance" writes James Harvey in *Romantic Comedy*. There's a unique kind of high spirits in Stanwyck's performance in many of her best scenes in *Eve*, so close to the bubbliness of an Irene Dunne or the lyricism of a Katharine Hepburn, but shaded with something more uneasy, more lethal. Harvey writes that her high spirits come out of a kind of "transmuted anger," and that's probably true. This anger never intrudes on Stanwyck's dual characterization of Jean, a delectable card sharp working on a boat with her father (Charles Coburn) and The Lady Eve Sidwich, a rapacious English noblewoman. But it informs every bit of the pleasure Stanwyck takes while rooking Henry Fonda's slightly rancid innocent, Charles Pike, a snake enthusiast and heir to the Pike's Ale fortune (it's "The Ale That Won For Yale").

Though Sturges isn't as fluid and visual a director as Leisen, a lot of the pleasures of this beloved movie come not just from its stream of words uttered by juicy character actors like Coburn, William Demarest, Eric Blore, and Eugene Pallette, but also from the sheer glamour of its settings. Edith Head outdoes herself on Stanwyck's wardrobe here, so that it's a sensual thing just to watch her being so beautifully presented in impeccably designed white and gold dresses and knit caps, and ornate little diamond brooches set against black and white suits (this is Stanwyck's anti-*Stella Dallas*, clothes-wise, a sort of reward). In many ways, it was a kind of holiday movie for Stanwyck. She said that the atmosphere on a Capra set was "like a cathedral," while on a Sturges set it was "a carnival."

"I wonder if I can clunk him on the head with this?" Jean asks, as she stares down at Charles from the bow of a ship. The question is barely out of her mouth before she yields to her low impulse and drops an apple onto his pith helmet. He's been up the Amazon for a year with his snakes (a frisky cartoon snake happily slithers down through the opening credits), and Jean seems to know, well before she should, that she has landed herself the prize chump of all time—or, as her father says, the ultimate "sucker sapien." Staring into her compact (which fills the frame), Jean hammers out sugar-high, wise-ass narration as Charles is assailed from all sides by hopeful females in the ship's dining room. Her dialogue could feel merely mean if Stanwyck didn't deliver it in such a rapid-fire, complexly layered way. Jean's hyper-articulation would have made Kay Arnold's head swim, and it could have intimidated Stanwyck only a few years earlier, but here for Sturges she has attained a total verbal mastery to match all of her other gifts. So many other directors asked Stanwyck to stare into mirrors and reveal damaging things about herself; Sturges gives her the mirror and the control over his film.

On the set of *The Mad Miss Manton*, where he was unhappy with the script, Fonda had been openly rude to Stanwyck, but he knew just how good a script *The Lady Eve* was and this time they got along splendidly. In his autobiography, Fonda writes that he fell in love with Stanwyck while working with her and always loved her afterwards, but she wasn't having his gush. "Yes, *Lady Eve* was a good picture," she said, sensibly, "but about the rest of Fonda's talk, he was single when I was single, and where was he?" Here's the straight-shooter, telling even this most plain-spoken and dignified of actors that if he had really been serious, he should have put his money where his mouth was and asked her out. Their mutual, unconsummated attraction to each other definitely helps the lingering scenes where Jean, wearing a black crepe dress with a tantalizing bare midriff, goes about seducing Charles, whom she calls "Hopsie," his childhood nickname.

"See anything you like?" asks Jean, leaning against her wardrobe. She senses that she can be as brazen as she wants with Charles, and he'll never catch on. It's his total obliviousness, his innocence, that starts to seduce her in turn, so that she's eventually a sucker in her own game. Charles is the ultimate con artist's dream, and she longs to give up her own worldliness for his innocence, or at least gain some relief in his uncomplicated presence. "Why, Hopsie," she purrs, when he confusedly leans in for a kiss, "you ought to be kept in a cage!" This is the flip side of the contemptuous, scarred Lily Powers; Jean is a woman who helplessly starts to love a man precisely because he falls for her manipulation so easily.

Jean seems genuinely scared of the pet snake in Charles's room (its name is Emma), but she smartly turns this scare to her advantage by screaming and running to her own room (Sturges speeds up the footage slightly so that Stanwyck and Fonda briefly look like they're in a Mack Sennett two-reeler). In the famous long-take seduction scene in her stateroom, which runs over three minutes, Jean idly plays with Charles's ear and musses his hair. "Snakes are my life . . . in a way," says Charles. Jean takes this in and says, "What a life," one of Stanwyck's mysterious conclusions about something or other, just like, "That's it. We're smart," in *Remember the Night*.

Jean leads Charles down a winding path of conversation about their respective romantic ideals. His is vague, and so she says, "It would be too bad if you never bumped into each other." It's a funny line, as Stanwyck says it, but also a sad one. Most people, she seems to suggest, never do meet the lover they imagine in their heads. Jean claims that she wants "a little short guy with lots of money," so that he can look up to her. Soon she has Charles cross-eyed with lust, and she even lets out a frankly sexual groan (Sturges smuggled a lot past the censors) before bidding her Hopsie goodnight.

Later, with her father, whom she calls Harry (he's known in the trade as Handsome Harry, so he seems to have been a ladies' man in his youth), Jean wakes up from a nightmare involving Charles's snake, Emma. The nightmare hints that she's subconsciously afraid of really giving herself over to him sexually because it might dig up some vanished, "ideal" romantic feelings from her youth. Harry deals some fifths on her bed in a way that surprises her: "You won't need it," he says, off-handedly, "it's just virtuosity." For Sturges, the secret aesthete, there's no such thing, of course, as "just" virtuosity. Otherwise, he wouldn't be filming Stanwyck's virtuoso cat-with-a-mouse comedic play with such love and delight (Fonda said that Sturges would uninhibitedly laugh at his own jokes, and that he was "a total egomaniac," but that this had "almost an endearing quality because he was so naïve about it").

When Jean tells her father that she's fallen for Charles and asks that he be spared at the card table, the old man demurs. She toughens up and boasts that she can protect him: "I'm not your daughter for free, you know!" Jean snaps. This constitutes another moment of deep recognition, coming fast on the heels of "What a life," in the stateroom. For Sturges, Stanwyck keeps hitting these gongs of verbal recognition so that they resonate so deeply they can hardly be explained, finally, with specific thoughts or words. *The Lady Eve* itself is slippery and resists the sort of "deep dish" analysis that Sturges always mocked in his work, while still offering as complex a sensory experience as any in the cinema. This movie was a hit, a honey, and a riot, and it's been loved ever since it was released, right when America needed to take its mind off the upcoming war, a war that barely impinged on Stanwyck's life on film (at one point, Demarest does a vaudeville-like imitation of Hitler, a reminder of the hell happening off screen).

"They say a moonlit deck is a woman's business office," says Jean, when Charles goes all mushy on her describing his love. Claudette Colbert would have said a line like that using all her earthy, racy common sense. Jean Arthur would have said it anxiously, as if she wasn't sure if she didn't sound silly. Irene Dunne might have said it with a tiny twinkle in her eyes, pressing the tip of her tongue to her palette, while Katharine Hepburn would have said it resentfully (or hopefully, if she was in her "femme" mode). Joan Crawford would have made it sound pushy and needy. Bette Davis would have said it ironically. Only Stanwyck could have said this line like she does in *The Lady Eve*, casting an eye over all of these possibilities, while never quite settling on one of them. It's clear that the idea amuses her, slightly. Jean doesn't take it too seriously. Or does she? Stanwyck makes it clear that Jean loves falling for her own act for once; all through this movie, Jean is at her most sincere when she's being most blatantly insincere with Charles. Surely this is a paradox of human behavior that a world-class actress like Stanwyck would intimately understand.

"A man that couldn't forgive wouldn't be much of a man," says Jean, with all the common sense maturity that Stanwyck can muster (and that's a formidable amount in 1941), after Harry warns her that she might be heading for a fall when she tells Charles the truth about herself. Sturges uses Fonda very cleverly in this movie, even more cleverly than he uses Stanwyck. When Charles learns that Jean and her father are gamblers and cons, he coldly rejects her, even pretending that he knew about her all along. Sturges brings out Fonda's rigid, priggish side, so that we don't feel quite so bad about laughing at him all through the shipboard scenes. Charles is such an uptight jerk when he spurns Jean that we glide into the final third of the movie completely on her side in any scheme for vengeance she cares to cook up for him.

Meeting fellow con Sir Alfred (Blore), Jean hatches a plan to imper-sonate an English lady and give Charles his comeuppance. "I want to see that guy," she snarls, in the hard, Brooklyn-nasal tone of Mae West. "I've got some unfinished business with him," she continues, her voice soften-ing slightly. "I need him like the axe needs the turkey," Jean concludes. It's a rather vicious line, but Stanwyck says it with her troubling brand of sadistic tenderness, an abstracted state all her own in which she consid-ers all her many unspeakable options and makes them blend and collide in her unreachable psychic depths.

Jean holds herself regally when she enters the Pike home as The Lady Eve Sidwich, charming Papa Pike (Pallette) with her tales of taking the subway (in these scenes, Stanwyck suggests an English accent by slap-ping together a bunch of inane, high-pitched vocal mannerisms and sketch comic impressions of Englishness). After Charles sees her, he's so befuddled that he takes a speeded-up pratfall over a sofa. When he gets back up, Eve rushes over to him and gently cleans him, Jean's love for her Hopsie breaking through. He goes upstairs to change, and Eve slips right through the narrow passage between a chair and a table without even looking down, a nifty visual detail that emphasizes how different they are and how they need each other. Charles takes another fall, pull-ing down some curtains this time, and Eve can't help laughing, like an audience member. Sturges then frames Fonda in a close-up, where he looks extremely attractive in his lost boy way.

Why doesn't he see through her right away? Well, Charles is pretty dim, but Jean has her own explanation. She says it's because they don't love each other anymore, though that's true only on the surface; that knife has cut deep into both of them. When she has Charles under her control again and he proposes marriage to her, Stanwyck glances down-wards and looks as if she's about to crack up as a horse keeps nudging Fonda in the head. (It took thirty takes to get the three-minute state-room scene because Stanwyck kept laughing, an unusual indulgence for such a famed professional, but one perhaps necessary so as to unleash the barely contained joy of this character, something that didn't come naturally to Stanwyck).

For all its fun, *The Lady Eve* also quite seriously describes the process of disillusionment in youthful nonsense romance, as well as the sort of constantly renewing attraction that is essential to any long-term sexual relationship after the first flush fades and is replaced by deeper knowl-edge. There's no such thing as too much information for real, devoted lovers (even if there are certain things that are definitely better left un-said, a point that Charles makes in the last scene).

Jean/Eve makes a strikingly skeptical-looking bride behind her flowing Edith Head veil, and she thoroughly enjoys disillusioning poor Hopsie
again on their wedding night, when the English lady she's impersonating
merrily admits to a string of husbands and lovers. "I was always taught
to be frank and honest!" cries her Eve, and Jean is honest too, of course,
about what really matters. When Eve gazes at him like a little girl as he
tries to forgive her, it's hard not to notice that this is the exact look Jean
gave her father when he was dealing his fifths; it seems like Jean is partly
working out her father issues here. Harry loves her and has his own code
of behavior, but he's also totally amoral. It's great to have a parent who
doesn't judge you, but Jean's father makes no judgments and thus has
no boundaries. She has to make up her own in order to really become a
full-fledged adult out from under his influence.

Charles keeps taking his pratfalls until she finally takes pity on him
and everything is wrapped up for a fragile happy ending that brings them
back to their original love boat, older and wiser, with promises of lots of
role-playing and sex games to come (the cartoon snake looks "morning after" sated as he hugs two apples that read "The" and "End"). *The
Lady Eve* is, in its way (and what a way), a perfect film, and it features
Stanwyck's funniest, most confident, and most unabashedly romantic
performance.

Before she was Barbara Stanwyck, Ruby Stevens was a teenaged chorus girl who came up the hard way.

Sincerely yours
Barbara Stanwyck

An early publicity photograph of a strikingly young-looking Stanwyck when she was under contract to Columbia Studios.

Adolphe Menjou and Stanwyck take their masks off for a moment in the Frank Capra tearjerker *Forbidden* (1932).

Stanwyck's young missionary falls under the nihilistic sexual influence of a Chinese warlord in Capra's *The Bitter Tea of General Yen* (1933).

Pawed daily by nasty men, Stanwyck's Lily Powers drowns in self-pity in one of the opening scenes of the scandalous *Baby Face* (1933).

A war-loving Robert Young tries to save Stanwyck from the corrupting influence of communism in the alarming right-wing comedy *Red Salute* (1935).

In the mid-1930s, Stanwyck was liberated from money and man troubles in a series of screwball comedies, including *The Bride Walks Out* (1936).

As her stardom grew, Stanwyck became more comfortable—and more beautiful— in glamorous clothes, often created by designer Edith Head.

In *The Mad Miss Manton* (1938), Stanwyck attempts to play a flighty Park Avenue debutante.

A rare photo of Stanwyck and her adopted son Dion (c. 1940). Courtesy of Photofest.

Stanwyck in her favorite role, the clothing-challenged Stella Dallas (note the fuzzy shoes).

William Holden is a violinist turned boxer in love with Stanwyck's Lorna Moon in *Golden Boy* (1939).

Stanwyck clings tightly to matinee idol second husband Robert Taylor.

Stanwyck in one of her greatest roles, Jean Harrington, a card-sharp brought low by love in the classic Preston Sturges comedy *The Lady Eve* (1941).

As singer Sugarpuss O'Shea, Stanwyck proves plenty yum-yum in *Ball of Fire* (1941).

Defiantly returning to her chorus girl roots, Stanwyck is a striptease artiste in William Wellman's *Lady of Burlesque* (1943).

Stanwyck plays it cool in perhaps her best-known role, blond-wigged sociopath Phyllis Dietrichson, in Billy Wilder's classic film noir *Double Indemnity* (1944).

Fate catches up with Stanwyck's spoiled heiress in her most flagrant Oscar bid, *Sorry, Wrong Number* (1948).

Appearing as a neglected wife in *East Side, West Side* (1949), Stanwyck gets some bad news over the phone.

A duplicitous Stanwyck cools her heels behind bars in Robert Siodmak's noir *The File on Thelma Jordan* (1949).

The end of an era: Stanwyck says goodbye to all that in Sam Fuller's masterful western *Forty Guns* (1957).

As an older woman, Stanwyck let her hair go white, but her face could still be as open and vulnerable as a girl's.

The young Barbara Stanwyck in all her glory, as Megan Davis in her best Frank Capra film, *The Bitter Tea of General Yen* (1933).

Stanwyck Soap and 1950s Drama

The Gay Sisters, Flesh and Fantasy, My Reputation, The Other Love, B. F.'s Daughter, East Side, West Side, To Please a Lady, Titanic, Executive Suite, These Wilder Years

*T*here were times when Stanwyck cast an envious eye over the kind of material Bette Davis was making her own at Warner Bros. She very much wanted to play in *Dark Victory* (1939), which went to Davis, and she also lusted for *Mildred Pierce* (1945), but her pal Joan Crawford snagged that one. Stanwyck wasn't especially suited to the woman's picture of this era, but, as was the case with many another genre, she got several chances to make this type of movie her own. As she had done in other genres, she tackled—and ultimately conquered—the soap opera on her own terms.

Davis and a few others had turned down *The Gay Sisters* (1942), a Lenore Coffee adaptation of a lengthy Stephen Longstreet novel, before Stanwyck took it on. The first ten minutes of this movie could make for a knockout drinking game; if you downed a shot every time somebody said the name "Gaylord," you'd be dead drunk before the first reel was finished. Papa Gaylord (Donald Woods), who is off to World War I, insists on "a Gaylord house, run by Gaylord servants, in the Gaylord manner," and he's just getting warmed up. He calls one of his three daughters a "good Gaylord" and then mentions that another is "a Gaylord, through and through." Of oldest daughter Fiona, a servant intones, "A Gaylord if ever there was one, and a redheaded Gaylord at that!" Just in case we don't get the picture yet, Father G cries, "You're not just a Smith or a Jones or a Brown, you're a Gaylord!" Counseling Fiona, he mentions, "You must always be a Gaylord," and emphasizes that, "The land is the Gaylord's religion." It's as if some Monty Python sketch had been sandwiched into the opening scenes; counting the readable names of the girls' dead mother and then the monogrammed hat that falls off of their dead father at the front, there are twenty-one instances of this "Gaylord" repetition mania in the prologue alone.

Jumping forward in time, it seems that the Gaylord girls, or "the Gay dames," as they're sometimes called, have been involved in litigation over their father's will for twenty-three years and counting. Stanwyck's "fighting Fiona" has some grudge against Charles Barclay (George Brent), a rich man in league with a charity trying to collect 10 percent of the estate, and Barclay has some grudge against her. Fiona has a small boy named Austin (Larry Simms), and we later learn that he is the result of Fiona's failed marriage to Barclay.

The intriguing thing here is Stanwyck's relation to her on-screen son. In his first scene, Stanwyck avidly watches this kid get picked on by a group of boys and then relishes the sight of him defending himself: "Fight back, punch him in the nose!" she snarls. Surely this attitude mimics the distant, tough-love way that Stanwyck tried to relate to Dion, who was too sensitive and awkward to be the little firebrand she wanted (Simms even looks a lot like a young Dion Fay). Later on, Fiona worries about where Austin will spend his vacations and briefly gives up custody of him over this issue, a sad on-screen contrast to Stanwyck's active avoidance of her own son off-screen whenever he had a vacation from military school.

The "Gaylord" madness lets up a bit in the first hour, but it comes creeping back in when you least expect it. "We Gaylords are a queer lot," says good sister Susanna (Nancy Coleman). Fiona herself gets in on the act: "Susie, Susie, what a Gaylord!" she sighs, and later makes reference to "an old Gaylord custom." To top off the Gaylord fever, when Fiona has finally given in to Barclay and sold the old homestead, she says, "Let's go down and drink to the end of the Gaylords," and Stanwyck is forced into another of her weirdly unconvincing drunk scenes. She's on much more solid ground when she sarcastically narrates a flashback to when she hoodwinked Barclay; it plays as a rip-off of *The Lady Eve*, but agreeably so. Stanwyck is fully aware here of the thespian implications of her contemptuous man trapping, referring to "my big acting scene" when Fiona pretends to get the vapors on her wedding night, then swooning ultra-falsely on a staircase. "Katharine Cornell couldn't have done it better," Stanwyck cracks, knowing full well that her modern style of performing is sweeping away the "back of the hand to the forehead" custard of Cornell and all her forebears.

Julien Duvivier's episodic *Flesh and Fantasy* (1943) was a follow-up to his earlier omnibus picture, *Tales of Manhattan* (1942). The last of the three tales here pairs Stanwyck with Charles Boyer. He plays a tightrope walker whose act involves pretending to be drunk and then finding himself on the high wire. We see him choke in the middle of this act (Duvivier was always expert at portraying moments of fear and humiliation), and then later, on a ship, he bumps into Stanwyck's elegantly dressed crook. Boyer's smooth-talking roué act makes an interesting contrast to her wised-up common sense, and she adjusts herself to him, becoming a bit more mercurial, a bit more continental. This pairing was an event, because Boyer was Stanwyck's equal as an actor, and it's a shame that they couldn't have found a good romantic comedy to do together, something more developed than this stylish but flimsy short story.

"*My Reputation* [1946] was what we classify as a good woman's picture," Stanwyck told John Kobal. "It is a problem throughout the world: the widow who is *comparatively* young, who does start to go out with eligible men, and then gossip starts." This movie, with its tacit wartime theme, was made in 1944 but only released in America in 1946. In the meantime, it was shown to serviceman overseas as a kind of dream of what they might be coming home to: a glorified suburbia, in this case Lake Forest, Illinois. Stanwyck plays Jessica Drummond, "a wife type" and widow of thirty-three whose former athlete/businessman husband has just died. It's a difficult role for Stanwyck, and she's uneasy in some of the early scenes as she tries to feel her way into this cloistered young matron dominated by a mother (Lucille Watson) who's been wearing black to mourn her own dead husband for twenty-five years. Jessica refuses to wear black, the first of many small rebellions that grow larger as the film goes on.

Jessica is the type who organizes picnics for her two young boys, driving around in her perfect station wagon with picture perfect silent dogs in the backseat. She's naïve and sheltered, and when a married friend (Jerome Cowan) makes a pass at her in his car, she's undone by the sleaziness of the encounter. Running to a female friend (Eve Arden), she breaks down. "I don't know what's the matter with me," she says, choking up, then smashing her arms into a couch. "I seem to be going to pieces!" she cries, and in this release of emotion, Stanwyck gains some control over her characterization.

She's shaky again when first dealing with a rather leering army major (George Brent). Encased in a tight white sweater, Stanwyck can't stop her eyes from looking a bit too knowing, but she's able to use her innate rebelliousness when Jessica begins to assert herself with her gossipy neighbors. Curtis Bernhardt, a minor but effective Warners stylist, gives the film a dark, velvety look, and he's capable of striking shots. When Jessica breaks away from her major, his shadow looms over her as she cringes against a brick wall.

My Reputation is often too polite for its own good; even Arden gets swallowed up in the chintz and candlelight. Stanwyck just seems miscast when asked to choke back hard liquor or to flinch when she sees the major's bed, but in the last half hour she comes into her own. The major tells Jessica that he isn't the marrying kind, and she's bold enough not to care. In one of the last scenes, staged quite beautifully by Bernhardt, Jessica stands in shadows while she relates to her boys how their father had been ill for two years before he died. She has had to go without sex for a while before meeting her major, and this revelation is an unexpectedly frank detail. Right before going in to talk to her sons, Jessica marches to the door and then hesitates slightly before opening it, an illuminating physical grace note that lets us see how closely Stanwyck has melded with her role after her early missteps.

In the fully charged ending, Jessica sees the major off at a train station and reacts gratefully when some passing sailors whistle at her, proving that she's still in her prime and more than just a mother and a widow. Stanwyck finishes Jessica's wave to the major, then just stays in her own feelings of relief and joy for a moment before squaring her shoulders and walking confidently out of the station. This isn't a major film, and Stanwyck strikes out as often as she hits the ball here, but the ending of *My Reputation* is certainly a keeper (Todd Haynes's melodrama pastiche *Far from Heaven* [2002] has a very similar climax, and this Bernhardt film can be seen as a rough sketch for Douglas Sirk's far more complex *All That Heaven Allows* [1955]).

Erich Maria Remarque wrote what would become *The Other Love* (1947) as a treatment for his inamorata Marlene Dietrich, but what wound up on screen was a lot more simplified than his original scenario, and it shares only certain surface similarities to his other work. The glossiest of soap operas, it's an anomaly in the career of André de Toth, who thrived on small crime films and westerns that he made as harsh as possible. And it's also anomalous for Stanwyck, in that she plays in a totally different style to suit this purple material, deploying an expert sort of feyness and quiet lyricism. As Karen, a concert pianist suffering from tuberculosis, she even pitches her voice much higher than usual, so as to sound as breathy and gaspy as possible (reviews of the time, however, noted that she made an absurdly healthy-looking patient).

The heroine looks better and better as she gets sicker and sicker, and Stanwyck shows up in a new (and becoming) Edith Head ensemble in practically every scene. The film has more clothes sense than dramatic sense. "There's been a lot of men in my life," chirps Stanwyck's Karen. "Bach, Brahms and Beethoven!" She plays the piano athletically, like someone digging ditches, and has David Niven as her lovelorn physician and Richard Conte as her rich racecar driver lover. Conte was a replacement for Robert Stack, who shot the film for a month before falling ill and dropping out. Conte acts more like a gangster than a playboy, while Niven is too lightweight for his role.

De Toth seems uninterested for most of the film, so that what should be a grand wallow in glamorous sickbed masochism seems more like a chore (Stanwyck was out sick for a while during shooting, unusual for her, and her illness added to the film's troubles). "At that time the motion picture industry was still shackled to Hollywood," de Toth later said. "We who were seeking reality not only in portraying characters but also in presenting real geographical locations had a great deal of difficulty and many obstacles to overcome."

Apparently Stanwyck shot a death scene. In the sixties, she talked about watching the film at home: "I have no will power. I watch all the old movies on TV, including some of mine . . . . But it does make me angry that they cut these movies. They cut key scenes. One of mine, *The Other Love* with David Niven, had a dramatic scene at the end, where I'm dying of consumption. Just before my death, Niven is talking to me. He knows I'm dying and I know it. It was very difficult doing. On TV, right in the middle of the scene, when David is talking and I'm gasping for breath, they end it, cutting out the death. I look like an idiot." IMDb lists the running time for this film as 95 minutes, but most circulating prints run 89 minutes, and a little-girlish Karen is still alive at the end of this print, cozied up to her doctor as he plays the piano for her.

The following year, Stanwyck cut her long hair short for *B. F.'s Daughter* (1947), an MGM adaptation of a John P. Marquand novel, and this haircut instantly made her look more severe and matronly. The early scenes are set in 1932, but no attempt is made in sets or costumes to suggest this period. Thus, Stanwyck's Polly, the devoted daughter of industrialist B. F. Fulton (Charles Coburn), meets her future husband Thomas (Van Heflin) in a staid-looking MGM cocktail lounge that's supposed to be a downtown speakeasy. Thomas is a Columbia professor with leftist ideas, but the film is generally vague on the subject of politics. At one point, Thomas mentions that he's written about B. F.'s "interlocking companies," but this is the only hint that her father might be up to anything crooked. Once married, Polly uses B. F.'s right-wing money and influence secretly to advance the lecture career of her leftist husband, a neat irony that the film is too wishy-washy to do anything with.

As *B. F's Daughter* goes on, the hugely wealthy, up-by-his-bootstraps B. F. is painted as a man so sentimental that he has kept several ailing companies going purely out of love. Unlikely, of course, but B. F. really is the swellest old capitalist you're ever likely to meet. This admission inspires Polly to fight for her dead marriage, which is the film's ultimate message—one that Stanwyck herself took too much to heart off-screen, I'm afraid. This is another film choice that reveals just how right wing Stanwyck was at heart (Keenan Wynn's opportunistic left-wing radio broadcaster here is a cartoon character to match the wilder excesses of *Red Salute*). It was shot quickly by old MGM hand Robert Leonard, and it was a cheerful set where a lot of practical jokes were played. The shrewd Bette Davis once remarked that happy sets rarely make for great or even good films, and *B. F.'s Daughter* is a case in point. This is a soap opera, one where a woman is finally forced to say, "I need you!" to a weaker-willed husband, and one masquerading at times as a glossy piece of right-wing agit prop.

Bosley Crowther, the film reviewer for the *New York Times*, could usually be counted on to get everything wrong, but he hit a rare bullseye when he wrote about Stanwyck's next MGM soap outing, *East Side, West Side* (1949): "A picture that just about hits the low-water mark of interest, intelligence and urgency." Like *B. F.'s Daughter*, it runs 108 minutes on very little story (at least Stanwyck's mid-thirties stinkers at Warner Bros. only lasted a little over an hour), and there's no feel at all for Manhattan on the clean studio sets. This is late studio filmmaking at its most barren and machinelike.

The film is filled with fine actors like James Mason and Van Heflin, but they're stuck in dull roles, and Stanwyck herself is saddled with the worst role as the kind of sniveling, stoic wifey who does nothing but worry about her husband's infidelities. She's up against young Amazons like Cyd Charisse and the ultimate big blond, Beverly Michaels, who acts as a deus ex machina in the last third. Sitting beside Charisse in a car at one point, Stanwyck is photographed like a grizzled old frontierswoman. The resplendent Ava Gardner, playing the hellcat trying to break up her marriage, dominates the whole stultifying enterprise through sheer physical splendor.

In her autobiography, Gardner admits to an affair with Robert Taylor when they made *The Bribe* (1949): "Our love affair lasted three, maybe four months. A magical little interlude. We hurt no one because no one knew." Stanwyck, who certainly could be counted on to know the score on things like this, was cuckolded in real life and then had to submit to the indignity of being cuckolded on screen by the same young woman that same year. In their one confrontation scene, Stanwyck goes into lockdown mode, so that Gardner even wins their exchange histrionically, and this isn't the end of the film's trials. Gale Sondergaard, who plays Stanwyck's mother here, was a noted victim of the blacklist. And the future Nancy Reagan, here billed as Nancy Davis, makes an uneasy impression in her few scenes as Stanwyck's loyal friend, as if she'd like to rush over and whisper, "Hey Barbara, let's name some names!"

More time and thought seems to have been lavished on the women's sculptural coiffures than on the script or direction. Their hair is twisted all over their heads into the most crazily elaborate shapes (Charisse in particular must have spent hours with the hairdressers in the morning). The only elements that compel attention here, finally, are these hair creations, a number of unaccountably ugly lamps, and the beauty of Gardner's body (especially her Louise Brooks-like back) in her clothes. Stanwyck is nearly a zombie throughout, looking like she's on some sort of medication, except in one scene where she displays a grand lady condescension to a short New York "type" that's as unattractive as it is uninteresting—even if it is theoretically right for the boarding school priss she's playing.

Close to twenty years after he menaced her in *Night Nurse*, Clark Gable was teamed with Stanwyck in *To Please a Lady* (1950), an MGM star vehicle that gets off to a rocky start. It opens with a poster that reads, "Regina Forbes, America's Leading Woman Columnist, 40 Million Readers, Fearless Exposés." And then Clarence Brown's camera prowls around a large office, settling on Stanwyck's Regina smoking a cigarette and looking cold and vindictive, as a shrunken Adolphe Menjou cowers in the corner of the frame. They're watching Gable's maverick racecar driver being interviewed on television, and it feels like the screenwriters have given Gable a character that he could have played in his barnstorming style in 1940, but is hard-pressed to put over as the older, much sadder man he is in 1950. There's a similar disconnect with Stanwyck's role in these early scenes, especially when she swaggers around a racetrack and has to listen to the drivers crow, "Take a look at that chassis!" and "Nice looking dish!" She seems embarrassed by this, not because she's lost her looks in any way (she never really did), but because their catcalls sound like they should be directed at a young bombshell, not a seasoned, attractive middle-aged woman.

The racecar sequence at the beginning and the one that ends the film play out as filler, but Brown often gives this movie a grey-toned, somber kind of melancholy that can't have been entirely intentional, as if he's taking his cues from his weathered stars. And stars they are, two of the greats—it's a pleasure to watch them together in a nighttime scene where her high heels sink into the dirt of the racetrack and he gallantly carries her around. Gable's driver intrigues Regina by slapping her face; Stanwyck takes the slap without flinching, as if her stoicism was so well known by this point that it's almost getting to be a joke.

Sometimes the young Gable enthusiasm rises back to the surface of his squinty blue eyes when he bothers to open them wide enough, and Stanwyck obviously enjoys being with a performer with charisma that equals her own, even when the script asks her to do a pixilated, Jean Arthur-type delayed reaction after he kisses her and consigns her to the stands for the last interminable racing sequence. As a team, at this point, Gable and Stanwyck would have been better off with an urban noir or a hard-driving western, but there are times in *To Please a Lady* when the film seems to know that just looking at the two of them sitting at a table together in a restaurant is enough for any reasonable audience.

Titanic (1953), directed by Jean Negulesco, is a missed opportunity all around, a forgettable film, neither as respected as the later British version of the 1912 maritime disaster, *A Night to Remember* (1958), nor as wildly popular as the James Cameron blockbuster edition in the 1990s. It has the morbid suspense of all the other Titanic movies, but little else. Charles Brackett produced, and he also had a hand in the script, which actually won an Academy Award for best original story, even though the fictional tale it tells before the boat hits the iceberg is neither original nor overly interesting. In fact, the whole thing is a bit distasteful.

Stanwyck's Julia is a society woman who wants to save her children from the decadent effects of an upbringing under their effete father, Clifton Webb. Her first close-up is quite striking, a mixture of melancholy in the eyes with a "what the fuck?" set to her mouth, making for a kind of curdled face. When she first sees Robert Wagner, she gives him a hungry look from an elevator, but the script has her gently picking him as a match for her pretentious daughter. Off the set, Stanwyck apparently picked him out for herself. They share one short scene together where she reads him a poem, and it's warm and suggestive. If this movie gave her nothing else, at least it gave her some pleasure in her personal life.

Webb has some amusing high-bitch moments, chiding Stanwyck about how he tried to "civilize the kind of girl who bought her hats out of a Sears Roebuck catalog," and spitting out his words with supreme contempt. He winces when Stanwyck yells at him and gets several laughs by chopping up his words: "You cra-zy woman," he snipes. When she tells him that their little boy is not his son, the revelation doesn't come as a shock; it's unimaginable that Webb could have had children with Stanwyck by any means other than artificial insemination. There's some arch writing on display when she tells him about the man who impregnated her, and Stanwyck delivers it archly. And she can't do anything with her scene with whiskey priest Richard Basehart, a wholly expendable character. Brian Aherne, as the dignified ship's captain, and Thelma Ritter, as the Molly Brown figure, give some energy to what is a fatally stiff first hour. By the second hour, there's nothing to do but wait and hope for this dull ship to hit that iceberg already. When it does, the movie comes to life, even though there are still a few snafus here and there.

In their parting scene, Stanwyck and Webb suddenly become a touching and believable couple. Lowered into the lifeboat, with her husband and son still on board ship, Stanwyck gives herself over to imagining the disaster: "I looked up at the faces lined along the rail—those left behind to die with the ship," she told Hedda Hopper, describing her experience of shooting these scenes. "I thought of the men and woman who had been through this thing in our time. We were re-creating an actual tragedy and I burst into tears. I shook with great racking sobs and couldn't stop." It took an event of this size to break the floodgates open for Stanwyck, so she couldn't stop once she'd started feeling and she couldn't regain her usual control. It's too bad that the film doesn't give her a proper frame for emotions of that size and depth.

Executive Suite (1954) is a crackling, if shallow, business drama, a kind of *Grand Hotel* of the boardroom in which Stanwyck took many of the unappealing aspects of her soap heroines and transfigured them through careful character layering mixed with unabashed going-for-broke effects. This is bloodless 1950s prestige filmmaking, and if it has its virtues, they're due to the overall neatness of the script by Ernest Lehman and the clear-cut direction by Robert Wise. In the first scenes, secretary Nina Foch introduces us to the film's main players when she sets up a board meeting: rogue Louis Calhern, emotional second banana Walter Pidgeon, Babbitt-like Paul Douglas (with mistress Shelley Winters), and bottom-line-watcher Fredric March.

Outside the office walls, there are many scenes with William Holden, who plays an idealistic, hands-on sort with a tirelessly (or is it tiresomely?) devoted wife (June Allyson) and perfect little boy. Enough time is spent with these men in grey flannel suits and their women that any sensible audience might wish that Lily Powers could saunter in and bust the place apart. But it's easy to see why Stanwyck decided to play Julia Tredway, the damaged daughter of the company's founder, even if she really only has about eight minutes of screen time to make an impact (in the last twenty minutes, she's confined mainly to silent reaction shots at an all-important meeting called to elect the next company president). Justifiably cocky, Stanwyck once said: "Put me in the last fifteen minutes of a picture and I don't care what happened before. I don't even care if I was *in* the rest of the damned thing—I'll take it in those fifteen minutes."

She does take *Executive Suite*—and by force at times. She has the flash part, the pay-off part, and it pays off in the expected histrionic ways, but it also lands deeper in several key moments. Twenty-one minutes in, when we first see Julia, she is staring out a window, her face flabby with preoccupation and worry (we later learn that her father committed suicide in 1933 by jumping out of a window). She's an abandoned woman, and she knows that her controlling stock in the company is the only thing that binds her to Bullard, the man who saved her from a breakdown and saved her father's company. A silly little hat sits forlornly in the middle of her graying head and she wears little white kid gloves. This costuming makes for a telling picture of a pampered girl gone sour and neurotic in middle age.

Stanwyck's transitions can be a bit abrupt here because she's playing for maximum impact to make each moment count, yet she also offers some interesting, subtle moments of almost humorous inertia. Julia Tredway is one of the few Stanwyck women to have a guilty conscience about being manipulative, and in the middle of making demands and exhibiting her self-pity with Pidgeon's understanding exec, she draws back several times into a wry self-awareness that lets us know Julia is a smart woman. She understands most of her own urges and miseries but feels she can do little to change them. Julia fondles Bullard's chair and then caresses his pipe; her romantic attachment to him is unavoidably part of her unresolved daddy issues.

Julia's second scene lasts less than a minute. The telephone rings and we see a woman's hand reach out to pick up the receiver. We hear a voice say hello, and it's the Stanwyck voice at its most cigarette-scorched. Wise cuts to her face when she hears of Bullard's death, and it stays completely still. Stanwyck makes us feel that Julia has somehow prepared herself for this moment, and she conveys all of this without moving her face at all. She doesn't even have a verifiable expression in her eyes, yet she somehow gets across exactly what Julia is experiencing and then closes her eyes, not fast, but not slow, as if a curtain is being lowered. Eleanor Parker was originally set to play this part, and if she had, she would have torn the scenery and maybe even the whole film itself to shreds, whereas Stanwyck has only to stare and smolder to place a whole blasted life right in your lap.

Foch and March do fine work in their own right, but no one can really compete with Stanwyck's bravura style here—not even her one-time golden boy, Holden, who shares the screen with her in a climactic confrontation scene. Julia is throwing away her personal papers into a roaring fire. Holden's Macdonald, who needs her support to take the top spot in the company, assails her directly, and she responds briefly, but then draws back into herself, the kind of "I'm watching everything from a distance" quality we saw in her first scene, times ten.

Julia retreats into a cold kind of remove, just as Stanwyck herself hid behind a mask in some of her poorer soap operas. But in *Executive Suite* this masking is revealed to be a necessary and even admirable survival strategy. Plunking down in a chair, her hands set in a sort of Zen yoga position, Julia concludes, "No matter how horrible things are, they can always get worse." This is an indelible moment, and it touches a very deep part of Stanwyck's creativity, the part that knows about depression so overwhelming that only the lowest energy level can possibly deal with it. She knows, and Julia knows, that if your energy is as low as possible, there's a good chance it won't sink any lower. A sudden rise in energy and Julia could go right out that window like her father did.

Holden's Macdonald keeps poking at her, and a lioness emerges, only to slink back to her cage. Stanwyck alternates between cold and hot like this until he draws blood. "I gave him ten years of my life and all my love, isn't that enough!" she cries, her eyes wide and credulous like a little girl, as she starts to pound on her accuser's chest. When he leaves her, Julia breaks down as she did in 1933, weeping brokenly over a desk and beating it with her arms, as she must have done many times before. She goes outside and she could easily jump off that executive tower, but then some bells start to ring (the film has no score), and this hard, massive sound sets something off in Julia. She lets out a fearsome howl and covers her ears with her hands, then shivers against a stone wall.

It's a bold choice. Joan Crawford covered her ears like this in many of her films, but with her it was too much a melodramatic surface gesture. With Stanwyck, it sets a visual capper on this volcano inside her character, and because the source is so genuine (and because we've been shown

Julia's mentality and life experience in such rapier-like thrusts), this ear covering is a flourish that feels justified, or earned. We can believe that Julia has had a life-saving epiphany in the last boardroom scenes because Stanwyck has prepared us for its possibility at every opportunity. Total self-knowledge doesn't destroy Julia, as it does Stella Dallas; it sets her free.

Such a role was even worth being second-billed to the unctuous Allyson, and Stanwyck might have won an Oscar for her performance if she'd allowed herself to be run in the supporting category. Foch got a nomination in that category. She remembered that Stanwyck kept hitting the desk after the Holden confrontation, bruising herself. "She showed off the bruises," Foch recalled. "It was as if she was proud of the pain." This is the dark side of Stanwyck, the deep-dyed physical masochist, but it offers an insight into her process and how it relates to her life.

Julia has to pound on that desk until she's bruised and until the bruises don't hurt anymore before she can put all of the baggage of her past behind her. Stanwyck was a woman who had battle scars related to events that were completely beyond her control, like the cigarette burns on her chest. But she dedicated her real life, her artistic life, to mastering self-inflicted hurts of her own in order to use them constructively—this time in the service of Julia Tredway's fall and rise. It's probably the smallest part she ever played, but it's also one of the most impressively virtuosic of all her performances.

It's a shame that Stanwyck was never paired with James Cagney—her male equivalent and then some—when they were both under contract to Warner Bros. in the mid-thirties. Instead, the two most exciting and trailblazing American actors of the time wound up in an end-of-the-line MGM adoption drama, *These Wilder Years* (1956), a poorly written and directed film that seems determined to act as a tranquilizer on their respective gifts. Between static takes, you can practically hear director Roy Rowland mutter, "Ah, I guess we should cut now, do a new angle on this scene, huh?" and the movie gives Stanwyck little to do but sip coffee from dainty cups and saucers and address envelopes. She's introduced holding a baby close to her grey curls and soon mentions the man who invented the safety pin. When Cagney offers that the inventor might have been a woman, Stanwyck chirps, "Women never invent anything, except men," which has to be a contender for the worst line of dialogue she was ever asked to utter.

Stanwyck would have been more at home as an unscrupulous baby broker than as the kind of noble bureaucrat who would never have

allowed her to adopt Dion. She tries to keep our attention here by doing clear "beats" in her relentlessly prosaic scenes, sitting down to her
kitchen table with a plop of exhaustion, or eating a meal Cagney has
prepared with quiet appreciation for the food. And there are a few precious two shots where the stars connect slightly and just riff with each
other without any defined goal. Who knows why no one thought to put
them in a crime drama instead, playing two tough old birds who turn
each other on by their mutual amorality. Or even a musical; these two
ex-hoofers delighted their crew with impromptu dances on the set. I'd
gladly give up all of *These Wilder Years* for a documentary short subject on
their remembered dance routines.

Wilder/Stanwyck

Ball of Fire, Double Indemnity

*B*efore moving to direction, Billy Wilder, like Preston Sturges, turned out a lot of screenplays (Wilder's were usually co-written with Charles Brackett). A prickly Austro-Hungarian refugee from Germany, Wilder's smart-aleck voice as a writer comes through loud and clear in his scripts for Ernst Lubitsch and Mitchell Leisen. Wilder had a weakness for lines of often-questionable taste; Lubitsch and Leisen could put some of these lines over, but not all. For instance, when Greta Garbo's Soviet commissar is asked about the Moscow show trials in Lubitsch's *Ninotchka* (1939), she solemnly intones that "there will be fewer but better Russians." It's a line that aims to get a gasp and then a bit of a laugh, a sort of stiletto jab, and it works. But then there's the moment in Leisen's *Arise, My Love* (1940) when a man says that he's anxious to get to war with Germany because, "I've always wanted to drop something on Hamburg after getting ptomaine from that hamburger." This isn't even remotely funny, or interesting, or anything. It's just a miscalculation of tone.

You never know which Wilder you're going to get in these early scripts or in his later movies. There's the man who completely understood Gloria Swanson's demented silent screen relic Norma Desmond in *Sunset Boulevard* (1950) and the changing gender mores of *Some Like It Hot* (1959), and then there's the clod whose camera tours the ruins of Berlin in *A Foreign Affair* (1948) to the strains of "Isn't It Romantic?" and who torments Ray Milland's drunk for showy fun in *The Lost Weekend* (1945). To quote his old boss, Samuel Goldwyn, with Wilder you have to take the bitter with the sour.

Critical opinion on Wilder has always fluctuated, mainly because it hinges on these highly subjective questions of taste, on deciding when he goes too far or when he doesn't go far enough. For the first movie he wrote for Stanwyck, *Ball of Fire* (1941), Wilder gleefully stresses what he sees as the vulgarity in her character, and she rises to the bait while maintaining an untouchable sort of shrewdness. Whatever his faults, Wilder had a keen talent for coming up with character names, and he gives Stanwyck a doozy here: Sugarpuss O'Shea, a gangster's moll forced to take it on the lam with a cadre of professors working on an encyclopedia.

There are seven of these old profs, just like the seven dwarfs, plus one young grammarian, Bertram Potts (Gary Cooper), who needs Sugarpuss to teach him the ins and outs of modern slang, the boogie woogie, the hoi toi toi, the corny and the cheesy. Potts too is well named, and his last name means that Sugarpuss gets to call him Pottsie, reminiscent of Stanwyck's name for Fonda, "Hopsie," in the vastly superior *The Lady Eve*, which had been such a hit earlier in the year. Cooper's character name thus feels like a nudge reminding people of another movie they liked. *Ball of Fire* is nothing if not commercial.

Stanwyck received her second Academy Award nomination as best actress for *Ball of Fire* (it really should have been for *Eve*, but the academy members had *Ball of Fire* more freshly situated in their minds), so it has pride of place in her filmography. While she's somewhere near her best in it—and certainly as sexy as she'd ever be in a movie—*Ball of Fire* is a flawed film, and there are several reasons why it never quite comes together. It runs one hundred and eleven minutes, which is rather lengthy for such a slim subject, and it has several scenes that go on far too long— especially a sequence where Dan Duryea's hood, Pastrami, is holding the professors hostage and they slowly work toward getting a heavy portrait to fall on his head.

Pastrami starts shooting things in their room at random, hitting a flower vase that explodes right next to the camera. This ostentatious shot is a good example of another problem here: Gregg Toland's deep focus photography seems much more suited to a somber melodrama like *The Little Foxes* (which he shot the same year). So many of Toland's shots are simply too heavy looking and deliberate for light comedy. When Potts confesses the deepness of his love for Sugarpuss, Toland has Stanwyck put on blackface so that only her eyes glow in the dark, and this trick is typical of his stylistic excesses, which never suit Wilder's material.

Then there's the question of tone. The scenes with the professors are just this side of cutesy, with a bedtime nursery score emphasizing what harmless old sweeties these guys are. The actors playing the professors generally follow suit. S. Z. "Cuddles" Sakall has many reasons to slap his hands on his shaky jowls to get a laugh, while Henry Travers does his blandly beaming Henry Travers thing. Richard Haydn (as Professor Oddly) is too much in love with the sound of his own overly fastidious voice, so that his speech about his own marriage seems to go on longer than it should. Only that memorable on-screen scoundrel Tully Marshall bothers to seem like a three-dimensional person as Professor Robinson, and the script doesn't give him enough to work with. If Marshall had played Professor Oddly, the speech about marriage might have had a chance of working.

As Miss Bragg, the old maid housekeeper who treats the professors like naughty children, Kathleen Howard, best known as the harridan wife to W.C. Fields in *It's a Gift* (1934), is stuck in an unlikable, go-nowhere role. At one point, Sugarpuss punches Bragg out to keep her from blabbing, and this feels like a mistake, not funny and not really deserved (Stanwyck's punch actually connected during one take, to her horror, and Howard suffered a fractured jaw for her trouble). Worse still, the coy professor scenes are intercut with a kind of gangster picture featuring Dana Andrews as criminal kingpin Joe Lilac. Andrews's scenes feel perfunctory, and at the end, he and his men are tossed into a garbage truck, as in a cartoon, yet they seem all too unpleasantly real in earlier parts of the movie. And Cooper is not as precise a comedian as Henry Fonda; his shambling delivery tends to get deliberately vague at times, as if he trusts that his own personal charm can get him out of thinking through his part.

Where is director Howard Hawks in all this? Critic Robin Wood, in his book on Hawks, sees *Ball of Fire* as an attempt to right the "wrongs" of Hawks's magnificent *Bringing Up Baby*, which Wood sees as troublingly anti-intellectual. But to my eyes *Ball of Fire* only reflects a stony lack of interest on Hawks's part. It isn't really a Hawks movie, either in terms of its look, which falls to Toland, or its attitude, which falls to Wilder. Perhaps the chief culprit, though, is producer Sam Goldwyn, who always managed to impart an overly dignified feeling to most of his movies, a heavy touch fatal to a brash comedy like this.

Considering all these obstacles, it's nearly incredible that Stanwyck is as good as she is here. There are classic moments, to be sure, not least Sugarpuss's first entrance. Potts is in a nightclub, researching his slang and jotting down colorful terms in a notebook (something I can imagine Wilder himself doing, so greedy was he for the low side of American culture to remind him of vestiges of his own lost Weimar milieu). We see a lacquered fingernail pounding out the beat to Gene Krupa's "Drum

Boogie" on a curtain, and the nail seems sexy, a little contemptuous, impatient. Even when she's only acting with the fingers of one hand, Stanwyck manages to give a nuanced performance.

Sugarpuss practically leaps out on stage, wearing a spangly-tatters outfit courtesy of Edith Head that shows off a bare midriff and Dietrich-caliber legs. Martha Tilton, a Benny Goodman warbler, dubs Stanwyck's singing. The voice may be a little too high, but it's still not a bad fit (it would have been better to have dubbed Stanwyck with Krupa's lead canary, Anita O'Day, whose spirited, libidinal, croaky style would have ideally matched the star). The best moment is when Tilton's voice cuts out and Stanwyck herself cries, "C'mon, Krup, knock yourself out!" and we see the manic, highly sexual Krupa do his inimitable thing with his drums. "Yeah!" Sugarpuss breathes—almost hisses—at the close, using Stanwyck's own voice again. There's a brief reprise where Krupa plays the boogie with matchsticks, spoiled by Toland's glossy concept shot of Sugarpuss's face gleaming down on a table as he saws away.

"Screw, scram, scraw," says Sugarpuss, trying to get rid of Professor Potts at her dressing room door, but she changes her tune when she realizes she'll need a place to stay to hide from the police. She makes another entrance, even more striking, when she shows up at the professors' domicile. Potts opens the door and she winks and says, "Heidi Ho!" clicking her tongue on her palette (there's elemental rain beating down behind her). When she hears the seven old professors scampering upstairs, she says, "Hey, what is that?" in a harsh, mean-sounding voice. Stanwyck is always alert to the moments when Sugarpuss lets her hard edges emerge.

Sugarpuss was an orphan, it seems, like Ruby, and ran away from her aunt, but her childhood is no bummer in this movie. Stanwyck tosses the single line about the aunt away as if an unhappy childhood couldn't possibly matter at this point. Unlike Jean Harrington, whose father insists that she be "crooked but never common," Sugarpuss can be downright dirty, as when she reacts to Potts's embarrassment at not being quite dressed, unsettling him with, "You know, once I watched my big brother shave"—one of those Wilder remarks that just skirts that line of upset stomach bad taste. The Wilder "note" is so different from Brackett's prep school elegance that it's easy to guess at who did what; the Oddly marriage speech, for instance, seems like pure Brackett.

"Wee, that's a lot of books!" exclaims Sugarpuss, taking in the large encyclopedia working room. "All of 'em different?" she asks. At a moment like this, I'm grateful that uncultured but ever-sharp Stanwyck is playing this Sugarpuss, and not, say, Ginger Rogers, who was originally pursued for the part but turned it down. Rogers would have played it "dumb," self-consciously, which is not something Stanwyck could ever do; witness the failure of her dippy heiress in *The Mad Miss Manton*. "This is the first time anybody's moved in on my brain," says Sugarpuss, almost seriously, plunking herself down in a chair and saying she'll work "all night." This is not an idle boast, of course. Sugarpuss is likely one of the best lays in the world—a little scary, maybe, but worth it. When Potts hems and haws, she lifts one of her legs up into his face and commands, "Alright, feel that," extending her foot enough so that Luis Buñuel or Quentin Tarantino would salivate. It's cold, says Potts. "It's cold and *wet*," she emphasizes, in a lower, more forceful voice, so that this simple statement sounds very rough and visceral, bristling with sexual possibilities.

She enlists the professors on her side, giving her hand to "Cuddles" Sakall and then cracking, "Can I have this now, kid?" when he shows no inclination to let it go. Stanwyck gives this movie what it so sorely lacks, speed and dynamism, and though she's still not too comfortable with sarcasm, she's professional enough to deliver the various wisecracks quickly and with aplomb. And she couldn't be more at ease playing the kind of woman who delights in toying with older men's fancies. "Any of you can jerk a zipper?" she asks, when she's trying to close a skirt, her manner not too far from outright hostility, yet willing to be taken by surprise, too. When Sugarpuss falls in love with Potts while manipulating him for her own ends, this romance is believable, even ordained.

Though she knows the score about most of the important things, this is in some ways a naïve woman. After she accepts an engagement ring from Lilac, Sugarpuss wonders if she will continue her nightclub career or "bust in on the Helen Hayes racket," an idea that doesn't seem either likely or sensible. There are several shots in this movie where Stanwyck is asked to walk slowly away from the camera. This is neither the exploitation stuff of *Mexicali Rose* nor the physical idealization of Capra, but rather the pro playing all of her cards, as if she's thinking, "Sure, I have a nice ass. Have a look, that's what it's there for."

"You're the one I'm wacky about, just plain wacky," insists Sugarpuss to Potts, with that curious vehemence Stanwyck often brought to love scenes. She puts several books down on the floor so that she'll be tall enough to kiss the towering Cooper. When his Potts asks her what she's doing, Sugarpuss says, "Oh, you'll find out," in a heated, offhand way that would get any heterosexual man's blood racing. Lilac tells Potts that Sugarpuss is a materialist who "sulks if she has to wear last year's ermine," but, like many Stanwyck women, she has a basic fineness that lets her see, finally, that there are more important things than fur coats.

When Sugarpuss realizes that she really loves Potts, Stanwyck gets her abstracted look and practically spits out, "I love him because he's the kind of guy who gets drunk on a glass of buttermilk, and I love the way he blushes right up over his ears. I love him because he doesn't know how to kiss, the jerk!" As the writer Sheila O'Malley put it in a tribute piece to Stanwyck, "His very innocence shames her. Yet she loves him. She loves his innocence. And yet there's that epithet at the end, 'the jerk'! She's got an edge. She's feeling as mushy as she's ever gonna feel, and that pisses her off." Sugarpuss gets sidelined a bit during the last third, but she's made her brassy "yum yum" presence felt in a movie that needs to get its act together for her and stop working at cross purposes between Wilder's Berlin sarcasm, Toland's pictorial solemnity, Cooper's mannered cuteness, and Hawks's cool indifference.

When I mentioned that I was writing a book about Barbara Stanwyck to people around my age (mid-twenties to mid-thirties), they usually didn't quite know who she was, unfortunately. If they asked me what movies she had been in, I always rushed right to *Double Indemnity* first, thinking they might have at least heard of *that*. Stanwyck probably made better movies, but none seem to have had the pop cultural impact of this Billy Wilder classic—even if some recent commentators have taken to making complaints about the blond wig Wilder had her wear.

Some even question her sex appeal in the film. Stanwyck was more than capable, of course, of turning on the sex appeal in both earlier and later movies, not least in the Wilder-scripted *Ball of Fire*, where she is as delectable a physical specimen as most men could hope for (and here, maybe, is where Hawks's influence might finally show itself). But in *Double Indemnity*, there's a damper placed on that sort of thing, and it has to do, in part, with Wilder's essential misogyny. So many of his movies evince a distaste for women, especially if they happen to be a bit older than an ingénue and still trying to peddle their sexual wares (just look at how he mocks poor Kim Novak in *Kiss Me, Stupid* [1964] or Juliet Mills in *Avanti!* [1972]).

James M. Cain first published *Double Indemnity* in serial form in 1936. Two years before, he had put out another salacious book about murder, *The Postman Always Rings Twice*, with intimations of carnal depravity (when the married Cora first couples with drifter Frank Chambers, she tells him to bite her lip and he does so until he draws blood). Both books were inspired by the case of Ruth Snyder, a Queens woman who

murdered her husband with the help of another man in order to collect
on the dead man's insurance.

Cain's *Double Indemnity* is told in the first person by Walter Huff (Neff
in Wilder's film), an insurance salesman in Los Angeles who walks will-
ingly into a kind of "House of Death" with blood-red drapes, the home of
Nirdlinger, an oil man, and his wife Phyllis. In the film, Wilder changes
Nirdlinger (a lingering nerd?) to Dietrichson (son of Marlene?), which
once again shows his talent for picking just the right character names.
In the book, Phyllis is "maybe thirty-one or -two, with a sweet face,
light blue eyes, and dusty blonde hair." Though she has "a washed-out
look," Huff sees that "[u]nder those blue pajamas was a shape to set a
man nuts." So, in Cain's book, we have a slightly faded dish with a great
bod. Not Stanwyck, by any means; more like Veronica Lake as she was
in 1952 or 1953.

"I like tea," says Cain's rather haughty Phyllis. "It makes a break in
the afternoon." She sounds like a bored housewife, but everything she
says might be calculated for effect, so it's hard to get a read on her. Walter
notices a few attractive flaws in Phyllis: two teeth that were "maybe a
little bit buck," and freckles on her forehead. Tiny physical flaws like this
can stoke a man's lust, and they definitely do the trick for Walter. Cain's
prose is tough and funny in these early scenes. It's not classic wiseacre
like Wilder's patter, but there are plenty of little laughs leading up to an
ellipsis; afterwards, we can tell that Walter has laid Phyllis.

When he asks about her husband, Phyllis says, "He treats me as well
as a man can treat a woman," which in retrospect sounds strange. What
is her standard for good treatment? She says she doesn't love her husband, but he's never done anything bad to her. Then, though, she reveals
her psychological buckteeth: "Maybe I'm crazy, but there's something in
me that loves Death. I think of myself as Death, sometimes. In a scarlet
shroud, floating through the night. I'm *so* beautiful, then." A sensible
man would have been out the door at "scarlet shroud," but Walter is a
little cracked himself.

Phyllis reflects that she would like to bring death to everyone, so
they'd be happy, and she begins to seem not human to Walter. "The
firelight was reflected in her eyes like she was some kind of leopard," he
says, employing a startling image in the middle of all the terse dialogue.
Phyllis used to be a nurse, and as Walter plans to kill her husband and
get a double payday from the insurance company, she often seems to be
living in a dream world, but there's also a sense that in her dreamlike
way she is pulling all of the strings.

After the murder, whatever feeling there was between Walter and Phyllis sours: "I loved her like a rabbit loves a rattlesnake," says Walter. This sentiment is far removed from the tough-love tenderness Stanwyck's Jean Harrington displays when she talks about herself as an axe that needs a turkey. It comes out that Phyllis deliberately killed the first Mrs. Nirdlinger. Then it comes out that she killed three children in the hospital where she was head nurse, one of them for money, and the others just to cover her tracks.

"She's a pathological case, that's all," says Keyes, an overweight insurance investigator. "The worst I ever heard of." In 1936, a flat-out sociopathic murderer like Phyllis was still an exotic thing, something undreamed of by most people. Today, she's one of the fictional firsts in a long line of genetic mutations with real-life killer counterparts. Cain makes it clear that Phyllis is incapable of feeling remorse, and in his scariest scene, her stepdaughter Lola remembers walking in on her when she was wrapped in red silk fabric "like a shroud," her face "smeared" in white powder and lipstick, standing in front of a mirror with a dagger in her hand and making faces at herself. (If Wilder had included this scene in his movie, it might have been Stanwyck's ultimate mirror moment in film, for she would have dared to look as grotesque as necessary while also doing what she needed to do to access Phyllis's ghastly, private playacting at murder). Cain's plot gets too convoluted, and his double-suicide ending on board a ship is neither very believable nor very likely, but he has laid down quite a template for any moviemaker.

Studios were interested in Cain's story right away, but the censors wouldn't let them touch it. In the early forties, the rule-breaking Wilder took the novel up in collaboration with Raymond Chandler, the hard-drinking creator of the detective character Philip Marlowe. It was a pairing of opposites, like Wilder's more storied partnership with the ivy league Charles Brackett, and it yielded a script that tarted up a lot of Cain's dialogue while shifting some of his emphasis—sometimes for the better, sometimes not. Wilder approached various actors with the script, and they were wary of it, for this was a new type of American movie, something that hadn't been seen before. There were precedents, like John Huston's *The Maltese Falcon* (1941), but this story was altogether nastier, more constricted, more pitiless.

Stanwyck admired *Double Indemnity* as a script, but she was nonetheless uncertain about it. "I had never played an out-and-out killer," she remembered. "I had played medium heavies, but not an out-and-killer." (I love her term "medium heavy," which suggests there is a kind of human scale for perfidy). She went to see Wilder. "I was a little frightened of it and, when [I went] back to his office, I said, 'I love the script and I love you, *but* I am a little afraid after all these years of playing heroines to go into an out-and-out cold-blooded killer. And Mr. Wilder—and rightly so—looked at me and he said, 'Well, are you a mouse or an actress?' And I said, 'Well, I *hope* I'm an actress.' He said, 'Then do the part.'"

Stanwyck told this story to praise Wilder, and she always had high regard for *Indemnity* because it caused such a stir, but I wonder if her initial hesitation to take the movie spoke to her instinctive sense of what was real and interesting in a role and what wasn't. Then again, maybe she was just plain scared of playing such a bad seed. Wilder took the right schoolyard tack with her and lightly taunted her, the equivalent of a bully asking, "You chicken?" He then placed that weird blond wig on her head; even he realized a month into shooting that the wig wasn't working. Buddy DeSylva, the head of Paramount at the time, took a look at the rushes and quipped, "We hired Barbara Stanwyck and here we get George Washington."

Wilder told Ella Smith that, "The wig was not much good, I admit," but later on he rationalized it as part of "the phoniness of the girl—bad taste, phony wig," as if his Phyllis is *supposed* to be wearing a wig. Is she bald, like Constance Towers at the beginning of Sam Fuller's *The Naked Kiss* (1964)? The effect is one of disfigurement, not exactly an aid to any sex appeal Stanwyck could have found for Phyllis. Cain's Phyllis is a looker but a monster inside, but Wilder's Phyllis has most of her flaws all on the surface, where we can't possibly miss them.

Still, on the level of pure craft, *Double Indemnity* deserves its status. Wilder has pruned away the unnecessary fat in the book's Lola section and also added some knockout suspense set pieces. The film feels, by and large, very modern, especially in the way it looks. We never seem to be on sets, and there's a vivid sense of Los Angeles in the exterior location shots (when Stanwyck's Phyllis enters a grocery store for the last time to scheme with Walter [Fred MacMurray], the sun is glaring down on her, and she's obviously on a real street in LA). Much of the movie's visual scheme, with all its Venetian blind shadows and cool Spanish-style architecture, must be credited to cinematographer John Seitz, who went to great lengths to achieve a dusty afternoon look for the Dietrichson house.

Under the opening credits, a man walks on crutches in silhouette to Miklos Rosza's throbbing, dissatisfied score. This image underlines a kind of impotence, both physical and moral. There are a few urgent shots of a car speeding through the dead of night, and this feeling of a deserted nighttime LA is amplified when MacMurray's Walter knocks on the door of his office building. An elevator operator lets him in and talks about how the company wouldn't let him take out insurance because of a heart condition. Walter deals with his chatter curtly, even rudely. But he's been shot, see, so he has to amble to his office and make his confession, which sets up the first-person narration that carries Cain's book.

This narration is often redundant. When he walks around the Dietrichson home, Walter tells us in words what we already see; such verbal reinforcement is Wilder's writerly weakness. There are several points in this movie when Walter is going about his business and we can see what he's doing and feeling (MacMurray is outstanding as this weak man corrupted by his job), yet when we see Walter bowling, for instance, Wilder has Walter's voiceover tell us that he's bowling, and why. Wilder doesn't quite trust the audience, and falls victim, sometimes, to over-explaining.

The question remains whether Wilder impedes or helps Stanwyck's performance as Phyllis. By my lights he sometimes does get in her way, not only with that blond wig, but in subtler ways, both visual and verbal—yet she barrels right through him anyway and does some of her most complex work. Her Phyllis is introduced standing at the top of a staircase, wearing only a towel and holding her sunglasses, so that Walter and the camera peer up at her. But there's nothing too sexual about this entrance; Wilder is too busy giggling. Walter is looking for her husband, he says, to discuss an automobile policy. "Anything I can do?" asks Phyllis, in a brazen come-on voice. "I'd hate to think of you having a smashed fender or something when you're not . . . fully covered," Walter smirks, almost laughing.

She's been taking a sunbath, she says. "No pigeons around, I hope," says Walter. To his credit, MacMurray's face falls a bit, as if Walter is embarrassed after saying this, and MacMurray's gesture is a good way of dealing with such a gross Wilder joke. Wilder himself said he used to taunt the puritanical Chandler with tales of his lively sex life, and there were women who responded to his brand of ribaldry, which is such a thin veil for contempt. These women must have said Wilder was "so funny," but humor comes from good places and bad places, and Wilder's humor is from a particularly bad taste neighborhood, one where you're probably going to get your gentler sensibilities mugged.

We see Phyllis's cheap shoes as she walks down the stairs; they have pom-poms on the toes, like something Joan Crawford would have worn in the early thirties (Wilder sets his tale in 1938 to explain why Neff isn't in the army). Walter makes a dumb joke about *The Philadelphia Story* (1940), and Phyllis, who has been applying lipstick in a mirror, snaps the lipstick shut to show her impatience with him. She sits down and crosses her shapely legs so he can see her anklet; he notices it, which was her intent, and she uncrosses her legs. When he talks about insurance, Phyllis paces back and forth, and we can see her weighing things in her mind, nervously.

It's never made terribly clear whether her nervousness in these first scenes is partly real or entirely feigned. Writer Nick Davis sees Stanwyck's "first sequence of coaxing Walter Neff into her murderous stratagems not as the first, purposefully amateur stage of a larger plot but as an imperfectly managed ploy; she doesn't harden or elevate Phyllis into a diabolical genius, but presents her as a woman who unmistakably dislikes her husband and dislikes her step-daughter." The Phyllis we see initially, Davis writes, has to work at being a monster. I think that Stanwyck is trying to complicate Phyllis in these first scenes, since she knows that the plot is going to box her tightly as a villain later on (it should be remembered that Stanwyck always learned the whole script and made a point of keeping the entire thing in her head at all times).

There's no doubt, though, about what she's doing in the famous foreplay dialogue that ends this first encounter, a scene that has been so endlessly excerpted on TV that it's tattooed on most of our brains. Its dialogue almost plays like a vaudeville patter routine. That tone might just be a clue to Stanwyck's basic approach to this part and this movie. Did the specter of career vaudevillian Frank Fay raise its ugly head in her mind while she was playing this woman who loathes her husband and wants him dead? She observed Fay's routines on stage during her formative years, and in 1933 she even sank her own money into a Fay revue, *Tattle Tales*, which marked the last time, regrettably, that Stanwyck acted on stage (she did scenes from her Capra films). Add a dash of Wilder's Weimar vinegar to this Fay training, and here it is:

"There's a speed limit in this state, Mr. Neff, forty-five miles an hour," says Phyllis, very fast, almost as if she's waiting for the next "Who's on first?" line. "How fast was I going, Officer?" parries Neff, the salesman incarnate. "I'd say around ninety," she says, with a lower inflection—heated, but a parody of "heated," too. "Suppose you get down off your motorcycle and give me a ticket," raps out Neff, quick as a shot. "Suppose I let you off with a warning this time," says Phyllis, suddenly a dominatrix. "Suppose it doesn't take," he continues (hit me harder, Mistress!). "Suppose I have to rap you over the knuckles," she purrs (Production

Code? What Production Code?). "Suppose I bust out crying and put my head on your shoulder," he ponders, a canny masochist. "Suppose you try putting it on my husband's shoulder," she snaps, just like she impatiently closed her lipstick in front of the mirror. "That tears it," he concludes, and the operative word here is "tears." Wilder is at his best when he turns his wordsmith glee to slang terms, the gaudier and more disposable the better. Phyllis has completely emasculated this man in one rapid-fire exchange, and he loves it. But she's weary of her own power, a feeling which maybe reads as the uncertainty we sometimes see in her eyes and in her movements.

Many later critics, most notably Parker Tyler, have seen Wilder's *Double Indemnity* as a love story between two men, MacMurray's Walter and Edward G. Robinson's Keyes. This feeling is made explicit in Wilder's dialogue. Walter tells Keyes he loves him several times, always sincerely, though there's no question that it's the love of a son for a father. Keyes, on the other hand, does seem to have the hots for Walter, subconsciously; he's always putting his hands on Walter's shoulders, and he jealously stays in the room when Walter takes a call from Phyllis. Walter lies to Keyes, says the call is from a girl named Margie, and Keyes says, twice, that he thinks that this Margie "drinks straight from the bottle." Keyes also lets us know about his one-time brush with matrimony. The "little man" that lives in his gut told him that something was crooked about his bride-to-be, and so he had her investigated and found out that she was a tramp on the take, so he feels justified in shutting women out of his life.

"You're not smarter, Walter, you're just a little taller," says Keyes, using this crack as an excuse to look Neff up and down, and he keeps saying he's going to tie up cases and wrap them in tissue paper with little *pink* ribbons on it. Keyes's life is mainly his job as an insurance investigator—all of his emotions run to Walter, who's deeply involved in Keyes's beloved line of work. Wilder, who knew his Freud, has Walter always lighting Keyes's cigars for him. Our wise guy director was hip to the fact that sometimes a cigar is just a cigar, and sometimes it symbolizes something else entirely. Thus, Keyes is a repository for Wilder's ill-concealed misogyny, and also provides Wilder with the framework for a naughty boy sketch of a repressed gay romance.

In her second scene, Stanwyck plays Phyllis just as nervously as she did before going into the "speed limit" patter. This is a telling choice because practically all of her other characters are seasoned manipulators—unless Stanwyck means here to suggest that Phyllis is such an evil genius that her feigned uncertainty is so expert that it looks real (this is a highly tricky area Stanwyck is operating in, a kind of actor's shell game to keep us as off-balance as her dupe, Walter). Phyllis reveals that she's a native Californian, "born and raised in Los Angeles." Many writers have commented that Phyllis obviously hates Los Angeles, but the way Stanwyck plays this line doesn't really read that way to me. When she says "born and raised in Los Angeles," her eyes gleam in an uncontrolled manner, like a little girl trying to please her daddy. They could be gleaming with hate, but it looks like pleasure, too. Then again, as we soon learn, Phyllis Dietrichson has a twisted relationship with pleasure, and this relationship is what makes the performance so modern, so much a leap forward from Cain's vivid but finally rather cardboard boogie-man tootsie.

Speaking of her husband, Phyllis says, "Sometime we sit here all evening and never say a word to each other." Stanwyck uses that flat, foggy Brooklyn tone in which "other" becomes "oth-uh," and it's hard to decide if the sound is Claudette Colbert classy or Susan Hayward guttural. It's really somewhere in between, in that grey, indeterminate area where Stanwyck creates and disturbs our expectations. No doubt Phyllis does spend empty evenings like this with her husband, but she isn't providing us with a real glimpse of her life; it's an act for Walter. At bottom, this Phyllis is the kind of sociopath who can't feel anything about anything except her own sick urges, and so Stanwyck empties out her arsenal of man-manipulation and comes up with this unsettlingly artificial mantrap, a kind of void, no soul inside. Phyllis lives in her head and in front of her mirror, and the rest is just show for the shadows surrounding her.

Stanwyck's face is made up so heavily that the effect is as unflattering as the Rumpelstiltskin gold of that wig, but Wilder allows her a white sweater so tight you can see her bra underneath it for the clincher seduction scene in Walter's apartment. This contrast of bad wig and revealing sweater makes her an angel of death under electric light outside his door, a creature of Los Angeles. When he wishes he had something fancy to give her to drink, she says, "Bourbon is fine, Walter," in a tired but grateful voice. Phyllis likes sex, and she hasn't been getting much of it at home; she might even be going without entirely (and Stanwyck could probably relate to this).

Mixing their drinks, Walter talks about some women who didn't get away with murdering their husbands, and as he does, Wilder gives Stanwyck a close-up where she unveils the monster Phyllis, obsessed by her own preoccupations—not a leopard, as in the Cain book, but a human animal that needs to go back to the warehouse, or the nuthouse, for repairs. As with Stella Dallas, Stanwyck takes the basic material of this character and deepens it. She brought a needed human dimension, among many other things, to Stella, and she also brings this dimension to Phyllis, but she's wrestling a tougher demon here. We can trust that Stanwyck knows exactly what she's doing, but she's never going to show you all her cards in this movie.

Walter talks about a woman who was executed for the murder of her husband. Lost in her fantasies, Phyllis says, "Perhaps it was worth it to her." Stanwyck's voice here is sensible, hushed, but uncommonly forceful; she's been saving this voice for the moment when it will scare us most. After this, though, Stanwyck gives us a few clues to what might really be happening inside Phyllis. When Walter suggests she divorce her husband, she says, "He wouldn't give me a divorce," in a fast, irritated tone that sounds like Phyllis is totally sure on this one point. Mr. Dietrichson beefs about her buying things; he had money when he married her, but that has dwindled. "And I wanted a home," Phyllis sneers, disgusted at her own momentary weakness (this, too, sounds genuine).

She was the nurse for Dietrichson's first wife, and she says she pitied him after the wife died. During those empty nights when they say nothing—or not much—to each other, Phyllis must always be returning to her fantasies of killing him, for we see her doing so in Walter's apartment with a diseased kind of Robert Ryan-like pride in her plans. "Walter, I don't want to kill him, I never did," she claims, so unconvincingly as to be ridiculous, but then she turns the screws on her victim by admitting, "Not even when he gets drunk and slaps my face." She says this in a slightly agitated voice that lets us know that this dominatrix doesn't mind switching to masochism every now and then (here, too, unavoidably, is a reminder of the drunk, abusive Frank Fay slapping Stanwyck's face in public, at Hollywood nightclubs—for an audience).

Phyllis says she's thought of leaving her drunk husband in the car with the motor still running and closing the garage door, like Bette Davis in *Bordertown* (1935) or Ida Lupino in *They Drive By Night* (1940). Phyllis is obscenely excited by the idea of this murder, and her excitement is sexual, so that Stanwyck is actually closer, at times, to Cain's Cora in *The Postman Always Rings Twice*, wanting to rut with her new man practically on the corpse of her dead husband.

Walter puts his large hand on Phyllis's white sweater and the camera pulls discreetly back; his voiceover says that she shed some light tears. When we get back to them in that room, they've definitely had sex, and it was probably pretty good in its animal way. Walter says yes, they'll kill her husband. Phyllis gets up off the couch, her face registering, "OK, it worked," but also a bit of nervousness; she isn't facing Walter at this moment, so this nervousness of hers is at least partly real. So many of Stanwyck's performances are about the almost non-existent dividing line between acting an emotion and really feeling it. She knew that the body and even the mind can't really know when you're "acting," which is why acting can be such a dangerous and depleting profession, an art form based on tricking yourself so convincingly that the "tricks" often dissolve, and what's left are real tears and real anger—even real happiness—on top of something troublingly hollowed-out.

We meet Dietrichson (Tom Powers), and he does seem like a crab, to say the least. He still treats Phyllis like an employee rather than a wife. Alfred Hitchcock often employed the same technique as Wilder uses here, getting us to identify with a would-be murderer and then confronting us with the moral implications of our identification. Wilder isn't making this picture to ponder questions of ethics, of course. He just wants to put on a good, "different" show and entertain an audience with depravity and its consequences, but Stanwyck is stalking bigger game.

When Walter insists to Phyllis that Mr. Dietrichson needs to die in a train accident in order for her to get a doubled insurance payout, Stanwyck makes Phyllis seem tickled by his enthusiasm, almost touched. She looks at him for a moment as if to say, "Wait a minute . . . are you my soulmate or something?" She does love Walter, in her way, while they're planning the murder and shortly afterwards, because he's made her fantasy real, and he seems like such an ideal partner that she can barely contain her admiring surprise at his resourcefulness.

When they meet at a supermarket to discuss their game plan, Phyllis bites her lip a bit to show that she's nervous, but she completely drops this act when Walter leaves her. The camera catches the monster Phyllis again, peering out like some hungry beast from behind boxes of food. Walter mentions that from now on it's "straight down the line" for both of them, and the monomaniacal Phyllis becomes obsessed with this phrase, repeating it, with variations, for the rest of the film, like a sinister mantra. Leading her husband to his car, she mockingly calls him "honey," and when he mentions coming back from his class reunion, Phyllis's mouth purses slightly, as if she's thinking, "You won't be back, buster." She stops the car and honks the horn, which is Walter's cue to strangle the husband. As he does this, Wilder gives Stanwyck a justly famous close-up to show how Phyllis reacts.

At first her mouth is open, excitedly, but then it closes again, tightly. In her eyes, there's a nearly unreadable look. It is at once childlike and sad, and there's a bit of self-recognition and a bit of satisfaction—and a bit of disappointment that the whole job is over, for she had so enjoyed the planning. "What comes next?" she seems to think, with the melancholy of a serial killer who knows that they can only really get off every once in a great while. There's even some joy in her face. So many things are blended together in this close-up that it has the visual effect of a full orchestra playing at full blast—probably something by Mahler.

Stanwyck takes you through every gradation of what a sociopath like Phyllis feels. Just how did she do this? It took craft, of course, and planning. I can only hope that she killed off Frank Fay in her head, and maybe Al Jolson—and every other man who did her dirt. But she needed to make a large imaginative leap here, too; anyone is capable of murder, if provoked, but some rare people need no prompting. Phyllis wants the money, as does Walter, but that's not why she does this, ultimately; she does it to satisfy urges that no animal has. She is the embodiment of a human plague, and it comes to us during the middle of a world war that would leave us with no illusions about the depths of human evil. Many of Wilder's relatives perished in concentration camps, and it doesn't take much thought to put a Phyllis in that context, a Maria Mandel of LA.

Wilder added a suspenseful scene, where their car doesn't start right away after Walter stages Dietrichson's death on the train. He makes another inspired addition when he has Keyes and Phyllis almost collide in Walter's hallway, with her perilously hidden behind a door. (Cain said afterwards that he wished he had thought of such a scene, yet it's purely a movie scene because, uncharacteristically, Wilder has thought it through in solely visual terms). The bits with Dietrichson's daughter Lola don't work too well, mainly because the actress playing this girl, Jean Heather, isn't as appealing as she needs to be, but we do learn from her that Phyllis did kill the first Mrs. Dietrichson (there are no murdered children in the Wilder version, which even he probably felt was a bit much).

Lola says that she saw Phyllis in front of the mirror, trying on mourning attire: "There was a look in her eye . . . I'll never forget," she adds. We know that look all too well. In the grocery store again, with sunglasses pressed into her wig, Phyllis talks like a zombie as she keeps Walter tethered to her. Then she takes off the glasses so that we see her overloaded, bleary eyes before she zaps him with an enslaving look and takes her leave. It's like a bump and grind, and then a move back behind the curtain.

In her last scene, waiting for a showdown in her darkened house, Phyllis is cool and tough. "We're both rotten," she admits. Walter says that she's a little more rotten, but that isn't true; he has a choice between righteous Keyes and bad apple Phyllis, and he chooses her way. She has no choice; she is what she is. When she throws a cigarette away, poised to go into action and shoot Walter, Stanwyck moves uncannily like a snake—an "Irrawaddy cobra," as Cain puts it—as she slithers up and fires her gun at her prey.

She hits Walter, but not fatally, and he sidles up to her. She can't fire the second shot to finish him off. Why? Is it, like she says, because she suddenly feels love for him, the same love she seemed to feel when they were planning to make her treasured murder fantasy a reality? He isn't buying it. "I'm not asking you to buy, just hold me close," she whimpers. He shoots her, and she falls limp in his arms in her white dress, a vanquished snake about to shed its skin, embodied by an actress who always makes "sincerity" seem a Byzantine concept. Now you see it, now you don't.

Stanwyck Noir

The Strange Love of Martha Ivers, The Two Mrs. Carrolls,
Cry Wolf, The Lady Gambles, The File on Thelma Jordan,
No Man of Her Own, The Man with a Cloak, Jeopardy,
Witness to Murder, Crime of Passion

Double Indemnity heralded a new era, one where Stanwyck dominated many a shadowy thriller, some of them failures, some of them overlooked gems, and some like *The Strange Love of Martha Ivers* (1946), which is a qualified success on its own limited terms. The ad campaign for *Martha Ivers* implores us to only "whisper her name!" If that sounds a little corny, it suits the serpentine, simmering yet often ramshackle movie itself, directed by Lewis Milestone, with a script by Robert Rossen, who later directed *Body and Soul* (1947) and *The Hustler* (1961).

Rossen worked his way up writing socially conscious Warner Bros. melodramas, and his tentative leftism sometimes shows up in *Martha Ivers*, with its schematic view of the greedy rich and the tough working class. The film starts out with an astringent sixteen-minute prologue, set in 1928, that acts as a kind of appetizer to the melodrama feast to come. Janis Wilson, the memorably neurotic little girl from *Now, Voyager*, plays Martha Ivers as an unhappy teenager longing to get out from under the influence of her aunt, Mrs. Ivers (a sinister Judith Anderson). The girl was born Martha Smith, the daughter of a working-class father and a rich Ivers mother. Mrs. Ivers has had her name legally changed to her mother's maiden name, but this authoritarian aunt can't change her niece's character.

Martha tries to run away with bad boy Sam Masterson (Darryl Hickman) during a thunderstorm, and Mr. O'Neil (Roman Bohnen), a schoolteacher ambitious for his son Walter (Mickey Kuhn), makes sure that Martha is caught and brought back to Mrs. Ivers. When Mr. O'Neil says that he wants his boy to go to Harvard, Mrs. Ivers wearily tells him that Walter would probably be happier driving a truck, a touch of 1930s leftism that sounds strange coming from her aristocratic lips. Mrs. Ivers, it seems, owns everything in town (it's even called Iverstown). After Martha is brought back to her, she slaps the girl and says that the best thing her father ever did for her was to die, whereupon Martha snarls out some hatred.

This is a heavy-spirited movie in which it always seems to be raining, as the characters circle their opponents steadily and slowly like boxers until they rush at each other and go in for the kill. Planning to run away again, Martha loses sight of her pet cat. When she sees Mrs. Ivers beating the animal with her cane, Martha pulls the cane out of her aunt's hand and bops her lightly on the head. Mrs. Ivers then falls down some stairs, dead. This sequence of events is all quite weirdly shot and put together, like a macabre silent film set to Miklos Rozsa's hard-driving, ever-percolating score, but it suits the movie's dreamlike unreality, putting us inside Martha's head and the way she sees and experiences things.

We jump to 1946 and our first course on the *Martha Ivers* menu, which involves the grown-up Sam (Van Heflin) and his relations with Toni Marachek (Lizabeth Scott), a sultry ex-con. Scott is one of those curious ersatz figures of this period who talks like she's seen a lot of movies and is trying to fit herself in with her hissing, sibilant line readings and curdled, tough-girl smiles and tears, both of which make her squinch up her face beseechingly. She's 100 percent artificial. Because of her lack of authenticity, she is the embodiment of some late 1940s films, a collection of movie signs that can only be read legibly if you are immersed in the style she's aping.

Heflin usually didn't play parts as cocky and lover-boyish as Sam Masterson, and he has a lot of fun here, especially when he's roughing up the grown-up, alcoholic Walter (Kirk Douglas), who's now a politico married to Stanwyck's Martha. This is Douglas's first movie, and he's expert at playing Walter's weakness, but he tends to be hammy and too aware of his own charisma (though he had wanted Heflin's role, he took to the weakling like a duck to water).

Martha Ivers was made during a set decorators' strike. Sometimes, in order to go on working, everyone would have to stay at the studio (they couldn't cross the picket line without the risk of being hurt), and Milestone sided with the strikers, so that some of the film was directed by Byron Haskin. *Martha Ivers* does have a patchwork quality at times; there are some careless, abrupt cuts here and there, and even some dissolves which seem uncommonly rushed. "Everyone had told me how nice Barbara Stanwyck was," Douglas wrote in his autobiography, *The Ragman's Son*, "so I was looking forward to working with her in this hostile environment. The crew adored her. They called her 'Missy,' and when she came on the set she went around hugging them, asking about their wives and children by name. She was a professional, she was there, always prepared, an excellent actress. But she was indifferent to me."

Later on, Stanwyck noticed that Douglas might be an up-and-comer. "I could see it happening," he wrote, "like the lens of a camera turning into focus. She looked at me, made eye contact for the first time. She said, 'Hey, you're pretty good.' I said, 'Too late, Miss Stanwyck.'" Off-camera, Stanwyck in this peak period could be as ruthless as the characters she played. At Milestone's suggestion, Heflin had worked out a complicated maneuver with a coin moving over his knuckles to show that Sam is a professional gambler, and Stanwyck took this in, warily. Then, like Martha, she went in for the kill: "Van, that's a wonderful piece of business," she said, "but if you do that during my important lines, I have a bit of business that will draw attention away from yours." Holding Heflin's eye, Stanwyck pulled her skirt well above her knees. "Any time you start twirling that coin, I'll be fixing my garter. So be sure you don't do that when I have important lines to speak."

Forewarned, Helfin only does the coin trick once in her presence, when Martha is supposed to be flustered by Sam. Assured of her power, Stanwyck also supervised her own lighting, for she had "her own favorite key light," at this point. She was now a far cry from the wholly vulnerable girl who let Capra take care of everything for her. The "pro" of *Martha Ivers* is estimable, of course, but sometimes one longs for the still unformed and open Stanwyck from 1930 to 1934 or so.

Stanwyck's first scene with Douglas inaugurates the main course of the movie, which starts a half hour into the running time. To counteract, or combat, Douglas's embroidering style in this scene, Stanwyck holds back and lets him manage everything, keeping a poker face and a ramrod posture (Edith Head costumes Martha in clothes that look suffocating and slightly off-center, with hoods and furs piled on for protection). Then, when she sees her opening, Stanwyck bares down on him, bending slightly at the waist and snapping out, "When did you get drunk, where did you get drunk, why did you get drunk," in one continuous, punching fashion: BOOM, BOOM, BOOM. When she's made her impact, this stiff, practical woman seduces him a bit, in Stanwyck's lightest, most distracted seduction mode; Martha knows that she doesn't have to expend too much energy keeping Walter in line. They're joined together by guilt: Walter's father, Mr. O'Neil, had them send an innocent man to the gallows for the murder of Martha's aunt, and when they learn that Sam is back in town, they worry that he's there to blackmail them.

Far too much time is spent on Scott's Toni, who looks less like she got out of the jug and more like she just came from the beauty parlor. And Stanwyck seems to sense that this isn't a particularly serious movie, so she mainly takes it easy and doesn't do any of the character work that might spoil the overall atmosphere of unreality. She sets off one tiny flare behind her eyes when Sam tells Martha that he doesn't really know her, and instead of the all-encompassing moment of recognition Stanwyck achieves in her heavy-hitter roles, she shows Martha thinking, "I hardly know myself." In her confrontation scene with Heflin, where Martha talks about killing her aunt and then realizes that Sam didn't see her do it, she makes her eyes shine like a wild animal as she comes at him with a burning branch. Stanwyck stays well within the parameters of her role throughout, using just enough of her talent to make us believe in Martha without overselling the part, which could have been disastrous. She's playing here for entertainment rather than acting out the reality of Capra or Ford or Vidor or Sturges.

In another slow-burning scene with Douglas, this time with Heflin standing between them as referee, Stanwyck excitingly chooses to shout him down and then pound on a desk and cry, "Then let go!" in a high-pitched voice. This action shuts everybody up for a moment. Walter at one point calls Martha "a little girl in a cage, waiting for someone to let her out," and the same could be said for Stanwyck the actress, who is only unleashed briefly at the end. Walter has fallen down the stairs (at least Milestone doesn't have another thunderstorm roaring in the background), and Martha encircles Sam with her spider-like arms. "Now, Sam, do it now," Martha urges, in Stanwyck's airy purr. "Set me free, set both of us free." She switches to a harsher tone: "He fell down the stairs and fractured his skull, everybody knows what a heavy drinker he was!" Then she goes back to purring, "Oh, Sam, it can be so easy . . . ."

Rozsa's score works itself into a fine frenzy as Sam walks down the stairs, and then the camera holds Martha in a close-up as she waits for him to kill Walter, her glistening lips open suggestively in anticipation of the crime. But her face falls in disappointment when she realizes that he won't do what she wants. "Your whole life has been a dream, Martha," Sam says. The best parts of *Martha Ivers* emphasize the dreamlike quality of the title character's mind, which Stanwyck physicalizes whenever she has the chance. She pulls a gun on Sam, but she can't shoot him; when he leaves, Walter holds the gun to her waist, and she pulls the trigger for him. "Ivers, Ivers," rings out a male voice on the soundtrack, and Martha murmurs, "No . . . no . . . Martha Smith." According to Rossen, Martha probably would have been happier driving a truck, or married to a truck driver. This isn't a movie or performance that can stand too much scrutiny, but both have their moments.

The same cannot be said for *The Two Mrs. Carrolls* (1947), a dreadful adaptation of a derivative stage chiller, non-directed by Peter Godfrey. Stanwyck was such good friends with Godfrey off-screen that she even helped bring up his three daughters when he and his wife passed away, so she may have been blind to his faults; his *Christmas in Connecticut* is often poor, but *Carrolls* reaches a whole new level of miscalculation and incompetence. It suffers from a precocious child (Ann Carter) who keeps spouting "adult-sounding" dialogue at a lugubrious pace, from Franz Waxman overdoing his stormy score, from Nigel Bruce overdoing his drunk friend, and from Humphrey Bogart embarrassing himself as a lunatic painter, widening his eyes amateurishly whenever he feels a crazy spell coming on. As his wife, Stanwyck is incongruously chipper in her first scenes, as if she thinks she can save some of this mess by being "starry." But she's also lazy here; when Alexis Smith starts coming on to her husband, it's hard to tell, at first, whether Stanwyck's character is amused by Smith's man-eating or just oblivious, or both. And later on Stanwyck gives some of her lines a distracted, stilted reading (you can't blame her if her mind is on something else, for she often seems to have wandered onto the wrong set and behaves as if she doesn't want to be noticed).

Bogart keeps trying to do her in with some poisoned milk, à la *Suspicion* (1941); he even offers some milk to the cops who lead him away, an insultingly obvious curtain line. It smells like a stinker from the start and only gets worse, and it's a crime that Stanwyck and Bogart couldn't have collaborated on something more appropriate. She would have made an ideal Brigid O'Shaughnessy in *The Maltese Falcon* (1941), though it's hard to begrudge Mary Astor one of her best roles.

Compared to the travesty of *Carrolls*, Stanwyck's third and thankfully last picture with Godfrey, *Cry Wolf* (1947), at least gives her something to do. As a woman trying to find out the secrets of an old dark house presided over by a seemingly bored or hung over Errol Flynn, Stanwyck rides horses, runs down dark hallways, makes use of a dumbwaiter to enter a secret laboratory, and skitters around on rooftops. There's an

effective scare or two, but the movie is mired in exposition and that
deadly Godfrey pacing.

In the immediate post-Code era, Stanwyck was a noble gambling lady,
but in the lost weekend of the late forties, in *The Lady Gambles* (1949),
she was asked to offer a case study in addiction. She does so admirably,
even daringly, all along the way, until the script descends into textbook
psychobabble (director Michael Gordon said that Stanwyck hesitated
about accepting this role and needed a bit of persuasion to take it, for
she had just run the histrionic gauntlet of *Sorry, Wrong Number* [1948]).
When we first see her Joan, she's a blondish woman blowing on some
dice in a dark alley, deep in noir land. The men she's with soon scatter,
and two other men beat her up, pretty violently. We see her wheeled
into a hospital on a gurney, passed out, her face bruised, as her husband
David (Robert Preston) tries to keep her out of jail by telling her story to
an indifferent doctor.

Flashback to Las Vegas, where Joan enters a casino looking all fresh
and dewy-eyed, her clothes neat and housewife-cute. Stanwyck pitches
her voice slightly higher than usual to portray this gullible, open woman, almost stretching her wide range to the breaking point in these first
scenes. But Stanwyck really starts to cook when Joan first catches gambling fever, embracing the illicit, clearly sexual thrill she gets from rolling
those dice. When she asks a big-time club manager (Stephen McNally)
for more money, Joan looks spent, out of breath and scared, like she's
just been through a disaster. When she gets upset about his initial re-
fusal, Stanwyck is desperate in the shamed way of a repressed, bourgeois
woman. This is knife-edge, exacting work, always specific to the person
she is playing.

The miracle actress who needed Capra's protection in order to give
her all on the first take had developed a formidable technique over the
years. In a scene where Joan tries to get money from a pawnbroker,
Stanwyck went even further with her character's outraged gentility and
sense of shame, and she did so under trying conditions. Gordon said,
"Houseley Stevenson, who played the pawnbroker, was getting along in
years and had difficulty remembering his lines. Because the scene was
so emotionally draining for Barbara—there were no fake tears in her
performance—after several takes I reconciled myself to settling for a less
than satisfactory performance on the old man's part rather than ask her
to keep repeating the scene. But Barbara insisted on my staying with
it until she knew I felt we'd gotten it right. The wear and tear on her
nervous system that day was considerable—but that's the way Barbara

worked." If you're going to shoot for being "the best of all," you must have flexibility and discipline. Stanwyck dug ever deeper into the reservoir of her emotions until it seemed, at times, that the rage and pleasure and agony she needed had no limit.

How did she learn to do this? In a bind like this pawnshop scene, when she had to keep repeating herself, Stanwyck may have used her own version of sense memories. When actors are dry and need a boost, they often have go-to images, thoughts, and visions from the past that can instantly call up what they need. Some of these spurs and triggers have a short shelf life, but the deepest of them can last for an entire career. What, I wonder, was Stanwyck using to come up with the scenes of Joan at the gambling tables, where she sweats and pants like an animal, her tongue sometimes sliding out of her mouth, followed by the "morning after" bliss when she wakes up in the afternoon? Stanwyck makes it crystal clear, and then some, that gambling is sexually stimulating for passionate Joan, so that there's no doubt that she isn't being satisfied by her husband (and Robert Taylor definitely wasn't satisfying Stanwyck at the time, if he ever had). Eying McNally's Corrigan, who exploits her needs, Joan says that gambling is "noisy and confusing and . . . just a little *dirty*"—and she doesn't mean the dirt that can be wiped away with a homemaker's dishrag.

Yet *The Lady Gambles* cannot bring itself to put the blame on Joan's good-hearted, dull husband and insists on introducing a red herring, Joan's older sister Ruth (Edith Barrett), a possessive sort who, like Stanwyck's sister Millie Stevens, raised Joan as her own child after their mother died. Bemoaning her spinsterhood, Ruth cries, "I should have put you in a home!" Stanwyck looks alarmed at this exclamation; her own sister did indeed put her in a home, several homes, in fact—most of them bad. Maybe this is part of the reason Stanwyck hesitated about taking this role, for these first scenes with her on-screen sister hit so close to home that they carry a nagging, unresolved tension.

Joan tries to reform, but she's soon gambling again. At this point, Stanwyck comes back from the tables looking like she's drunk, but in the best possible way, hyper-aware and liberated. It's scenes like this that make me wish we could liberate Stanwyck from this well-meaning but somewhat sterile movie and install her into something like Jacques Demy's *Bay of Angels* (1963), where platinum blond Jeanne Moreau makes a religion of roulette and offers it to us like a vision of paradise.

Joan looks like a startled little girl when David catches her gambling again, then sinks down into a chair like a ruined middle-aged woman (it's often extreme age transitions like this that separate the great actors from the merely good ones). She goes back to pimp-daddy Corrigan with childlike misgiving on her face—this is a movie that suggests a lot, but never follows through on its promises. Joan winds up in a low dive, with blond hair, dancing and rolling customers for money. When a low-life forces her to blow on his dice, Stanwyck makes this moment look deeply humiliating, as if Joan is being forced to give head.

In the last scenes, set in the hospital, Ruth is set up as the villain, but Stanwyck and Barrett (who's quite good) play against the script, so that when Ruth tells Joan that she killed their mother, it seems like there's a deeper trauma at play. In a few moments here, as David tries to comfort Joan, Stanwyck transcends her material and hits a deep well of fear and remorse that feels bruisingly personal. This performance is the opposite of her Megan Davis in *General Yen*: too Method, too Lee Strasberg, too much. The doctor uses laughable reverse psychology to talk Joan out of jumping off a ledge, and the film ends with Joan and David looking out at a new day and a new beginning. But Stanwyck has shown us too much hurt and nervy excitement to make us believe that this woman will ever go back to being a housewife.

When the American Film Institute gave Stanwyck its Lifetime Achievement Award in 1987, Walter Matthau remembered her in *The File on Thelma Jordan* (1950, also known as *Thelma Jordan*), particularly the way she sighed, "Maybe I am just a dame and didn't know it." Matthau then went on to knock her co-star, Wendell Corey, an unprepossessing actor who was good when he was doing a menacing type in Budd Boetticher's *The Killer is Loose* (1956), but who was hard-pressed to hold his own as a leading man opposite Stanwyck. *Thelma Jordan* has a fine director in Robert Siodmak, a past master of film noirs like *The Killers* (1946) and *Criss Cross* (1948), and he brings a solemn, German expressionist look to the first scenes of *Jordan*, where Corey's assistant DA Cleve Marshall staggers into his office, drunk, trying to avoid a dinner with his wife and hated father-in-law. "Fed up," he says to his co-worker. "You ever heard that phrase? No, you wouldn't, you're not married."

Siodmak frames a long hallway behind Cleve, and he does the same thing in Cleve's house, where Cleve's slightly whiny wife nags at him over the phone. The director is trying to set up the same sense of gentle disillusionment he found in Charles Laughton in *The Suspect* (1945) and in George Sanders in *Uncle Harry* (1945). But Siodmak is defeated by Corey's limitations and also by the extremely wordy script by Ketti Frings, which always goes out of its way to dissipate any momentum with tangents and unnecessary exposition.

Still, Siodmak works up to a fine entrance for Stanwyck's Thelma, who is revealed in a slight shock cut near the office door, breaking into Cleve's dreamy inebriation with her direct look, her white Edith Head dress and gleaming gold necklace, and her somewhat ritzy manner (lots of British "a's" in these first scenes). Cleve and Thelma get to know each other at length, and as their scenes plod along, it's hard not to wish someone like Dana Andrews were playing Corey's role, someone with some charisma and presence. Andrews could have kept *Thelma Jordan* from descending into the doldrums, as it often does during its first half hour or so.

We get lots of chatty dates between Thelma and Cleve, yet the screenplay barely establishes Thelma's rich aunt (Gertrude Hoffman) before having her shot off-screen. The narrative is more interested in "whodunit" than character, and Stanwyck puts the brakes on, merely walking us through Thelma's back-story, which involved being a hostess at a gambling house and dreams of becoming an actress, both of which sound promising but get little follow-through. When Thelma and Cleve run around the scene of the crime, things start to get unintentionally comic because they keep panicking. "Touch the safe!" he tells her. "Wait, what about the window?" she asks. "I left a note!" she remembers. They wipe fingerprints off things, put new fingerprints on other things, turn the corpse over, and so on. Stanwyck's "fear" feels lazy, or at least unconvincing—which might be the point, but couldn't Thelma show *some* acting talent?

Siodmak told an unsettling story about working with Stanwyck on this film. "Barbara always had the character completely worked out," he said. "Before we started shooting, she would be sitting in her chair, her eyes closed and her concentration on the scene she was to play." This sounds like her, but then he added: "One day, before a very difficult scene, I tried to give her some last minute advice. That was the only time she showed any temper. She brushed me impatiently aside. I didn't mind, for I was sure she knew what she wanted to do." Judging from her rote work in *Thelma Jordan*, it's a shame that Stanwyck gave Siodmak the brush-off. He was often an exceptional director of actors, and he could have helped her deepen parts of this character that needed deepening, especially the sense that Thelma is a frustrated actress, which never really comes through in Stanwyck's performance. You'd think it would be catnip to her as a performer who, at her best, was always aware of the levels of role-playing everyone engages in.

Things improve slightly when we get to court, where Thelma is tried for murder, even if there are unwelcome echoes of *Remember the Night*, a far superior film, as Cleve deliberately throws the case out of love for his mistress. When Cleve shows Thelma a photo from her gambling girl past, we see Stanwyck in a blond wig, usually a scary sight, but here it looks so fake that this photo reveal gets another unwanted laugh. There's a good scene with Thelma's crooked lawyer (Stanley Ridges), where he details his crookedness from the shadows; this is the only point where Stanwyck seems genuinely engaged in the film. The climax gives her a nasty bit of business with a cigarette lighter in a car, and then a tearful bedside confession where she talks about her good/bad nature and wonders, "You don't suppose they could just let half of me die?" before expiring. We are left to wonder what Stanwyck might have accomplished with Siodmak if she had been more open to him and if Frings's script had been more concise.

As it is, *Thelma Jordan* is the kind of movie that can be viewed several times without any memory of past viewings. Perhaps Stanwyck was suffering from noir fatigue: "My God, isn't there a good comedy around?" she asked at the time. "I'm tired of suffering in films. And I've killed so many co-stars lately, I'm getting a power complex!" Screwball comedy with feelings, for Preston Sturges, had been much more agreeable to her than noir and its restrictions, but she never did get another comedy role (it's a shame she didn't work for Hawks again in the early fifties, or for Blake Edwards in the early sixties).

Stanwyck had much more enthusiasm for *No Man of Her Own* (1950), which reunited her with Mitchell Leisen. Director Leisen, who got such exceptional work from her in *Remember the Night*, gave her a book he was interested in called *I Married a Dead Man* by Cornell Woolrich (written under the pseudonym William Irish). She was so taken with its morbid plot that she insisted to Paramount that it be her next picture for them. Woolrich stories have been made into many fine films, most notably Hitchcock's *Rear Window* (1954). This Hitchcock-type material is sometimes not in Leisen's comfort zone, yet he manages to personalize a lot of it (Woolrich was gay, as Leisen was, and there's a sensibility at work here that makes their outsider status plain).

The opening scenes, which were written by Catherine Turney, are inventively done: Leisen begins with an image of an idyllic suburban street, as Stanwyck starts to talk to us on the soundtrack: "The summer nights are pleasant in Caulfield. They smell of heliotrope and jasmine, honeysuckle and clover." She pitches her voice higher here, which suits the woman she's playing, Helen Ferguson (the same name as that of Stanwyck's longtime publicist and special friend, a former actress who sometimes lived with Stanwyck and protected her from the press).

Helen urgently describes the hush of the evenings, the stillness in a place like this. "The summer nights are pleasant in Caulfield," she says, "But not for us. Not for us." She will repeat this "not for us" mantra again. It refers specifically to her and her boyfriend Bill (John Lund) as they ponder what to do about an inconvenient murder. But in Stanwyck's reading the line also speaks to the outcasts of this world, the people who aren't welcome in homes like this, the Lee Leanders, the Mitchell Leisens, the Cornell Woolrichs—and the Barbara Stanwycks, of course. She was as secure as she'd ever be in Hollywood in 1950, and as socially accepted. She was politically conservative, so she had no fear of the blacklist of that time. But some worldly people can only go so far in their pursuit of a happiness that stems from a feeling of unthinking security, and her Helen Ferguson discovers as much—just as Lee did, and just as Stanwyck did.

Leisen takes you inside a large, comfy house, and Helen talks about the cleanness inside ("the smell of *wax*," Stanwyck emphasizes, so forcefully that you begin to smell it). We see Helen sitting across from Bill with a blond-headed baby boy in her lap. The couple seems to be at the end of an argument, locked in stalemate. "This is a thing apart," says Helen, "this is murder." She goes upstairs to put the baby to bed, and Leisen darkens his frame so that we can only see Stanwyck's eyes glowing from the shadows. Helen's voice continues on the track, leading us into a flashback. She says she was desperate, and we see her in a phone booth, down to just a few pieces of change, pregnant and stranded in New York.

In this flashback, Stanwyck makes her face into a stony mask with a shining forehead; she wears little or no make-up. We see Helen dragging her pregnant bulk up some stairs, and then she begins to cry desperately at a closed door. We see her betrayer, Stephen (Lyle Bettger), and his new woman, a blond (Carole Mathews). Helen has begged there before, for she has nowhere else to go, and Stephen slips some money into an envelope and slides it under the door to her. Helen opens the envelope and pulls out a train ticket to San Francisco. She thinks for a moment and finally accepts the situation with Stanwyck's familiar stoicism, grown a bit grim with time. Leisen shows us Helen lumbering back down the stairs of the rooming house, then pulls back so that we see the money left on the landing. She still has some pride, it seems.

Leisen and Stanwyck create an intense mood of static despair in this first flashback sequence, and they keep to this mood when Helen gets on her train. She's seated in an uncomfortable position and looks old and tired until Hugh Harkness (Richard Denning) offers her his more spacious seat. Responding to his offer, her face seems to grow years younger, so that she seems like a grateful little girl: Ruby Stevens at twelve or thirteen, surprised by some bit of random kindness. When Hugh's wife Patrice (Phyllis Thaxter), who is also pregnant, asks about Helen's husband and finds out that there is no husband, she's embarrassed. "Funny, you never think, do you?" Patrice asks, so polite, so cheerful, so unmarked by life. "No, you never do," Helen murmurs, in a way that takes in her own foolishness and Patrice's radically different ignorance, seeming to measure the enormous distance between the two and then melding the women together so that they can somehow share the same small space. It's as all encompassing a line reading as her, "That's it, we're smart," from Leisen's *Remember the Night*, only much more beaten down and resigned. Lee Leander is still young enough to wonder at life, but Helen Ferguson is old enough that she has to do the hard work of continuing to exist, even though her existence has been given over to sordid repetitions that she can no longer truly learn from.

In the ladies' room, Patrice comes out with hearty American bromides like, "Don't let anybody tell you that Europe is cheap," and she insists that Helen try on her wedding ring. There's a real ambivalence in these scenes: Leisen is alert enough to how grating Patrice can be, but he also sees how her basic kindness is something that everyone longs for, the kind of kindness that leads a man to not only give up his more comfortable seat to a pregnant woman, but also try to be friendly with her because she so obviously needs a friend. It's a more complex attitude, finally, than the Leisen/Sturges representation of the perfect family in *Remember the Night*, even though it doesn't last for long. We can intuit Leisen's ultimate feeling about this all-American couple, these non-outcasts, by the gleeful, abrupt way with which he dispatches them. Trying on Patrice's wedding ring, Helen looks into a mirror, and no sooner has Patrice insisted, "I couldn't have bad luck," than the mirror shatters (upsettingly, given the consistent relationship on screen between Stanwyck and her mirrors), and the train flips all the way over.

The restroom set where Stanwyck played this scene with Thaxter was built inside a steel wheel. Leisen suspended a camera from a catwalk, and when the train was supposed to be hit, he rotated the wheel all the way around with both actresses inside doing their own stunts. The effect is unnervingly realistic in its violence. Helen is taken from the wreck on a stretcher, which leads to a shot from her perspective looking at a ceiling as doctors cut off her coat and save her baby through caesarian section. When she wakes up, Helen is suffering from a concussion, which Stanwyck suggests by making the emotions behind her eyes seem liquid, unmoored to her mind. Leisen gives nearly Capra-esque attention to Stanwyck's plain, intensely girlish face in the hospital bed. After Helen realizes they've mistaken her for the dead Patrice, she tries to tell them the truth, but she's too ill and upset to do so. Stanwyck allows herself to be extremely vulnerable in these scenes, and Leisen is sensitive to every small shift in her expression.

Going to meet Hugh's well-off parents, Helen says, "It isn't too late, I can still back out!" several times in voiceover to the rhythm of the train's wheels on the track. Just as she spoke to us so tantalizingly after the opening credits, Helen's voice reappears every so often to tell us her thoughts. This is an interior sort of cinema, and it's saved from gimmickry because its experimental nature isn't stressed. Stanwyck's voice isn't exactly in sync with the train wheels—as it would be, say, in a Rouben Mamoulian movie from the early 1930s. It's enough here to suggest a correlation between things like outside sounds and inside worries.

Helen is met at the station by Hugh's mother, played by the stage star Jane Cowl (whose popularity in the twenties meant that Ruby Stevens became Barbara Stanwyck instead of Jane Stanwyck, according to the former Miss Stevens herself). Given that this is a Leisen movie, Helen's baby boy is soon placed on a plush satin pillow. It must be said that when the plot starts to get more contrived and improbable, the director seems to retreat into his own distinctive set design and lighting, which—because this is a melodrama with a noir patina—is much darker than usual.

Helen keeps making mistakes, of course; she's never sensible enough just to say as little as possible to Hugh's family (but maybe her concussion hasn't worn off yet). Helen is "passing" in these scenes, as Leisen and Woolrich had to, as Stella Dallas tried to. Helen Ferguson, living a lie! (Whatever the truth of the lesbian rumors about Stanwyck and her publicist, Helen Ferguson, who could be very motherly and controlling with her best client, Leisen may have had a private laugh over this character name). Everything up to the train wreck and hospital stay is effectively dreamy, but in this perfect house where Helen is passing, and where family members sit around the piano just as they do in *Remember the Night*, things start to get sleepy rather than dreamy. A part of the problem here is Lund, one of those movie actors from this period who seems to have been employed precisely because of his stolidity and lack of charisma. He's playing a man whose motivations throughout are a mystery, and Lund can do nothing to enlighten you.

Helen gets a threatening telegram. Of course, Stanwyck has to read it to us again on the soundtrack after we've read it ourselves, but it's more dramatic when she reads it, so we can forgive the reiteration. The unsa-vory Stephen turns up to blackmail Helen, and Stanwyck has little to do but look worried. (Leisen shot a scene where Stephen slaps her around, and Stanwyck insisted on Bettger actually hitting her, naturally. But this scene was cut, probably because it was too rough, and so we're missing perhaps a key example of Stanwyck's masochistic "hurt me when I tell you to" streak). Stephen forces Helen to marry him (she's set to inherit money). Stanwyck gets a bright idea as she hears the section about "til death do us part" in the marriage vows; you can almost see a thought balloon that says, "I know, I'll kill him!" at this moment. Stanwyck milks the moment as if she's decided to play this one scene comedically—if they weren't going to give her comedies anymore, she'd just have to make her own opportunities. This wild choice punctuates the overly lan-guorous mood of the film quite nicely.

Helen goes to kill Stephen. He's already dead, it seems, but she fires the gun anyway and then gets the weirdly loyal Bill to dump Stephen's body off a bridge. This is another shot, like the train crash, where Leisen sur-prises us by not cutting away when we expect him to; he lets us see the corpse as it flops over in the air on its way down. "God forgive me," Helen whispers, finally, and Leisen lets her off the hook with an ending in line with the blonds equal danger theme running through Stanwyck's career. Like many of her movies of this period, *No Man of Her Own* is uneven, but it deserves a lot more exposure and comment than it has received.

Actor Joe DeSantis remembered that there was much tension and "personal unhappiness" on the set of *The Man with a Cloak* (1951), an atmospheric period thriller shot right after the ordeal and humiliation of Stanwyck's divorce from Taylor. It begins promisingly, with David Rak-sin's ominous score under the credits and some tense low angle shots of 1848 New York, where the saturnine Dupin (Joseph Cotton) observes the arrival of gamine Madeline (Leslie Caron), a French girl who has come to win some money for her fiancée from his reprobate grandfather Thevenet (Louis Calhern). Stanwyck makes her star entrance walking down some stairs in the Thevenet household, her face a mask with little glimmers of contempt burning away underneath, her voice precise and false. She plays Lorna Bounty, a once-celebrated stage actress reduced to keeping house. Lorna is a schemer, almost a Mrs. Danvers type, a stone butch eying young Madeline's Paris lingerie with Sapphic bemusement. Stanwyck parcels out some of her behavioral modes here like individu-ally wrapped gifts, then pulls back into a steady, watchful look.

Recalling her work on this film, Caron remembers the star as a steely pro who tried to deliver the goods on the first take. "Barbara Stanwyck was very steady and always ready with her lines," Caron says. "She was sure of herself and acted with conviction. She had chosen her interpretation and stuck to it—I don't think she ever needed more than one take or two. The second take might have been for the soundman or the camera operator, but rarely for her. Of all the actors I've worked with she was probably the one who had the least nerves. She was immensely disciplined."

At times in this film, there's almost a feeling of a pretentious Albert Lewin movie, but *The Man with a Cloak* is really only interested in being a mystery story with an inane twist at the end, one which reveals Dupin's future identity as a famous writer (an increasingly bored Cotton gives no indication whatever that he might be playing the author of "Annabel Lee"). In its first half hour, the movie has a chamber music quality that is not uninteresting, and Stanwyck's own sorrow on set deepens some of her effects while making others muddier; when she sizes up Dupin, this familiar Stanwyck action is opaque and unreadable. Fletcher Markle, the director, reported that Stanwyck rejected a change that would have made her sinister character more sympathetic, clinging to the integrity of her original conception.

There are some exchanges here where all Stanwyck plays is, "I'm a cool customer." But this choice pays off in a scene toward the end (which must be the one Markle was referring to) where Lorna explains herself a bit and tells some of her sad history in a way that's so crisp and good-humored that it becomes briefly exciting, delivering a small frisson of "the past can't hurt me" that might have given Stanwyck herself some relief from her own suffering. A scuffle between Dupin and DeSantis's butler at the climax verges on slapstick, but there are moments of value in this picture.

Jeopardy (1953) was originally a twenty-two minute radio play, and it was expanded enough to make a sixty-nine minute feature, directed for no-frills action and impact by the reliable John Sturges. "Traveling the United States is wonderful," says Stanwyck, in a voiceover at the beginning, and she goes on to extol the highways and then Tijuana as a travel destination. There's a faint air of condescension in this narration, but to the film's credit, it's this same condescension that will get Stanwyck's character into a jam. She plays Helen, a happy wife and mother of a small boy, for the first pedestrian fifteen minutes or so, but once her husband (Barry Sullivan) gets caught under some pilings from a rotting peer, Sturges and Stanwyck leap into action.

In a few hours, the tide will be coming in and the husband will be drowned. It's been established that this woman doesn't react well in emergencies. When she tries to ask for help from some Mexican locals, she mispronounces the Spanish word for rope, which her husband had told her; the locals want to assist her, but they can't understand what she's saying. Arriving at a rest stop, Helen runs around a bit (Stanwyck is compellingly panic-stricken) and finally finds some rope. She turns, and as she does so, Sturges frames a hulking man (Ralph Meeker) behind her. Helen runs to him—she sees that he's an American and blindly trusts him, but he turns out to be Lawson, a killer on the run.

Sexy/scary Meeker gives the film a boost of energy. He gets a rise out of Stanwyck, trading slaps with her in his car and leering at her until she realizes that the only way she can save her husband is if she can seduce Lawson. Helen wonders aloud if "every wife" wonders what she would do in a situation like this, a query she repeats at the end of the movie. Earlier, looking out at their deserted vacation spot, she had said, "I hated that jetty the minute I saw it." These lines reek of bad radio drama—and that isn't the only problem here.

When this woman starts lighting her cigarettes and staring down the convict next to her, Stanwyck loses whatever character she was playing and substitutes one of the strongest aspects of her mature star persona, the Tough Broad Who's Seen It All. This persona doesn't remotely gibe with the weak-willed woman we've seen up to this point; in fact, the gap between where she starts and where she ends is so great that it winds up being rather funny, while also confirming just how large Stanwyck's range was. So she got tired of playing this mousy '50s wife; who can blame her? "Savin' your kisses for your husband?" snarls Meeker, as he takes Stanwyck roughly in his arms. Helen puts out for this guy, but we get no sense of what she really feels about this capitulation and what it costs her. The last scene features two unlikely changes of heart for both Helen and Lawson, so that the only thing left to do is admire how Sturges puts over the suspense mechanics of this skimpy drama.

There are several pluses attached to another skimpy movie of this time, *Witness to Murder* (1954), an independent production by screenwriter Chester Erskine for United Artists. The biggest plus is George Sanders's hilarious villain, Albert Richter, an ex-Nazi still spreading fascist propaganda in post-war Los Angeles. In the peremptory opener, Stanwyck's interior decorator, Cheryl, awakens from a restless sleep, goes to her window and gives a start. In a reverse shot, we see Richter across the way strangling a blond, ringing her neck until she falls down dead. Erskine's name then appears over the murder window, and his name has pride of place in the end credits, too; he's listed before director Roy

Rowland, who stages the various scenes set in offices very lazily, having the actors just line up in front of desks to spout their boilerplate lines.

If anyone, aside from Sanders, deserves some credit here it's cinematographer John Alton, who expertly frames the shadows in the opening scenes as Richter tries to hide the body, then startles the eye with a bright shot through a chandelier when the police, headed by Lawrence Mathews (Gary Merrill), come to investigate Cheryl's story. "Writer, huh?" asks Lawrence, when he spies one of Richter's books. "That's one crime of which I am guilty," Richter replies (Sanders gives him a hoot-worthy little shiver of false modesty).

"A mash of Nietzsche and Hegel," says Lawrence of Richter's work after having him investigated. When this villain's true colors come out toward the end, his ideas sound like a mish-mash of something, but of what I can't be too sure. Alton lights Sanders satanically as Richter confronts Cheryl in her home, and the naughty actor actually widens his eyes with bloodlust before going into a paroxysm of shouted German (you really do have to see this to believe it). He then grabs Cheryl up in his arms and natters on about how there is hate in love, or love in hate, until she struggles free and runs shrieking for the door.

Stanwyck does a lot of shrieking and running for the door in this picture, and she doesn't get to have even a fraction of the fun that Sanders is having. Cheryl is so weak-minded that Richter easily railroads her into a stay in the bughouse, where she encounters a fearsome Juanita Moore, nursing slashed wrists and a broken heart, and an exhibitionist blond played by Claire Carleton, who can't remember taking her clothes off in the street. Even these cameo players are given more to chew on than Stanwyck, whose character foolishly runs away one more time so that we can have a climax atop a half-finished skyscraper. Her docility with an insulting asylum doctor is particularly hard to take, even if Cheryl is trying to please him to get away from the scene-stealing lady crazies. This is a woman who needs to put on her white gloves before rushing out to find clues about her tormenter, and Stanwyck looks like she knows what a simp she's playing.

Crime of Passion (1957), a confused but often intriguing crime thriller, comes toward the end of Stanwyck's starring career in movies, and she seems rather burned-out in it—even if there are still some smoldering embers looking for a place to rest and singe us. Her face looks much heavier than usual, even swollen, and when she goes into one of her trademark hysterical tirades, it seems like she's just switching on a faucet and letting the water splash wherever it will.

We first see her character, Kathy Ferguson, reading over some mail. She's a newspaper writer who specializes in advice to the lovelorn. "There's gotta be some happy people left in San Francisco," says her flunky, also reading her mail. To which she croaks, "Not if I can help it." He reads her a letter from "Foolish 17," who is in love with a married man; what should she do? "Forget the man, run away with the wife," says Kathy boldly, setting up the next few scenes, where this Stanwyck woman is as close to a lesbian character as she gets before *Walk on the Wild Side* (1962).

Her last name is Ferguson, of course, the last name of Stanwyck's publicist den mother, Helen, so that it seems like scriptwriter Joe Eisinger might even be coding this role and throwing a bone to Stanwyck's Sapphic fans. When Kathy gets involved with a murder case (a husband killed by his wife), she comes up against the sexism of policeman Alidos (Royal Dano), who bluntly tells her, "Your work should be raising a family, having dinner ready for your husband when he gets home." Kathy reacts dreamily and uncertainly to this chauvinist junk, but she still manages to get back at the cop by obtaining the address of the murderous wife, and then withholding the information from Alidos. We expect a little more feistiness from Kathy in these early scenes, but Stanwyck needs to prepare us for what's coming, so she walks a shaky line between satisfaction and skittishness (in the newsroom, director Gerd Oswald gives her several close-ups to register her distracted unrest with the boss at her paper, who runs articles twice because he thinks no readers will care).

Oswald then delivers a montage of women reading Kathy's column. We see a wife in bed, staring unhappily at her sleeping husband in the twin bed next to her, followed by an image of two girls cuddled up together blissing-out over Kathy's woman-on-woman copy: "Where can we turn, except to the heart and understanding of another woman?" Where indeed? Two B-girls at a bar commiserate over Kathy's newspaper come-ons, and two extremely butch female cabbies nod their heads over it, as if Oswald is about to stage a lesbian revolution.

No such luck, of course, but at least the film includes such options in its opening half hour. When cop Bill Doyle (Sterling Hayden) talks to Kathy over dinner about the virtues of a home and family for a woman, Kathy quite rightly shuts him up by saying, "Propaganda, not for me." Oswald then gives Stanwyck a lingering close-up, as Kathy talks about wanting to go to sea (just as Lee Leander did in *Remember the Night*). In this scene, where she looks so sad, so heavy with sorrow and marking time, Stanwyck gets across an entirely new and very painful sense of nihilism and foggy hopelessness, a far too strong and upsetting emotional coloration for the larval narrative that follows.

Kathy marries Bill, for reasons that seem purely self-destructive, and then she tries to adapt to being a housewife. She says that she wants to be "a good wife," as if the repressive mores of the time have finally gone to her head, and she's grabbing at them like a drowning woman grabbing at a lifejacket. Maybe she's gone a little crazy; how else to explain a Stanwyck character who says, even in the late fifties, that she wants nothing more than to darn a man's socks?

Right away, Kathy is completely lost in Bill's working-class milieu. The women chatter inanely about their TV sets, while the men talk about salary hikes. The worldly Kathy is knocked like a pinball between two opposing hells, not at all right with the women and not accepted by the men. Neither group is worth trying for, but Kathy's identity crisis has her gravitating naturally to men—even unworthy men—over women. Is Kathy a completely repressed, never-active lesbian? And could Stanwyck identify with that uncomfortable state?

Crime of Passion raises all kinds of questions like this, but it can't begin to answer them; to do so would have been impossible in 1957. So why does Oswald set up those obviously lesbian cabbies as a kind of visual alternative for Kathy? In the pre-Code *Ladies They Talk About,* the film sets up the presence of a butch lesbian who likes to wrestle and Stanwyck's layered, almost impressed reaction to her. These characters and her relation to them set Stanwyck up as a lesbian icon; it doesn't matter if she never did anything sexually with a woman off-screen. On-screen, especially as she got older and her voice lower, Stanwyck could sometimes throw subliminal, perhaps subconscious hints out to the girls. To be a great actor and a great star, you need androgyny—not too much, but just enough to keep everyone on their toes.

Another montage shows how the vapid talk surrounding Bill's friends and their wives makes Kathy sick, and *Crime of Passion* begins to seem like a feminist nightmare, short on sense and rhetoric, but long on suggestions of despairing mood and feeling. Kathy rails against the "mediocrity" she sees around her, and it's easy to feel that this is Stanwyck herself passionately condemning a conformist culture that is about to put her out to pasture on television—that little box that all the dull housewives here chat about. But when Kathy starts to scheme and wheedle to get Bill promoted, it becomes an open question whether she is "unnatural," in this film's terms, because of her drive and her need to work, or if the sexist society she lives in is entirely to blame.

The film wants to have it both ways, so that most audiences in 1957 could see Kathy as just a misfit, yet when we see this film now, it's impossible not to think she's being driven crazy by a sick, unfair society. What is Kathy's damage? We never really learn, and when she tangles with Raymond Burr's police bigwig, this encounter further muddies the waters. He lays Kathy (which is almost laughably unconvincing, given their lack of chemistry), and then says he's going to give a good job not to Bill but to the odious Alidos, who started this whole mess with his sexist challenge. It all ends in murder, of course, and the incarceration of a woman who would have been far happier meeting up with, say, Agnes Moorehead or Jan Sterling at a bar and setting up house afterward.

Ordeal for Oscar

Sorry, Wrong Number

*B*ecause Stanwyck never worked at one studio for long, she never had studio backing in the annual Oscar race, and so she went home empty-handed four times, the last time for a movie version *Sorry, Wrong Number*, an expanded adaptation of Lucille Fletcher's well-known radio play. Stanwyck made no bones about her disappointment at not winning an Oscar. When she lost in 1937 for *Stella Dallas*, she was quoted as saying, "I put my life's blood into that one. I should have won." Certainly she should have won over that year's winner, Luise Rainer, for her mostly silent, victimized Chinese wife in *The Good Earth*. But Greta Garbo never won an Oscar either, and I'd probably give it to her for her career-best work in *Camille* that same year. Stanwyck's 1941 nomination for *Ball of Fire* was a surprise and must be counted as a nod for her work in *The Lady Eve*, too. She lost to Joan Fontaine in *Suspicion*, an uncertain performance that was rewarded to make up for passing over Fontaine's far superior work in *Rebecca* the previous year. At least Stanwyck's Phyllis Dietrichson lost to Ingrid Bergman in *Gaslight* (1944), a performance that was at the very least competitive and given by an actress who was in the same league, talent-wise, as Stanwyck.

Stanwyck's work in *Sorry, Wrong Number* strikes me as an attempt to do something the Oscar voters might like, for the showy role of bedridden neurotic Leona Stevenson calls for something more along the lines of the scenery-chewing style of a Bette Davis or a Joan Crawford than it does Stanwyck's best life-or-death realness. She lost to Jane Wyman's sweet, victimized deaf mute in *Johnny Belinda* (1948), the polar opposite of Stanwyck's strident Leona, who mostly victimizes herself. If I had my druthers, I'd give Stanwyck an Oscar for *Ladies of Leisure* in 1930 (Norma

Shearer could definitely do without her award for *The Divorcee*), and another for *The Lady Eve* in 1941. As for her high-pressure work in *Wrong Number*, I'm glad she didn't win for this atypical, sloppy picture; it's not at all representative of her talent, her artistry, or her overall style.

Agnes Moorehead began her career in radio with Orson Welles, and she started her film career with him in *Citizen Kane* (1941), playing the mother of the future tycoon. She also appeared in Welles's *The Magnificent Ambersons* (1942) as the hysterical Aunt Fanny, one of the greatest performances in film history. Moorehead is huge and histrionic in *Ambersons*, but she makes us painfully aware that Aunt Fanny herself knows about her own self-indulgent shortcomings and can't do a thing about them. That awareness, too, is key to her performance in the radio version of *Sorry, Wrong Number*, first broadcast on a show called *Suspense* on May 25, 1943, and then reprised on the radio, by popular demand, seven times before 1960.

Fletcher's play runs a little over twenty minutes, and it makes spooky use of telephone sounds; every dial tone and rotary click ups the chiller ante. Moorehead's original performance in 1943 is her most human and relatable; she emphasized the shrewish nature of Leona as she continued to perform the role over the next twenty years, but she usually began on a quietly whiny note, as if Leona talks just to hear herself speak. Her voice sounds thin, like a querulous spinster's, and she scolds her interlocutors like a prim spinster would after accidentally overhearing a murder plan over a crossed telephone wire.

Leona is given to telling everyone that her health has been poor for twelve years (so that we quickly suspect she's suffering more from a psychosomatic or psychological ailment), and she is easily flustered, a weakness that will be her ultimate downfall. Her thin voice rises up to high, fluting tones when Leona gets imperious; Moorehead excitingly adds some quivers to her middle register as Leona starts to get scared (the best, or at least the most virtuosic, performance she gave of this play was the one she did in 1945). When she calls the police, they reason with her, but she hangs up on them, and then says, "Why did I hang up the phone like that? Now he'll think I *am* a fool."

Moorehead's Leona is capable of briefly seeing herself for what she is, a professional nuisance, but she's unable to change—not in the twenty or so minutes she has left before she's murdered by the same man she overheard on the crossed wire. She's sick, all right, but sick in her mind, and we can't blame her husband too much for wanting to murder her; she is obnoxious, and exhausting. The achievement of Fletcher's play, which was written purely as an exercise in radio suspense, and Moorehead's tour-de-force performance, is that we don't want Leona to be killed, no matter how annoying she is. We recoil from her, then identify with her rising panic—quite a feat to pull off in such a limited amount of time.

Moorehead is more than a little hammy, but this part doesn't call for restraint; the role of Leona requires an actress to go as all-out as Moorehead does, with her symphony of gasps and rasps and arpeggios of hysteria up and down the vocal scale. It's a tribute to her work that it's hard to imagine seeing this Leona; she exists as a voice, and Fletcher taps into the fear associated with this disembodiment. On the telephone, we're all verbal consciousness and no body, just as radio voices are Beckett-like instruments talking to themselves, just as Leona does.

It's just you and her in the dark, as Leona finally descends to desperate whispering, sure that a man is in the house and about to come up and stab her to death. The people on the other end of her line get less and less helpful, until she's finally disposed of, her almost sexual scream blending into the shriek of a train whistle.

Moorehead's career was rather unfulfilling after her Welles films, but how do you follow those two seminal movies? She's probably most known now as Endora on the 1960s TV show *Bewitched*, but she's really the archetypal radio actress, a performer who could do pretty much anything with her voice, best restricted to extremes of short duration.

Leona Stevenson, then, is a part for an actress who can get full mileage out of playing a neurotic. This type of role goes against Stanwyck's grain, her aspect and image of total, widespread knowledge. For her screenplay, Fletcher opens up her radio script with flashbacks, and sometimes flashbacks within flashbacks, and this strategy weakens her original conception to the point of almost total incoherence.

Under the credits for *Sorry, Wrong Number*, we see a phone and its shadow, and Franz Waxman's stormy music gives way, momentarily, to an ominous telephone busy signal. So far, so good, but when a title card comes up under the image of girls working a switchboard, it's easy to predict trouble ahead. "In the tangled networks of a great city," reads the card, "the telephone is the unseen link between a million lives . . . It is the servant of our common needs—the confidante of our inmost secrets . . . life and happiness wait upon its ring . . . and horror . . . and loneliness . . . and . . . *death*!!!" Those three exclamation marks after "death" set the unfortunate, "Step right up!" carnival barker tone of this picture, and this crudeness remains consistent from first to last. Anatole Litvak directs *Sorry, Wrong Number* as if his audience is both stupid and greedy for lurid detail, and the effect is one of thoughtless confusion.

The camera takes in a nighttime interior and a phone off the hook; we then see Stanwyck's Leona, crying, "Opera-tuh, opera-tuh!" from her bed, her diamonds glinting on her fussy lace nightgown. Stanwyck pats her hair and dabs at her face with a lace handkerchief to get across how pampered and cloistered this woman is in the heat of summer (so much of the performance that follows will be predicated on surface indications such as these). After Stanwyck hears the murder plan, she furrows her brow and actually shakes the phone in frustration—a weak choice, borne more of a performer's desperation than a character's frustration.

It becomes instantly clear just how wrong it is to see Leona in this first scene when we should really only be hearing her on the phone, on the radio, in the dark; Stanwyck has to make impossible physical transitions as a real woman in a real bed. What to do? She falls back on invalid clichés (panting, obsequious looks), and decisive body movements, but there's no emotional throughline to what she's doing. Litvak keeps moving the camera away from Stanwyck to look around the apartment so that she can just be a voice like Moorehead was, but he always has to come back to her, and nothing can hide the sketchiness of this character and this situation as visualized.

Stanwyck's version of this woman's high-handed foolishness is painful to watch because it's all on one note, all done in a monochromatic style that doesn't have the jittery fun of Davis's emoting or Crawford's heartfelt reaching for effects. Stanwyck can't make herself over into that kind of showboating actress at this late date, so she just heedlessly blasts her way through, putting lipstick on while staring at her grotesquely preening face in a mirror (it's enough to make you imagine Capra shouting, "Barbara, stop this hamming! You can have one of my Oscars!").

Glamour shots of a 1930s Stanwyck peer out from behind furniture belonging to Leona's father (Ed Begley), who tells his daughter that maybe what she heard was just a gag on the radio (an in-joke from Fletcher). Leona talks next to Miss Jennings, secretary to her husband Henry (Burt Lancaster), and this woman is an Agnes Moorehead type, a skinny old maid played by Dorothy Neumann as if she were doing a dreary comedy sketch. Things get worse with the introduction of Sally Hunt, Henry's old girlfriend, played by Ann Richards as a dippy blond who seems to be trapped in a Carol Burnett-style parody of phony 1940s acting.

Lancaster is ill at ease in his role—great to look at but still green as an actor. He lets Stanwyck push him around in their scenes together until we get the feeling that she doesn't like her rich girl hypochondriac one bit. Bette Davis could seem to despise some of her characters, and yet still be exciting to watch because of all the effort it took to put them together. But Stanwyck can't get by on this kind of technique; it feels too shallow for her. In her scenes with Begley, always a crude actor, Stanwyck does fast-sell work without grace or thought—this from an actress who even in some of her worst movies always seems to be thinking, weighing her options, considering.

"But that's what acting is, it's *re*-acting," she told John Kobal in the 1960s. "When youngsters ask me how to act, I say, 'Don't. Re-act! *Don't act!*'" World class advice, and yet in *Sorry, Wrong Number,* one of her best-known movies and the occasion for her last Oscar nomination, Stanwyck does nothing but "act" in Litvak's half-assed vacuum, where everybody shouts for no reason and strides around. It's as if the base of her talent had been dynamited away.

A honeymoon montage featuring wealthy Leona and poor, ambitious Henry only serves as an occasion for Stanwyck to cement the "she was too bossy and that's why she lost Robert Taylor" publicity narrative that would cling to her for the rest of her life. The interminable flashbacks keep coming. Genteel-voiced Sally calls Leona and tells her about a trek she made to Staten Island because of some suspicions she had about Henry. "I waited there for about an hour," she says. "Nothing happened." No kidding! (Non-fans of Richards might be interested to know that she retired from acting shortly after this, thankfully, and devoted herself to poetry, publishing a collection in 1971 called *The Grieving Senses.* I kid you not.)

Sally keeps talking and talking at pay phones and crying, "Wait, I know I have another nickel!" while we pray that she doesn't, and finally she's all out of money to gab on the phone with. Hearing a doorbell downstairs, Stanwyck's Leona gets up from her sickbed and cries, "I can't come down, I'm on the top floor and I'm sick!" with her voice breaking on "sick," in that pure emotion way of hers. This role doesn't need that emotion, though, which is why we see so little of it.

Litvak cuts next to a floor show with a female dancer being twirled and twirled upside down by her partner (it seems like he'll bring on some jugglers next to pad the running time a little more). Dr. Alexander (Wendell Corey) breaks the news to Henry that Leona is "what we call a cardiac-neurotic," and when he hears this, Henry winds a phone cord around his wrist until the phone falls to the floor (broad foreshadowing of the end, of course). After hearing this diagnosis, Leona screams, "Liars!" about ten times, as she collapses on her bed.

Following this fresh blast of hysterics, Litvak unwinds an even duller flashback involving Waldo Evans (Harold Vermilyea), a tediously mousy type who went in with Henry on a scheme to embezzle money. The film goes right to sleep for a long time owing to Vermilyea's measured, Edmund Gwenn-like voice. And Fletcher does Lancaster a real disservice; we are told in dialogue everything his character is supposed to be feeling, when it would be so much better to just show a few short scenes of him becoming discontented with his marriage and his own lapdog status. The actor rushes through this movie with scarcely veiled impatience.

Stanwyck bypasses the few occasions when she might have made this cardboard woman more complex—even moments when she could have made Leona at least a quasi-recognizable human being, such as the scene where she has her first psychosomatic attack in front of Henry after wondering if he's only married her for her money. We get no sense of Leona's insecurity or her relation to her father, only the same "shoot the works," hard-edged emoting; there's no vulnerability, no humanity, just bulldozer acting. We learn that Henry has set Leona up to be killed for her insurance, as if this whole project was penance for *Double Indemnity*. This time, the actress who played the murderer is on the receiving end; this movie is a steep price for Stanwyck to pay for Phyllis Dietrichson.

So, finally, we come to the main event, Leona's final act fight for life. For twelve days, Stanwyck played her scenes in bed in order, and she took them seriously. Litvak had her do take after take, and she trusted him, even when the crew started to get angry and told her that she had done enough. I wonder if better, more nuanced takes might not have been left on the cutting room floor; nothing in Litvak's career suggests that he was a good judge of performances. In fact, he had a knack for making a hash of promising projects (see particularly his enervating collaboration with Vivien Leigh in *The Deep Blue Sea* [1955]). I'm willing to make Litvak the villain here because nothing in Stanwyck's work before or after this movie suggests the dumbed-out flattening that occurs in this picture.

Taken purely as an exercise, and detached from the preceding hour or so, the last reel of *Sorry, Wrong Number* contains some colorful work from its star—not serious or first-rate Stanwyck, but definitely colorful. We see Leona's shaky fingers on her white phone, and when she finds out that she's calling the morgue, she throws herself all the way down out of frame while Waxman's music goes nuts. His scoring really helps, and it deserves a lot of credit for making these last moments what they are (Fletcher herself was married to the Hitchcock composer Bernard

Herrmann, so she knew the importance of a musical score). Leona thinks to call the police, then quickly calls the hospital to get a nurse. This kind of stupidity will be exhibited in many a horror film to come, where the audience yells at the screen and gets to feel superior to the dopey victim.

Her husband calls: "Did you say Mr. Steven . . . Mr. Stevenson from New Haven?" Leona asks, and Stanwyck's hesitation between "Steven" and "Stevenson" displays the naturalistic talent that's been missing in action all through this movie. Stanwyck makes Leona look like a little girl now, even with her messed-up, gray-streaked hair. "Evans said that you wanted me to . . . to-die," she says, strategically using that wooden "to" of hers to get across the stuttering simplicity Leona has reached. She apologizes for being so "awful" to her husband, but we should have felt this ambivalence earlier. Now it's too late, for us and for Leona.

Waxman's music steadily builds as Henry tells her to get out of the house (the insurance money is unnecessary now, a too-cute twist by Fletcher). "I can't move, Henry, I . . . I'm too frightened," she cries, believably paralyzed. Then she looks up, and her face freezes. "Henry," she says, quietly. "Henry," she repeats. "*Henry*, there's somebody coming up the stairs!" she screams, building up to that third "Henry" until her voice crescendos and breaks into terrified little pieces flying around the room (this magnificent vocal flourish, with Waxman's music, has never failed to raise gooseflesh on my arms whenever I've watched this). Finally Leona is pleading with an unseen assassin, promising to give him anything, then screaming hoarsely as he goes in for the kill (I assume he strangles her). The curtain line is just a terse, "Sorry, wrong number," and this is the one improvement on Fletcher's original play, where the killer was wordier after the murder.

Stanwyck did this part for Lux Radio Theatre in 1950, but she didn't do the Moorehead version, unfortunately. The Lux broadcast runs about an hour, and it does play better than the film, but it still doesn't have the concentrated sting of the Moorehead original. After caterwauling her way through the finale, Stanwyck has to come back on and sputter about how she just loves Lux soap, I'm afraid. It isn't acting, what she does in *Sorry, Wrong Number*, but it is classic awards-baiting, and it is, like that Lux plug, pure, unadulterated show business.

Two for Sirk

All I Desire, There's Always Tomorrow

$\mathcal{T}$here is no cinema reputation that has made a more dramatic turn-around in recent years than the work of Danish-German émigré Douglas Sirk. In his most productive period, the 1950s, his Universal soap operas and melodramas were looked down on as tearjerker money makers marked with the opulent vulgarity of their producer, Ross Hunter. But in the seventies and ever since, audiences and writers have looked closer at Sirk's supposed lowbrow "weepies" and discovered their irony, their levels of social criticism, their flamboyant consciousness of sex and neurosis, and their magisterial, often downright icy visual style that traps people in architectural cages (a later German auteur, Rainer Werner Fassbinder, was profoundly influenced by both Sirk's technique and his radical pessimism). A highly intellectual, cultured European of the Thomas Mann school, Sirk favored broken, "in-between" type characters who move helplessly in a kind of circle, never able to break free of the wheelhouse of American society. He was most interested in portraying failure in all its permutations. In the two films he made with Stanwyck, he came as close as he ever would to analyzing his obsession with failure, aided in both cases by his star's willingness to imagine and experience a theme that she herself was not invested in.

"The mirror is the imitation of life," Sirk told an interviewer, Jon Halliday. "What is interesting about a mirror is that it does not show you yourself as you are, it shows you your opposite." And so, in his two films with Stanwyck, he holds up that mirror that she was always looking into in her movies and shows her her opposite, and the result is her deepest and most unusually inflected work since Capra's *General Yen*. Sirk understood her almost as well as Capra did: "She gets every point, every nuance without hitting on anything too heavily," he related to James Harvey. "And there is such an amazing tragic stillness about her at the same time. She never steps out of it and she never puts it on, but it is always there, this deep melancholy in her presence."

"And the way she acted between takes was very different," Sirk remembered. "Most people, as soon as the camera stops, you know, go straight to the mirror to check. But every time, she would go to a corner of the set, hardly talking to anyone—until we were ready to shoot again, and she was always ready and always perfect." (Maureen O'Sullivan, a supporting player in Sirk's first film with Stanwyck, *All I Desire* [1953], found her "a cold person," because of the way she isolated herself on set. Stanwyck needed to do this to get into character, for Sirk had stimulated her most creative impulses). "She impressed me all the time as someone who—what can I say?—someone who had really been touched deeply by life in some way," Sirk concluded. "Because she had depth as a person . . . ."

Sirk favored the title of Carol Brink's source novel *Stopover*, and considered it far stronger than the final title of his initial collaboration with Stanwyck, *All I Desire*. Concession to popular taste was something he always had to work against; even so, these concessions to Ross Hunter stimulated Sirk's creativity. After the credits, we see a placard with, "Naomi Murdoch, Direct From Broadway," billed fourth on a theater bill. "Naomi Murdoch, that's me," Stanwyck says, in voiceover, "Not quite at the bottom of the bill yet and not quite at the end of my rope."

Her voice sounds beyond exhausted, like an empty cornhusk, as she tells us about the stale air in theaters during the summer months and how she's never really impressed an audience. She has dyed blond hair and is dressed like a showgirl. We later learn that Naomi used to do Shakespeare and the classics, but, like Sirk, she's been boxed into giving the public what it supposedly wants. She was probably not a very good actress, Naomi says, but maybe she just tells herself that because she's tired of feeling badly about the downward trajectory of her career. "Brother, there's not much to look forward to," she says, continuing the voiceover in her pleasantly weary voice. "Well, I guess some people might say maybe I asked for it." Stanwyck stresses the "I guess" and the "might" and the "maybe." She's drawn to such escape-hatch words in all of her interviews, and they add to that "in-between" feeling that Sirk is focused on.

In an overhead shot, Sirk frames a large wooden beam running across Naomi's head as she enters her shared dressing room, the first of the prison bar shots he so favors in his interiors. Her dressing room crony tells Naomi that she should "go back to legit," where you don't have to worry so much about getting old. Sirk frames Naomi in a mirror as she opens a letter and reads it, then moves to her actual body and then back to her image in the mirror when she gives the letter to her fellow vaude-villian (a mirror shot in a film, an image of an image).

"It's a laugh, that's all," Naomi says, in an agitated, slightly panicked voice. "Dearest mother," the vaudevillian reads, and Naomi says, "I told you it was a laugh," in Stanwyck's fastest, most scaldingly self-loathing delivery. She's in a mirror again, narrating her character's life for a direc-tor who will leave her with no illusions whatever. Naomi thinks about visiting the husband and three children she left behind years ago in a small town; her daughter Lily (Lori Nelson) is in a school play and is ask-ing to see her. When the vaudevillian encourages her, Naomi murmurs, "I've done it on the stage," as if she thinks she can just act the part of the glamorous absentee mother.

Naomi narrates for us again, talking about her hometown, Riverdale, Wisconsin, and about "the lawns the husbands were so proud of." River-dale is a place you leave, and Riverdale is a place to come back to when you're close to the end of your rope. Her older daughter, Joyce (Marcia Henderson), is a prim, hypocritical type who is always scolding Lily, who takes after her mother. Naomi's husband, Henry (Richard Carlson), is a school principal; when we first see Henry, he's being told by a school supervisor not to go teaching any "progressive ideas." Henry doesn't flinch one bit at this. The way he keeps O'Sullivan's spinster school-teacher character on tenterhooks about their relationship feels mean; he practices the type of well-intentioned meanness that can't be called out for what it is. This is a town where all anybody ever really cares about is how things look. "A woman comes back with all her dreams, with her love," Sirk said, "and she finds nothing but this rotten, decrepit middle-class American family." (This is a far better and more integrated movie than Lang's Clash by Night, which had a similar theme.)

As Naomi approaches her old house, Sirk shows us her shadow on the pavement; there are some discreet violins playing on the soundtrack. When he cuts to a close-up of Naomi moving forward and looking all around the outside of the house, Stanwyck is so deeply involved in this woman's nostalgia and regret that the scene almost feels pornographic, as in her best Capra work. This is acting at so high a level that it doesn't even seem like acting; it seems like we are watching a real woman on a real street. Stanwyck is able to achieve this level of exposure partly be-cause Sirk is so stylized and chilly and distant.

Never before or after does Stanwyck's face look so much like an open wound, an open battlefield. Her mask is dropped in this close-up, and we seem to be seeing the engine room of her talent, the bottom of her being. What she was always able to do with her voice to get an orchestral effect she is now skilled and daring enough to do with her face. And the Sirkian irony is particularly brutal here, for Naomi is looking with such longing at a house that all but broadcasts a sense of complacent, prison-like security. Sirk uses low angles inside the house to give us a sense of entrapment as this prodigal mother enters. After she's greeted her children and they've gone upstairs, Sirk cuts to an overhead shot and divides the frame between Henry and Naomi with an ornate banister.

When the German housekeeper asks Naomi if she can still do a high kick onto a box that holds cigarette butts, Naomi cheerfully does her chorus girl kick and the butts explode all over her disapproving daughter Joyce as she enters from the landing (this image says more about their relationship—and even Naomi's relationship to this small town—than any dialogue could have). The usually gentle Carlson is surprisingly forceful when he gets into an old argument with Naomi, which spurs Stanwyck to turn on a dime into resentment. "That's all you care about, isn't it? Appearances and what other people will think?" she asks, spitting out the words as fast and contemptuously as possible.

She says that she won't laugh too loud anymore and embarrass him or "speak to the riff-raff I knew before I married you," which lets us know that Naomi used to be a bit of a Stella Dallas. She had been too loud, uneducated, from the wrong side of the tracks, but anxious to improve herself with this beautiful young man, this schoolteacher who taught her the classics that didn't go over so well when she escaped to the commercial theater. It's an open question whether Naomi's lack of talent is at the root of her problem. She can be seen, however, as a stand-in for Sirk, an artist, a director of the classics of German theater, forced to flee the Nazis and give up his cultural heritage and to struggle to express his creativity through the medium of Hollywood melodrama.

In the early scenes of *All I Desire*, Stanwyck is so sensitive that she almost vibrates with barely controlled feelings. She's especially touching when she watches Lily in the school play, a bit of trash called *The Baroness Barclay's Secret*. Naomi's voice comes on the soundtrack again as she describes her delight in seeing how promising her daughter is; it's as if she's being confronted with her own youthful self, before bad luck and the realities of the theatrical marketplace tore apart her dreams.

Gradually, Naomi begins to get control of herself, and Stanwyck lowers the carapace of her own "tough/smart" performing style onto Naomi's festering disappointments and tiny hopes. "Don't wait too long, Henry," she says, knowingly, about his delayed relations with O'Sullivan's teacher. But Naomi can't help returning to all the mixed emotions this confrontation with her hometown and her youth keep digging up in her. The love between mother and daughter here (created partially by the distance afforded by a theatrical setting) is finally more real and convincing—more mature, more coherent, more deeply felt and imagined—than the entirety of *Stella Dallas*.

At the after-party for the play, Naomi dances the bunny-hug with Joyce's fiancée. It looks grotesque at first, but then Sirk cuts to an overhead shot and Stanwyck starts to transform the novelty steps by doing variations on them until the dance begins to look beautiful. Naomi is out of breath when she finishes (the film always reminds us of her age and of time running out), but she catches it long enough to read Elizabeth Barrett Browning to the guests. "And if God chooses, I shall but love thee better after death," Naomi recites, staring straight at Henry. Stanwyck opens her mouth and lets her tongue flutter near her teeth on the "th" sound in "death," so that it sounds almost lascivious, a hint that a big part of Naomi's problem is her sexual drive, which couldn't be satisfied by Henry and had to be condemned by small town mores.

Sirk has his actors constantly move in and out of confined spaces that keep them from really reaching each other. The Murdoch house is a trap, and so is the small town of Riverdale, but Sirk has shown us that what lies outside of middle-class strictures is no better. In fact, the rootlessness of city life might even be worse for a single person. Naomi needs to find her happiness where she can, and it rests, finally, in this jail of a home. "You don't know how unimportant success is until you've had it," Naomi says. Stanwyck doesn't shrink from this line, even if it's the one line here that might have caused her some personal pain. Disillusioning Lily, Naomi says that there has been no glory and no glamour in her life. She then recites a litany of soul-destroying show business work and winds up with, "And I know a pawnshop in every town on the circuit." Stanwyck makes Naomi sound almost proud as she goes over this laundry list of failure. It's the pride of sheer survival.

Sirk sometimes loses the thread of his argument in some of the later scenes. He's stymied by journeyman players and errant script choices, and he's forced to tack on a Hunter "happy ending," so that Naomi stays in town (she leaves in Brink's novel). Still, it isn't really a happy end for anyone; Henry will never satisfy her, and the town gossips are obviously out for blood after Naomi accidentally shoots her old lover Dutch (Lyle

Bettger). But there is one thing that Naomi has found that might sustain her, a love for her children. Stanwyck never played a more poignant scene than the one she enacts here with her young son Ted (Billy Gray), trying to explain to him how people aren't perfect and warning him, in an archetypally maternal way, about the pain he's about to experience in adolescence and all the rest of his life. Stanwyck arrived at this purely motherly place for this scene in a major Sirk film, but she couldn't get there for her own son. There are some people who can only express their feelings through the work they do. I would hope that if Dion ever saw this movie, he could feel the "imitation of life" truth in his mother's words.

Stanwyck was top billed in her second movie for Sirk, *There's Always Tomorrow* (1956), but this incandescently angry film belongs to Fred Mac-Murray and to Joan Bennett, who excels in her role of housewife as monster. MacMurray plays Cliff, a successful toy manufacturer in California, and we first see him in his large workroom filled with toys in various stages of development. Sirk foregrounds various toys in his frames so that they look a bit menacing, as if they're rebuking their maker. Cliff's new product is Rex, the walkie-talkie robot, a small talking toy that sits on a long table waiting to be animated. When Cliff goes home, Sirk creates an even more stark-looking prison, a house filled with pools of dark shadows, puritan-style wooden furnishings ,and three bratty, selfish children Cliff's wife Marion (Bennett) dotes on. It's Marion's birthday tonight, and Cliff has planned a date with her, but she's not having it. At her age, she says, birthdays are a time to turn the mirrors to the wall. Marion is the "I want to see nothing" opposite of nearly every Stanwyck character.

Completely rejected, even by his own cook (Jane Darwell), Cliff sulks in the kitchen until he hears the doorbell ring. He opens the door and there in the dark is Norma (Stanwyck), an old flame, walking toward him into the light. Gratefully, he asks Norma if she'd like to accompany him to the theater, and she seems delighted to go. Stanwyck makes it look as if Norma doesn't have anything definite in mind when she goes to see Cliff and is just following her instincts blindly. She and Cliff used to work together, but she went away and started her own dress business in New York. "Blue Moon" was their song; she's so glad that he remembers that. Back at his workroom, Cliff shows her how he's incorporated their old song into one of his toys. Norma tells Cliff that she married once, out of loneliness, but then shrugs it off as having happened a long time ago. Time is now Stanwyck's ally against pain, for she can say about anything, "that doesn't matter now."

One of Cliff's daughters hurts her foot (she cries like a much younger child), so Marion refuses to accompany Cliff on a little vacation he's
planned for them. The novel (and perilous) theme here is that of a father
who dislikes his own children. Cliff seems right to dislike them, but he
never quite sees just how complacent and destructive his wife Marion
is, and she's the real problem here, not the kids, who just need some
discipline. Cliff goes by himself on the vacation, and what do you know?
Norma is there, too. Did she plan it, or did they really just bump into
each other accidentally? Most likely, Norma planned on running into
Cliff in such a way that she didn't even know herself what she was doing. All the people in this movie tell lies to themselves and refuse to see
what's in front of them. Appearance is all in this rotten society that Sirk
dissects like a surgeon. "I've never been one for casual acquaintances,"
says Norma at dinner, and that was true of Stanwyck, too; she had only
a few close friends and didn't let anybody else get near her. Love? Cliff
asks. Norma replies, "I guess I just kept myself too busy." And that, too,
could be something Stanwyck might have said about herself.

Cliff's son sees his father with Norma and immediately jumps to conclusions. He's rude to Norma when Cliff invites her over for dinner. Afterwards, when Cliff tries to get through to Marion to tell her about his
discontent, she reveals the full extent of her passive-aggressive bitchery.
He wants a little adventure in their life, like when they were young! "If
life were always an adventure, it would be very exhausting," Marion
says, with a smug little smile. She's right, of course, in a way, but Marion uses this "sensible" attitude to keep her husband's feelings totally in
check.

And Marion is murderous about Norma, saying that she pities the
poor childless career woman. Cliff counters that Norma has had excitement and success, but Marion insists that those things "don't mean so
much to a woman." When Marion goes to get a dress at Norma's new LA
flagship store, Norma looks slightly disappointed when Marion manages
to insult her in that infuriating "oblivious" way we've seen so much of
in her marriage to Cliff. The people here are so stuck in the roles that
they're supposed to be playing that they can't react in any natural way.

By this point, any sensible audience would like nothing better than
to see Marion's queenly humbleness punctured, but the conventions of
society (reflected, of course, by the conventions of the movies), won't
stand for that, and so Sirk is left furiously signaling the hypocrisy of
middle-class life with his images, while the script takes several sharp
right turns in order to make everything come out the way it needs to. In

one triumphant, shocking moment, Cliff sits down to read the newspaper and notices a framed family photo looming up in front of him from a table. Fed up, he blocks the photo with his paper (MacMurray makes this movement in just the right measured, "fuck you" way).

We see Norma hopefully putting on some perfume in front of a mirror before Cliff's children confront her. Instead of being ashamed, she tells them off, as if she's been watching Sirk's movie herself (she certainly couldn't have found out all the bad things she mentions about this family from one dinner, unless she has the discernment of a great novelist). Rain from a windowpane is reflected on her face, so that Sirk makes visual the tears that Norma cannot afford to cry. Meeting with Cliff, she says that they couldn't be happy together, even though we've seen quite enough to know how miserable they'll both be without one another. He'll have a wonderful life with Marion and the kids, she says—and, most tellingly, she falls back on what she thinks people will say, how they'll gossip about Cliff deserting his family. This is the sort of soapy, "the status quo must be maintained" writing that the movies of this time made us accustomed to.

Sirk, though, manages to make us realize that Norma's familiar argument against change is based on a pack of stiff 1950s bourgeois lies that the upheavals of the 1960s would try to sweep away. "Be happy, Cliff . . . you *will* be happy," Norma insists, before running away from him. But of course he won't be happy, and neither will she. Given boilerplate soap to work with, Sirk fashions a genuine tragedy and an early Capra-esque call to arms, a call to self-actualization. It is a call to the 1960s, a decade when Stanwyck found herself relegated to TV as a western mother who, in stray glimpses, bears a certain resemblance to Bennett's Marion, the domestic tyrant par excellence.

Wild West Stanwyck

Annie Oakley, Union Pacific, California, The Furies,
The Moonlighter, Blowing Wild, Cattle Queen of Montana,
The Violent Men, Escape to Burma, The Maverick Queen,
Trooper Hook, Forty Guns

When asked about the western, which was probably her favorite genre, Stanwyck sighed happily, "Oh, I love to do them. I just love to do them." She owned ranches for most of her life and also raced horses. Wide-open spaces agreed with her. "Well, I'm particularly fond of reading about the early West," she said. "I think it was a very romantic era in our country." In the heyday of her initial years of stardom, the 1930s, westerns were usually relegated to B and Z picture programmers and were rarely major features, but that started to change in the mid-to-late forties. By the fifties, the western in America was one of the most challenging and complex of film forms. In the hands of directors like John Ford, Howard Hawks, Anthony Mann, Raoul Walsh, Budd Boetticher, Allan Dwan, André de Toth, and many others, it was characterized by any number of fresh ideas and attitudes, politically, morally, and aesthetically.

George Stevens's version of the early life of *Annie Oakley* (1935) is about as sophisticated politically as you can expect from a film of its era. This is a movie that often hints at a more developed content but usually retreats into period charm and the kind of comedy routines that Stevens learned at the Hal Roach studios while photographing the best short subjects of Laurel and Hardy. "No fiction is stranger than the actual life of Annie Oakley who came out of a backwoods village half a century ago to astonish the world," reads a title after the credits. But the film does indeed fictionalize parts of her story to suit the conventions of the time.

Stanwyck actually does look a lot like photos of the real Annie, who stood barely five feet tall; Stevens makes sure to film her in such a way that she looks small, even dainty, in his over-packed frames.

We first see Stanwyck's Annie riding in a carriage with her mother. "Gosh, ain't he pretty," she says softly, looking at a picture of Toby Walker (Preston Foster), a renowned sharpshooter (in real life, Stanwyck had a helpless respect for male beauty). "That's not for ladies," says a barkeep to vaudevillian Vera Delmar (Pert Kelton), trying to keep her out of his barroom, but she cracks, "I'm no lady" and barges right in. Stevens does some fast cuts to nonplussed male faces. "Next thing you know, they'll be smoking cigarettes!" says one man, while another wonders if there's nothing sacred anymore. There's no heat in their objections. Stevens situates his audience so that they can see what relative progress has been made for women since the nineteenth century.

Throughout, Stanwyck is wearing far too much lipstick to play a country girl, and her Brooklyn smarts sometimes don't match Annie's more simple common sense, but she has some fine moments early on. Jeff Hogarth (Melvyn Douglas), a scout for Buffalo Bill, offers her his arm, and when she hesitates, her mother nods her approval of his alien, chivalrous gesture. Stanwyck's Annie takes Jeff's arm, finally, but her face definitely registers that she thinks such exaggerated deference to her sex is silly.

The real Annie competed with marksman Francis Butler and beat him. Butler retired and soon proposed to her, and they lived out their lives together happily. In this film, Annie goes up against the fictional Toby, and when she and her mother see that she's going to ruin his career if she beats him, Annie throws the match. Before Stanwyck does this, she looks down for a moment, as if she's thinking, "Well, life is unfair, we knew that going in." She didn't have the heart to beat Toby, she tells her friends: "He was just too pretty," she repeats, matter-of-factly.

After Jeff brings Annie to the attention of Buffalo Bill (Moroni Olsen), they go out into the waning sunlight so that Bill can introduce her to his mostly male troupe, which responds with confusion and disdain. This sequence is done with a truly evocative series of magic hour shots that highlight Stevens's eye for pictorial effects. The best parts of *Annie Oakley* seem to be about a moment in American history when the demarcation line between the sexes was blurry. In the world of this movie, men are too pretty and famous gunfighters like Buffalo Bill have Stanwyck's 1940s-style hair, while the women are as hard and saucy as Pert Kelton and as capable as Stanwyck herself.

Yet the script and direction ask Stanwyck to be too sweet in too many scenes. There's not enough of the down-home grit that made Annie a legend in her own time and ours, a precious alternative to Barbies and beauty queens for the tomboys of the world. Foster does well in the most fleshed-out role here, but Douglas is just a dim point in the eternal triangle. "Aim at a high mark, and you will hit it," said the real Annie, and that's the spirit that Stanwyck embodied as an actress, desiring and often achieving the crown of "the best of all" in her chosen profession. Both Annie and Stanwyck deserve better than this contrived version of Oakley's story. For all its ingratiating qualities, this ensemble movie loses all urgency in its final third (for a more daring version of this material, look no further than Robert Altman's still underrated *Buffalo Bill and the Indians* [1976]).

The little girl who dreamed of being Pearl White relished acting the tomboy heroine in Cecil B. DeMille's *Union Pacific*, a railroad epic that begins with *Star Wars*-style unrolling credits and a rousing score that segues from workin' on the railroad to my darlin' Clementine without missing a beat. This is the kind of action movie that kids could see and then act out afterward; in all of its scenes, it only matters what's happening in the moment and not why it's happening, particularly.

DeMille, much derided by his fellow directors but an unstoppable force in his industry, was a showman who never quite lost the simplicity of the silent films from the teens; he himself was a contemporary of Pearl White and an important rival to D. W. Griffith. His movies almost always made money (one wag called a picture of his "a movie for De Millions"), and that's because his hard-driving, circus-like sensibility was close to the confused emotions and instincts of the American public, especially on the issue of sex, where he proved a master at arousing prurient interest, having his cheesecake and eating it too by condemning licentiousness with biblical but slightly winking fervor.

Stanwyck appeared often on DeMille's radio show, and he was impressed with her lack of temperament on *Union Pacific*, calling her "a good workman," his sincerest compliment. As Mollie Monahan, a postmistress and all-around spitfire, Stanwyck is introduced atop a train, shouting happily for her pa and crinkling her nose at him. She delivers her lines in a heavy Irish brogue that announces, "Yes, get used to it! I'm going to try an accent!" This Irish accent, unlike her more effective light one in *The Plough and the Stars*, "comes and goes," as people like to say. But Stanwyck is obviously having so much fun physicalizing her role, hitching up her skirts, and throwing up her arms, that she fashions a wholly new, animated style to suit DeMille's specific needs. For the first half of the film, Stanwyck's acting is akin to action painting; she throws her colors around vigorously, but if we step back, there's an order to what she's doing. In repose, Stanwyck gives Mollie her own watchful urchin look, and she makes a smooth transition to sentiment when asked to lament, to the strains of "Danny Boy" on the soundtrack, the needless death of a man in a saloon.

With her frequent partner Joel McCrea, a man who moves with tough, contained manly grace, Stanwyck has a sisterly chemistry. Rather unexpectedly, she plays out a most revealing scene with him in *Union Pacific*. "You think I'm an outrageous flirt," says Mollie to McCrea's Jeff, as they rest for a moment on the tracks. "Did you never know that flirtin' gets into a woman's blood like fightin' gets into a man's?" she asks, her face taking on a lyrically high-energy yet contemplative look. "Now, a girl begins coquettin', to discover if she has the power. Then she goes lookin', like a fighter after a bully, for the hardest man to conquer. But tis never the man she wants, tis the pleasure of bringing him to her feet!" Mollie concludes cheerfully, less for Jeff than for herself, as if she's worked something out.

This is a classic explanation of Stanwyck's relation to men on screen. *Union Pacific* had many writers, so we can't be certain who wrote this speech, but it really rings a bell for her. The man she dreams of, Mollie/Stanwyck continues (aided by McCrea's horny prompting), will give her the spanking she deserves. This isn't just sexism, but something else, something having to do with the tender roughness that Stanwyck wanted on screen from men and perhaps, to an extent, in her personal life. She got only roughness with Fay, and a bit of tenderness, but little else, from Taylor, so she never really found the combination she craved—except with Capra, mainly in movies.

California (1946), a Paramount western directed by John Farrow (Mia's father), was the first film Stanwyck made in color (she only made six in total and remains for most of us, in memory, a creature of lustrous black and white). The film begins with shots of California's natural scenic wonders, narrated by a bewildering variety of voices (this opening is so goofy that it suggests a parody of one of the "sight-seeing" shorts of the time). We see some wagons circling on a town's main street, and Farrow's camera moves to the left until we catch a group of women throwing Stanwyck's shady cardsharp into the street. It's quite an entrance (and it looks like she takes the fall herself, frustrated stuntwoman that she was). When Farrow cuts to a closer shot, Stanwyck raises herself up out of the dust and says, "Thank you," to the women, "thank you very much," her mouth wide open and her teeth bared in a sneer.

She tries to vamp Ray Milland to get him to take her to California, the state that Stanwyck so loved that she practically never left it from 1929 on. But Milland isn't buying. Instead, saintly Irish winemaker Barry Fitzgerald lets her tag along with him. The pioneers ostracize her, and Fitzgerald tells her not to take their cruelty to heart. She stares off into space and begins to recite a litany of places she's been to with pretty names: Natchez, Memphis, Savannah, Biloxi. And all of these cities hurt her, it seems. Stanwyck's anger in these first scenes is too harsh for the movie to handle; she provides this candy-colored western with a strong belt of bitterness, and suggests that her character, Lily, is a hopeless case. "A woman gets tired knowing too much," she says. It's an archetypal Stanwyck line, but when she doesn't react after Milland slaps her, only to touch her face with pleasure after he leaves, it seems like the screenwriters are just trotting out a familiar routine for her without adding anything new.

Lily gets lost in the shuffle when the narrative settles down and introduces the villain, Pharoah Coffin, played by George Coulouris. Coffin is a lunatic slave trader (the role needs a George Sanders or a Claude Rains to really put it over), and Lily's motivations for taking up with him aren't clear. Stanwyck stops sneering and gives the rest of her performance with her red lipstick, which glistens obscenely in some of Farrow's extreme close-ups. Though Farrow's camera movements can be extremely elaborate (he favored takes that often lasted close to five minutes or more), they can't disguise or enhance the perfunctory quality of most of the acting and writing. Toward the end, Fitzgerald has been shot, and we see Stanwyck hurry over to him from the left. The camera glides away to the right and picks up Milland, then glides left again so they can stand over his body, then follows Stanwyck as she exits left. It's quite a complicated single take, and it must have taken all kinds of time for preparation, but it's like a long, beautifully written sentence that finally doesn't say all that much.

Robin Wood, in his admiring but ambivalent essay about *The Furies* (1950), called it a "hybrid" picture that brought together the western and the woman's melodrama. But this rich brew of a movie also partakes of daring elements of screwball comedy in its treatment of the blatantly incestuous, tough-funny battle of wits in 1870s New Mexico between T. C. Jeffords (Walter Huston, in his last role), a rip-snorting, jocular cattle baron with a shock of thick white hair, and his blond, lovingly competitive daughter Vance, played by Stanwyck.

When he directed *The Furies*, Anthony Mann was coming off a string of talent-displaying noirs like *Railroaded* (1947) and *Raw Deal* (1948), and he had just made his first western with James Stewart, *Winchester 73* (1950). Always drawn to the most upsetting implications of violence and revenge, Mann in his best work could sometimes be a bit heavy-handed, which is why the light, almost Sturges-like opening scenes of *The Furies* come as such a surprise. Maybe Huston and Stanwyck managed these interactions themselves, for she clearly felt some of the same admiration for Huston as an actor that Vance feels for her father.

Like many of Mann's westerns, this is a Shakespearian sort of film, with T. C. as King Lear and Vance as a Regan or Goneril with a wide streak of Cordelia love. Vance is introduced trying on earrings in her dead mother's room. Her face is sly yet secretive, her feelings deeply hidden, though we can see that Vance has some private source of amusement that keeps her continually tickled (an unusual mode for Stanwyck). As she chats with her handsome, stooge-like brother, Clay (John Bromfield), Vance idly plays with a pair of scissors that have been lying on a dressing table.

T. C. has kept his dead wife's room exactly as it was, and Vance is staking her claim to her father by invading it and wearing one of her mother's old dresses. When she hears T. C. riding up to the house, the knowing Vance, with her hard, adult laugh, suddenly becomes an excited little girl, eager to see and please her daddy. T. C. eyes her from the stairs: "You were in her room," he says. "That's right," Vance replies, testing him. "Her gown befits you," says T. C. This is a highly-charged moment, and there are a lot of things working to create a queasy mood: the razor-sharp tightness of the framing and editing, the usage of the odd word "befits," and of course the actors, who are set on their own often bizarre course together.

If this film had been made later on, in the late 1960s or 1970s, it probably would have been more open about the incest theme, and may even have suggested sexual abuse as its basis (this line of attack turns up frequently when modern writers delve into the myth of Lear and his daughters). Under the strict censorship laws of 1950, Mann and his gifted collaborators can only hint at what goes on between T. C. and Vance, and these hints make the film sometimes impenetrably ambiguous. The original slant here is that Mann seems to be positing the relationship that T. C. has with his daughter as a lively and even natural thing, at least in these early scenes.

Vance kisses T. C. happily and unashamedly on the mouth, and there's no suggestion that she wants to actually go to bed with him, even when he asks her to "scratch my sixth lumbar vertebrae" and she cheerfully obliges. "Pretty good, huh?" asks T. C. in his barroom manner, standing in front of his own portrait; he's a rampaging egomaniac who dares us not to like him. *The Furies* is a great movie because it doesn't demonize this power-mad, instinctual man. It understands that his charm is like a hurricane and that his energy is essential if you want to get anything done. He's a life force, and the film respects him. Maybe this represents another strand of Stanwyck's innate right-wing leanings, this mixed admiration for such a crazed capitalist.

Vance thinks and feels so much from moment to moment, in her subterranean way, that it's often hard to keep up with her, and Stanwyck never makes it easy to understand this character, one of the most multi-faceted she ever attempted. She banters with T. C. in their nearly newspaper comedy style, but then we see her vulnerability with her childhood friend Juan (Gilbert Roland), a man she loves—but not in the romantic way he loves her. Juan and his people have been reduced to being regarded as squatters on their own land, an empire T. C. calls The Furies, and Vance is always having to bargain with T. C. to keep him from burning them off the land permanently.

T. C. has his own currency printed as IOUs, and he thinks his money is better than the government kind because his has some cheesecake value (there's an image of a girl riding a bull on his illegal tender). T. C. is a man of huge appetites, performing his own life and legend for us. It's clear that he's sleeping with his Mexican maid, Chiquita, which Vance approves of, even if she doesn't take the same pleasure in Juan (in the source material, Niven Busch's novel, Vance is more involved with Juan, but their platonic love in the film is in many ways more interesting).

"You won't have it easy, finding a man," taunts T. C., eying his daughter. "I've spoiled most of 'em for you." Vance puts her boots up on T. C.'s desk, and he asks her to scratch his itchy vertebrae again. But there's a chasteness in Mann that thankfully stops him from going too far with their father-daughter attraction (nor will he conjure the evil that Huston's son John found in the incestuous Noah Cross of *Chinatown* [1974]). A lot of different elements make *The Furies* what it is, not least Charles Schnee's tangy script and Victor Milner's low-light, sunset-time black and white cinematography, with its evocative use of grey silhouettes, but it's Mann that keeps all these potentially explosive elements in line. You can see his acuity at work in the way he chooses his outdoor landscapes so that every bare, runty tree and towering cactus seems to express the inner lives of his characters.

The framing is just as precise indoors, too. When Rip Darrow (Wendell Corey) invades Clay's wedding party, Mann has Darrow and T. C. stare each other down across his composition, framing Vance coming down the stairs in a tiny sliver screen right, so that she looks like she's sliding down Darrow's shoulder. In this one expertly composed shot, the whole narrative of the film shifts, even if Corey is not at all up to his manly-guy role, unfortunately. When Vance dances with Darrow, she asks him if he thinks he's top man of God's green earth, the exact same question that she asked T. C. earlier in his office. Vance and T. C. both use other people as chess pieces in their game with each other, and woe betide anyone who gets between them. Observing the budding romance between Vance and Darrow, T. C. rings them out of the room with a large bell (Huston is always game to introduce broad comic touches like this, which Mann observes just dryly enough for maximum tension).

T. C. offers Darrow money to break off his relations with Vance; he had earlier offered her a dowry of fifty thousand dollars if she married a man he approved of. When Darrow accepts the money, Vance stiffens with affronted pride, and Mann cuts to a close-up of T. C. looking lovably boyish and triumphant, as if he's won back the girl he loves. In this shot, Mann starts to get at the deep-dyed sickness in the repressed, or at least misdirected sexuality in T. C. and Vance. After Darrow leaves with his money, T. C. takes up his old bantering tone with Vance, who has her back to us. When she turns, we see that she's in tears. T. C. goes in to hug her to him, and a tear shoots out of her right eye onto his shoulder—at this point, their relationship doesn't seem vital and amusing anymore, just pitiably unhealthy. *The Furies* works a twisted new template for Stanwyck, who weakens for love as she's done in the past and then has to strengthen for vengeance, as if this were some Freudian *Lady Eve* on the range mixed with *Electra*.

The movie then introduces an alarming new element: Judith Anderson as Florence Burnett, "Flo" to T. C., a widow with connections who makes no bones about her designs on both The Furies and the man who rules over them. Sipping her favorite drink, a cognac with orange juice, Flo brags to Vance about how she got T. C. a meeting with the president, and at one point condescendingly taps Vance's chin with her black fan. The film takes on a fresh level of excitement now, because Anderson is as formidable an actress as Huston is an actor, and their stage training is of an entirely different order than the one Stanwyck received from Willard Mack. Anderson and Huston aren't on the same modern, internalized wave length as Stanwyck, but they both have such authority that

Stanwyck begins to seem hemmed-in and even routed in her scenes with them. This corralling is something that has never happened before and will never happen again to Stanwyck on screen. Luckily, this upstaging exactly suits what's happening to her character.

When T. C. asks Flo to scratch his itchy lumbar, Vance absorbs this request as the ultimate insult. Mann gives Stanwyck a pause as she goes upstairs, where we can see Vance experience a moment of recognition about her true feelings for her father. Vance wants to be T. C.'s wife, which is why she put on that dress in the first scene. In her own mind, her relationship with her father doesn't need to involve sex; we learn later that T. C.'s dead wife was "a lady," who found it distasteful to fornicate except to conceive children.

Flo is nothing if not bold; she even dares to look at the books on T. C.'s empire Vance has been keeping. Her every "My dear," when spoken to Vance, fairly drips with aggression, and when she taunts Vance about her failure with Darrow, telling her that she needs to leave The Furies and take the grand tour of Europe, you can practically see Vance on the boat already. Flo Burnett is as steely an enemy and rival as anyone could imagine, and Vance sees no way around her. Sex is one thing that she can't offer her father, and sex is what Flo is giving him—while also being an unimpeachable "lady" with useful friends in high places. And so *The Furies* works up to its primal scene, the scene that everyone remembers after they've seen it.

In Vance's dead mother's room, armed with hot tea, Flo tells Vance that she's going to marry T. C. Retreating to her mother's vanity table, Vance asks, "Why? Why do you marry him?" Her voice sounds drained of energy, almost zombie-like, and this isn't the "I'm not going to expend energy on you" tone that Vance takes when she's insulting someone. She's genuinely at her wits' end. Flo is straightforward and honest, even calling herself "an adventuress" and admitting that the marriage is "perhaps for love of the man, or perhaps for love of The Furies!" (Anderson uses her full Shakespearean iambic pentameter rhythm for this thrilling line reading.)

Vance turns, and her eyes cloud over as Flo tells her that she's to be relieved of managing The Furies (for her own good, of course). Juan and his people, Flo continues, will finally be thrown off their land. This last bit is what really enrages Vance past all endurance. We see her reach behind her back for the scissors on the vanity table, and after a short, remorseless buildup, aided by Franz Waxman's steadily boiling music, Mann cuts to a close-up of Vance's contorted face as she leaps forward with the scissors in her hand. We hear a shrieking, bird-like cry off-screen, and Mann cuts to the scissors falling to the floor, dripping blood, then cuts to Flo's face, which sports two splotches of gore. Then, in the most gruesome shot, we see Flo covering the left side of her face, blood gushing out between her fingers.

Vance has been backed into a corner, utterly vanquished. And so she does the only thing she can think to do, lashing out with childlike fury and destroying this woman's face so that T. C. will no longer want to bed her. Stanwyck makes us understand, beat by beat, how a person could be driven to such a vile act, and when she actually strikes out with the scissors, her face says, "Yes, I *will* dare this." After that, we've crossed a line with Stanwyck artistically that can never be uncrossed. Vance is not a sociopath like Phyllis Dietrichson; this is a mixed-up but industrious woman, and to see her descend to such savagery is more truly disturbing than viewing the remorseless actions of an aberration like Phyllis.

This act of violence presages all-out war between father and daughter. T. C. hangs Juan and then confronts Vance on horseback, provoking one of Stanwyck's most vivid tantrums. Vance practically spits at T. C. as she vows to take his world away from him, but the film relaxes a bit after this stand-off (it couldn't possibly continue at such a pitch of intensity). Vance goes around the country buying up T. C.'s IOUs. She has a memorably bitchy exchange with a good-time girl named Dallas (Myrna Dell), who acts friendly and says, "I'm new in town, honey," only to be met with Vance's scalding reply: "Honey, you wouldn't be new anyplace." Stanwyck gets a laugh by rattling off the line as fast as possible and, crucially, not bothering to even look up from the ground as she says it, a perfect example of her strategically "lazy" way with an insult. Stung, Dallas looks at Darrow when he enters the room, then looks at Vance and says, "I never could see what they see in the thin ones." Vance quickly says, "It's not what they see," a radical statement about the superiority of inner quality over outward charms. Fun as this scene is, it doesn't fit with what's gone before; it's as if the film can no longer deal with the Pandora's Box it has opened up and is blindly striking out in random directions.

There's some fetching S & M sex comedy when Vance tells Darrow that he'd like to hit her (he does, and she keeps on smiling at him), and then tells him that he'd like to kiss her. He answers yes. "What's in it for me?" she asks, exiting the scene by biting lustily yet with feigned disinterest into a chicken leg. This comic scene suggests that Vance has begun to transfer her "bad girl" tendencies from her father to Darrow

(Lord knows she'll probably be a handful in the bedroom). But where does that development leave poor dead Juan, or Flo, both casualties of this father-daughter drama? The film doesn't forget about Flo; when we last see her, she is covering her disfigured face with a handkerchief and drinking cognac and orange juice to excess. A bankrupt T. C. asks her for money, and she politely refuses. "Money is the only thing that makes loneliness bearable to some slight degree," Flo says. Anderson gives this line its full weight, especially in the way she lingers on the "some slight degree" and then chokes the words off.

Anderson was the definitive Medea of her time on stage, and in *The Furies*, she offers as fine a performance as could be wished for in this important role. Her last scene, especially, haunts the movie, putting the lie to its attempt to simply celebrate T. C. and what he has wrought in the final reels. Cast as Juan's mother, another famous stage actress, Blanche Yurka, shoots T. C. down in the street after father and daughter have reconciled in their own way (Vance has total control now of The Furies, and T. C. admires her dedication, so like his own). What *The Furies* seems to be saying about American expansionism and the diseased hothouse of the American family romance gets lost toward the end, but that's because these issues can't really ever be resolved. This is a movie that presents a large, active, deadly world of its own, and Stanwyck is at her fully committed best in it, stimulated to reach for her highest heights by her fellow actors and by Mann's scrupulously tactful direction.

Stanwyck made three of her very best films opposite Fred MacMurray: *Remember the Night*, *Double Indemnity*, and *There's Always Tomorrow*. Her fourth film with MacMurray, a 3-D western called *The Moonlighter* (1953), has a poor reputation, but it boasts a smart script by Niven Busch, who provided the source material for *The Furies*, and an effectively dramatic opening. A lynch mob, looking for MacMurray's moonlight cattle thief, hangs the wrong man (a black prisoner sings and weeps, upsettingly, in his cell as this drama plays out). At first, Stanwyck's role as MacMurray's loyal girlfriend seems thankless, but she gets in on some serious action later on, shooting it out with Ward Bond and then doing some rough stunt work when her character falls over a waterfall, and her chemistry with MacMurray gives depth to the script's sketch of their troubled relationship.

Stanwyck then went south of the border for Argentine director Hugo Fregonese, who has a minor reputation in some auteurist circles. David Thomson has written of the small pleasures of Fregonese's *Blowing Wild* (1953), a film shot in Mexico but set in some unspecified country in

South America where oil wells keep pumping and bandits are ever lurking. This movie seems to have been made in a hurry, and it leans on *The Treasure of the Sierra Madre* (1949) in its opening, with Gary Cooper and Ward Bond as down-and-out male friends who meet up with a third friend (Anthony Quinn), a successful oil-driller who has captured the hand of Stanwyck's lusty Marina (her part was originally intended for either Katy Jurado or Dolores del Río). They make an odd couple in their first scene, Quinn and Stanwyck, and she treats him dismissively, complaining of his stench, until he forces her into a scorching kiss. Though at first she resists him, she finally responds with gusher-like physical passion (it's like a cartoon version of the grappling over the sink she does with Robert Ryan in *Clash by Night,* and it shows that Stanwyck's sexuality, once awakened, is as incendiary as ever).

Stanwyck trots out her sexy/mercurial mode when she kisses Cooper and then lets her mouth open on his arm for a sensual moment or two. Riding roughshod over hubby Quinn, who has a cowardly streak and has his first oil derrick pumping right outside his house for reassurance, Stanwyck explodes, "Those pumps are driving me nuts!" She soon gets her revenge. Kissing Quinn, she stares up at the derrick and then shoves him right underneath it, first with a sort of "Hah!" expression, and then a blank, "What did I do?" face—junk food acting for a junk food movie. "I committed murder to get you, mur-dah!" she howls at Coop, in a singed voice that sounds slightly Ida Lupino-like. He strangles her for a bit, then leaves her alone, and she covers her ears and pulls back her face with her hands until it looks like a distorted, grotesque mask. It's a totally ridiculous gesture, and totally right for this tasty pulp fiction.

Cattle Queen of Montana (1954) finds its star at loose ends. As Sierra Nevada Jones, a would-be settler in Montana, Stanwyck wears a red wig that makes her look, at times, like a grown-up Little Orphan Annie—yet several characters remark on this unfortunate hair as if it cinches Sierra's attractiveness. Bathing in a mountain stream, she's spied on by Ronald Reagan; the TV-wise charisma he exerted to get him through his eight-year role as commander and chief is in short supply here. There isn't one interesting scene in this movie, and even the cinematography by the estimable John Alton isn't up to par; some day-for-night work is so egregious that it looks like its flaws might be deliberate, as if Alton was trying to get a blue sky/black tree Magritte-type effect that doesn't gel. As Stanwyck herself said of such efforts: "[Y]ou do the best you can—and you privately hope that nobody goes to see it." The Blackfeet Indian tribe in the cast made her an honorary member after admiring her hard work performing stunts. She didn't use a double for the skinny-dipping scene (the water was cold, in the mid-forties), and she did most of her own shooting and riding. The name the tribe gave her was Princess Many Victories III. Even in this film, I'd amend that to Queen Many Victories, Second to None.

As a girl, Ruby Stevens went to the zoo to study the way the animals walked, especially the cats in cages, the panthers and tigers, and she adopted their coiled slinking as a way of protecting herself. Of course, "animal exercises" have long been a staple of acting classes; students are entreated to do just what Ruby did to pick up interesting physical behavior that may enliven or reveal the characters they will one day play. In *The Violent Men*, a well-made Western loaded with sex and violence, Stanwyck plays Martha, a woman who plays at being "the loyal wife" and "the gracious lady" to Lew (Edward G. Robinson), the owner of a vast cattle empire. If her blond hair isn't a tip-off to her real character, Stanwyck's stealthy, panther-like movement through a room lets us know this is another of her duplicitous women, anti-heroines who play at false roles in order to get what they want. Once again, Stanwyck is the actress as villain and sociopath.

In Martha's case, she's pretended to love her crippled husband for twelve years, but has secretly carried on an affair with his own brother, Cole (Brian Keith). Lew speaks of being only "half a man," and it's clear that his crutches are meant to symbolize impotence, but Martha isn't particularly interested in being sexually satisfied. Instead, she wants Cole around for back-up in the range wars that always seem to be heating up. When she tries to keep Cole away from his Mexican sweetheart, Martha's eyes get hungry, but she isn't hungry for this man. Like Lily Powers, she's a Nietzschean superwoman who lives for power.

Lew's grand house is set on fire, and this fire leads to the film's most memorable moment. Lew and Martha appear at the top of some stairs as fire balloons up around them. He loses his crutches and looks to his wife: "Martha, my crutches," he cries, a once-dominant man reduced to the level of helplessness. Martha grabs the crutches, and Stanwyck freezes in a masterful hesitation as she considers her options. Will I? she thinks. Do I dare? *Yes!* She chucks the crutches into the fire with fiendish energy, her mouth opening wide, as if her own daring excites her sexually. But Lew somehow survives his wife's colorful vengeance, and Martha gets her just deserts when Cole's girlfriend shoots her. Stanwyck does a marvelous fall to the ground when she dies, stiff, straight down, THWACK! It must have killed her bad back, but it was worth it, visually.

In 1945, cinematographer John Alton wrote a book on his craft called *Painting With Light*, and that's just what he does in Allan Dwan's *Escape to Burma* (1955), presenting a constant series of delights for the eye, especially when experimenting with shadows. There are exciting visual effects achieved throughout with smoke and firelight and an attention to the gradations of color. When Stanwyck's matriarch, Gwen, moves through a darkened room to turn on a light at one point, the red of the red lampshade practically pops out at us three-dimensionally. Alton shows similar attention to the actors; amid various thrills and spills, Stanwyck is romanced by an unusually relaxed Robert Ryan, and when he first kisses her, Alton has her move in and out of shadows as she wonders if she likes it.

On a script level, *Escape to Burma* is nonsense, which is why it has a reputation as one of Stanwyck's worst movies ("Why would a woman like you want to spend her time in a teak forest?" is one of Ryan's more laughable lines). But Dwan puts this small adventure over with gusto; it's certainly miles ahead of the same team's misbegotten *Cattle Queen of Montana*. Alton goes too far sometimes with the filters on Stanwyck's close-ups, and the ending resolution is particularly silly, yet on a purely stylistic level there's a lot to enjoy here. There's an amusing photo of Stanwyck on the set where's she's holding a leopard in her lap; if anything, it's the leopard who looks intimidated. "She could have been a great animal trainer had she wished," said Dwan.

A singer named Joni James (she sounds like her name) warbles an insipid theme song under the credits of *The Maverick Queen* (1956), which is based on a Zane Grey book that might have been finished by Grey's son. For fifteen minutes or so, we take in some poor acting and some poor editing and some poor framing as the Wild Bunch makes a robbery. Included in this bunch are Butch Cassidy and the Sundance Kid (Scott Brady). The latter makes a lunge for the film's ingénue (Mary Murphy), then comes back to his main woman, Stanwyck's maverick queen, a saloon gal who's butcher than Butch and Sundance put together.

"Oh, for heaven's sake, take a bath first!" she snipes at Sundance, still dealing with smelly men and their smellier advances. She looks good with light reddish hair, but in her early scenes here, Stanwyck treads perilously close to late Crawford dreadnought camp, putting men down in her low, cigarette-deepened voice. The film has echoes of Crawford's *Johnny Guitar* (1954), with none of its quality. Hack director Joe Kane keeps the camera running until people have finished their dialogue, then leaves it on out of sheer inertia once they've left the frame. There's action stuff to keep us awake, including Stanwyck's climb up a hill after a fall off a horse, but her death by shooting is so indifferently staged that it's hard to tell if she's been shot before she quietly expires and the film ends, with more Joni on the track.

"A Chronicle of the West," reads a card that appears on the screen before the credits come up for *Trooper Hook* (1957), Stanwyck's sixth and last movie with Joel McCrea. Given its charged subject matter (Stanwyck plays a white woman who has been held captive by Native Americans and has a child by a native chief), it's a surprisingly blah film. Stanwyck herself doesn't seem invested in her role; when, in close-up, her face is first pulled up by the hair by a soldier, she does "stoic" and "inward," but she just isn't feeling it. The movie has a cramped, dusty look and suffers from very awkward editing; when Stanwyck is finally reunited with her husband (John Dehner) toward the end, director Charles Marquis Warren dissolves away from him right in the middle of a sentence. The script is vaguely racist—at one point, McCrea tells Chief Nanchez (Rudolfo Acosta) that maybe "you're more white than you know," when the chief shows that he cares about whether his son by Stanwyck lives or dies. *Trooper Hook* has lots of possibilities, and Stanwyck has a good moment or two—shyly responding to a friendly stranger who waves at her, or staring into one of her eternal mirrors and saying her name out loud— but the film needs more dynamic direction and thoughtful writing.

That same year, Stanwyck's period of western doldrums suddenly ended as she entered into the wild world of total auteur Sam Fuller, a tough-talking former newspaperman who wrote, produced, and directed her in *Forty Guns*, her last major movie. *Forty Guns* is a source of dizzying stylistic excitement, and a kind of farewell and tribute to Stanwyck's film career. "To work with Stanwyck is to work with the happy pertinence of professionalism and emotion," said Fuller later. "She's superb as a queen, slut, matriarch, con girl or on a horse. . . . Her form or class or appeal or whatever you want to call it stems from tremendous sensitivity and thousands of closeted thoughts she can select at will, at the right moment, for the exact impact."

Fuller knew what he had in his star and he tailored his film to her measure. He dared her into her most dangerous stunt, where her character, Jessica Drummond—a Catherine the Great of the West who makes her own law with her forty hired guns—catches her foot in the stirrup of her horse and is dragged across a landscape during a twister. The stunt men wanted Fuller to let them control the drag so that they could undo their own feet if the horses' hooves came too close to their heads. Fuller refused them, so Stanwyck offered to do the stunt herself, Fuller's way (she did it three times, demonstrating her Lillian Gish-like dedication to the movies). It's quite an image, seeing her dragged across the plains in steady, unbroken takes—she's become so elemental by this point that she seems fully the equal of both horse and cyclone.

Forty Guns is a Cinemascope marvel, Stanwyck's only real widescreen movie, if we don't count Sirk's *There's Always Tomorrow*. It begins with a view of the sheer immensity of the western landscape; in another shot, we see the hugeness of the sky, reflecting Fuller's lust for size and hinting at all the happy jokes to come at the expense of male pride. We hear the thunder of hooves; the editing has a kind of musical rhythm as Jessica and her army of men rumble down a hillside to intimidate the Bonnell brothers, whose leader, Griff (Barry Sullivan), has come to clean up Jessica's empire. Fuller uses every inch of the Cinemascope frame to grab and hold not just our attention but all of our senses (this film really needs to be seen on as large a screen as can be found).

The brothers ride into town, and Griff talks to a man who's being menaced by Jessica's bad seed brother, Brockie (John Ericson). The man is nearly blind, and Fuller shows us several frames from his blurred perspective, providing an alienation effect that contrasts with the clarity of those opening shots out on the prairie. Fuller soon switches moods again; we hear a man's voice singing the theme song, "Woman with a Whip," crooning about how Jessica is "a woman that all men desire," but no man can tame. Songs were standard on the soundtracks of movies in this period, especially westerns, but Fuller confounds our expectations when Barney Cashman (Jack "Jidge" Carroll) walks into the frame, and we see that he's singing the song for us—or lip-synching it, at least—as the camera follows him in one of the film's first punishingly long tracking shots. The tone here is blunt and outrageous, close to that of Mel Brooks's *Blazing Saddles* (1974), yet it's married to the most sophisticated visual technique imaginable. Fuller possessed exactly the sort of dichotomous sensibility to make a grand filmic swan song for Stanwyck, who made so much of her career by verbally bridging yawning gaps between disparate ways of living and looking at the world.

This is a film about sex on the range; every gun is phallic, and a lot of the dialogue consists of impudent double entendres. "Ah-yah!" Jessica cries off-screen (it sounds guttural and ugly every time she does it). We then see her striding into jail to ask about her brother Brockie, who has shot the nearly blind man. Stanwyck has a wolfish look here and she speaks harshly, but her long ponytail provides a fetchingly incongruous physical touch (Stanwyck lost a lot of visual mobility after she cut her hair in 1948).

When Griff intrudes on a dinner set for Jessica and her forty guns, Stanwyck puts on such a knowing face that she's obviously decided to play these next moments for laughs—and she gets them. Fuller frames her sitting very still in her chair, and she dominates the wide frames with her stillness, just as Robert Ryan does playing the criminal mastermind of Fuller's *House of Bamboo* (1955). The hair around Stanwyck's face is its by now familiar grey, but something about Fuller's direction has clawed away all the cobwebs that had grown over her on-screen sexuality, so that she's as hot-to-trot, don't-give-a-damn sexy here at fifty as she ever was in her twenties (what a contrasting double bill this movie would make with Capra's *General Yen*). Her Jessica is a totally plausible matriarchal dynamo and born ruler, and we can feel Stanwyck's relief at finally being cast correctly for her age and fully ripened experience (Fuller wanted to make another movie with Stanwyck as Evita Peron, and surely that would have been potent stuff, too).

Jessica asks Griff what he's heard about her and then bites her lower lip and lowers her eyes before ordering all of her men out of the room. Once they are alone, Jessica offers Griff a job; he says that such a job wouldn't be his size. "It could be any size you want it to be," Jessica purrs, and Stanwyck leaves no doubt about what she's really getting at. Griff takes out his gun. "May I feel it?" she asks. "Uh-uh," he demurs, not willing to give over control to her. "Just curious," she says, tauntingly. "Might go off in your face," he warns. "I'll take a chance," she near-whispers, relishing Fuller's absolutely filthy double entendre (this is the best dialogue she's had since *Double Indemnity*). She lets out her "whatever" sigh when she handles his gun, tossing it contemptuously in the air. This is a woman who outright owns the guns and the manhood of forty men, and she's not easily impressed.

Later, on the range, Griff wonders if Jessica feels "naked" without her army, and then tells her that one of her men has been misbehaving. "You want to spank him?" he asks her. "I just want to see if you can *take it*," she says. There seems to be no end to their sex talk, all done barely in code. He tells her she looks upset. "I was born upset!" she declares, one of Stanwyck's best lines, a line that shows just how deeply Fuller understood her; it reverberates back over the whole length of her against-the-odds career and life.

After she's been dragged by her horse and survived that twister with Griff, Jessica rests up in a barn and outlines her past in some detail. As a kid, she had to deliver her own brother, and when her mother died in childbirth, Jessica buried her and then took care of Brockie. At fifteen, a man "tried to get rough" with her, and when her father intervened, he got shot. At eighteen, Jessica says, she was "the boss of my own spread." Stanwyck delivers all this back-story in the most matter-of-fact, Olympian of tones; she's a winner, "the best of all," and so is Jessica. There's no room here for the self-pity of Lily Powers, or what's left of Ruby Stevens.

"You've come a long way," says Griff. He could be talking to Stanwyck herself, but Jessica is done cantering down memory lane. "My throat's dry, I'm talking too much," she croaks, leaning in for a kiss, as if to say, "Screw the past, lets grab what's good *now*." This is Stanwyck's last hurrah, her summing up, and it is indeed a long way from Capra's gentle early talkie world to Fuller's curious modernism. "They don't normally write parts for women my age because America is now a country of youth," she told a reporter who asked her about the four-year gap between *Forty Guns* and *Walk on the Wild Side* (1961). "Something is gone," she said, rightly, and spoke of her more "romantic" films. "Now we've matured and moved on. The past belongs to the past," she said, sounding like Jessica Drummond.

Forty Guns is mainly a rollicking western sex comedy for about the first hour of its running time, but then Fuller switches gears, in his ballsy way, into something more serious—all in one dazzling six-minute take. "Am I talking too much?" asks Griff, as he sits with Jessica at her piano; they're both worried about boring the other with small talk about the past. He keeps telling her how he feels about killing, and she listens to him with an abstracted look on her face as the camera starts to prowl ominously closer. Shots are fired from the back of the room; they take cover. Jessica's loyal retainer, Ned (Dean Jagger), walks in and says that he had to shoot Griff, and then Griff moves forward and disarms him. After this embarrassment, Jessica stands stock still at the right of the frame as Ned pitifully confesses his love to her. Jagger, never the most subtle of actors, opens himself up very purely and simply both to the camera and to Jessica.

Jessica listens to Ned talk so intently that the film seems to be holding its breath with her, taking in his words. She sits down to write Ned a check to pay him off. "I'm sorry, Ned," she says, her face impassive, her voice stony and unforgiving. This is a telling choice for Stanwyck; it would have been so easy to act touched by Ned's sorrow. But she makes us see that Jessica, and people like her who have made themselves winners, can't afford to sympathize with such abject weakness, even needing to look on it as a kind of contagious disease (it should be remembered again how much Stanwyck admired Ayn Rand and her objectivist philosophy, and how much Lily Powers learned from Nietzsche).

Ned exits from frame left, dropping the check on the ground. Jessica goes to Griff and kisses his hand, mouthing her devotion to him. They hear a thudding noise and move to investigate; Ned has hung himself. Denied love and sex and given money instead, he sees no more reason to live. Is he somehow a necessary casualty? I can imagine Stanwyck answering "Yes." It's survival of the fittest: first in Brooklyn, then in an abusive first marriage and a humiliating second attempt, and then in that most embarrassing of roles, the aging actress, lucking into one more seminal film, a film that was loved and admired by the burgeoning French New Wave.

Brockie kills Griff's brother as he walks out of the church with his bride. Barney croons another song as the now-widowed bride stands in her mourning black on a hillside; he sings that "God has his arms around me, and I'm not afraid," another drastic switch in tone that works because of Fuller's "take it and like it" long takes. As the plot starts to resolve itself, Fuller freezes Stanwyck's Jessica into a still photo under a dissolve to her forty male guns on horses and zooms slowly into the lingering photo, a surprisingly lyrical effect (this movie is always surprising us). "You could still be the boss, if you wanted to," says her lawyer, but Jessica is about to abdicate, just as Stanwyck herself is pretty much at an end as a star performer.

The lawyer tells her that she'll lose everything, "everything you've built up," and Stanwyck stares out at us, plunking a melody out on a piano with her finger. At this point, we're ready for one of those looks of recognition she used to honor us with, but those are gone now. What's left is an indescribable look, something so deeply personal and labyrinthine that there's no following it or guessing where she could possibly be in her mind; there's a kind of psychic wilderness in her face. Stanwyck was always smart enough to perceive what was coming for her, but who can really be truly ready for death, which to her meant retirement from the movies? In this scene, her face says all of this and more that can't be ascertained, no matter how long we think about her trajectory as a woman and as an artist. "There was a scene loaded with a page of monologue and she knew it perfectly," said Fuller. "I asked her, before the take, to eliminate the gibble-gabble and show the words in her face." I'm willing to bet that this is the scene he was talking about.

Fuller had wanted to kill Jessica off, and that would have been more than appropriate, but the studio insisted that she live. She survives a gunshot (crying out, "Oh!" in an orgasmic way as she takes a bullet), and is last seen inanely running after Griff. The more telling moment in these last scenes is when Jessica tries to comfort the blond widow: "You have one thing in your favor," she says, "Youth." A reviewer for *Picturegoer* saw *Forty Guns* and wrote, "Even the most tactful of picturegoers would have to admit that Barbara Stanwyck is no longer a youngster," bestowing the kiss of death on her career. It would only be resurrected, in an often bastardized, sentimental form, on television, a cruel kind of shrinkage after the Cinemascope glories of *Forty Guns* where, Prospero-like, her powers were celebrated and then relinquished.

Aftermath

The Barbara Stanwyck Show, Walk on the Wild Side, Roustabout,
The Big Valley, The House That Would Not Die, A Taste of Evil,
The Letters, The Thorn Birds, The Colbys

*W*hen film roles started to grow sparse in the late 1950s, Stanwyck was eager to get into television with a western series. She appeared on several Zane Grey Theater presentations, but the networks wanted her to parrot Loretta Young's successful anthology show, where Young swirled on camera in a designer gown, introduced each episode, and then proceeded to act in most of them. For the 1960–61 TV season, Stanwyck succumbed and attempted a similar format with *The Barbara Stanwyck Show*. The worst part of the format was that she had to introduce each story as Young did; deprived of mobility. Stanwyck turns to the camera in a stiff model's "pose" before the title comes on, and the effect is less Young-hostessy than taunting-forbidding, as if Stanwyck is saying, "I dare you to watch!" She had to read her intros off a teleprompter and was expected to make little jokes and plug the sponsors; she was very unhappy doing this. There were thirty-six episodes in all, of which she appeared in thirty-two. She won her first Emmy for the show, but it was cancelled after only one season.

Almost all of the episodes are so poorly written that Stanwyck can't sustain much interest in them. She's hit with more than a fair amount of sexism on this show, playing a lot of "career women" who have to learn their place. And she deals with lots of juvenile delinquents played by Method actors like Vic Morrow; she looks at them as if she'd like to understand what they're trying to do, yet she's the one who seems natural and real, while their Actors Studio style has dated. There are several episodes where Stanwyck has to interact with actors who are so inept that they would never have been employed for a motion picture; it's distressing to see her try to perform with these amateurs.

When she does get a good subject, as in "Confession," a murder story that pairs her excitingly with Lee Marvin, the half-hour format leads to jerky writing and abrupt editing that mitigates both the sexual chemistry she has worked up with Marvin and the convincing degeneration of her character as she's holed up in an apartment overlooking a noisy merry-go-round. "She lives only for two things, and both of them are work," said Jacques Tourneur of Stanwyck (he directed a few of these shows for her, including "Confession"). In several episodes, she plays Josephine Little, an import/export dealer in Hong Kong who does battle with Red China. "You keep your cotton-pickin' Red hands off my country!" she cries in "Dragon by the Tail," which was praised in Congress by Francis E. Walter, chairman of the House Un-American Activities Committee. When she was cancelled, Stanwyck made some cracks at her sponsors' expense: "I never even got a free shampoo," she complained.

Finally, Stanwyck got a movie offer, a featured role in *Walk on the Wild Side* (1962) as a lesbian madam. At first, she was jubilant: "Chalk up another first for Stanwyck!" she crowed. But when gossip columnist Louella Parsons called her and claimed to be shocked that she accepted such a part, Stanwyck got defensive with her. "What do you want them to do, get a real madam and a real lesbian?" she asked. The role was juicy, but perhaps its air of exploitation made Stanwyck uncomfortable (and it definitely added fuel to the fire of the lesbian rumors surrounding her bachelor woman private life at the time). The script, which was based on a Nelson Algren novel set in Depression-era New Orleans, was worked over by many hands, and the film suffers from two miscast and uncharismatic leads, Laurence Harvey and Capucine, the mistress of producer Charles K. Feldman. Capucine is such a weak and bored scene partner that Stanwyck has to work in a kind of void, which can be seen as appropriate, since her character, Jo Courtney, is unrequitedly in love with Capucine's prostitute Hallie. The movie featured a frustrated dynamic that Stanwyck had never been asked to play before.

Stanwyck enters *Walk on the Wild Side* with plummy confidence, even doing a literal "star turn" before going upstairs to see her beloved star hooker—she almost laughs, maybe with the sheer joy of just being in a movie again. Hallie says that Jo should stop trying, that she "can't change" for her. But Jo replies, "Sometimes I've waited years for what I've wanted," in a ghostly, absent voice. She's a predatory hawk, a woman who swoops down on unhappy or destitute girls and installs them in her elegant New Orleans bordello, but Stanwyck makes sure we can see Jo's genuine, tender love for Hallie. She's aged visibly since her last on-screen role in *Forty Guns,* and Edward Dmytryk photographs her harshly, as if Jo is a greyed, narrow-eyed bird of prey ("Take your claws off me," Hallie says to Jo at one point).

Jo is saddled with a legless husband who scuttles around on a pulley. In a scene late in the movie, she reveals her disgust for men. "Love," she sneers, quietly. "Can any man love a woman for herself without wanting her body for his own pleasure?" This is a lady who despises yet profits from male lust, and this is the one quality that makes her interesting in relation to Stanwyck's other characters. But Jo Courtney is a shallow conception, a woman who needs to be "explained" by some Penguin Freud, a lesbian who doesn't even get to be a real lesbian because that would be too threatening in 1962. Instead, we're made to understand that she's frigid.

In her big early scene where she slaps and manipulates Hallie, Stanwyck performs an expert, almost campy pyrotechnical display, startling us with some decisive movements and step-on-the-gas shouting to keep the girl in line (her exhale on an "Ah!" sounds like the hiss of steam heat from a radiator). The scene plays rather like an audition, or an advertisement for her talent: "I'm tired of sitting at home with the TV, hire me!" she seems to be signaling. *Wild Side*, turgidly directed by Dmytryk, is anything but wild and is only enlivened by a baby-faced Jane Fonda, shaking her chassis as a runaway-turned-hooker named Kitty Twist, and by a sinuous credit sequence by Saul Bass involving a kingly black cat slinking along to Elmer Bernstein's jazzy, amusing score. Stanwyck obviously put thought and skill and honest emotion into this smallish role, but it led her nowhere. She hated flying, so she was stranded in Hollywood when most movie production at that time had moved abroad to Europe.

Two years later, producer Hal Wallis, a trusted link to an older Hollywood, offered Stanwyck the opportunity to appear in an Elvis Presley movie. She was understandably skeptical at first. "But I thought this might be very interesting," she told John Kobal, "this would give me an entirely different audience, a very young audience." (Her reasoning is close to the thinking that Bette Davis used to talk herself into accepting *Return from Witch Mountain* [1978], a Disney feature). And so she's billed below the title in *Roustabout* (1964), one of the legion of assembly line Elvis movies that make for such a depressing day of programming when they habitually get run back to back on television. Stanwyck plays Maggie Morgan, the owner of a struggling carnival, and she's endorsed in the film as an emblem of personal feeling amid financial failure—even if this whole enterprise is just one more moneymaking venture for Elvis's manager, Colonel Parker. "I think he's smooth, and sexy," says a female audience member as Elvis sings the first of many interchangeable songs. But the King looks bored and stale.

After a fight, Elvis finds himself working in Maggie's carnival, where he draws in teenage customers with his lazy, open-mouthed leers. Stanwyck is still slender and attractive in her blue denim and white and grey mane of hair. She underplays and generally takes it easy, but there's one scene with Elvis where she can't help herself—she has to be an artist. Fed up with his selfishness, Stanwyck purrs, "Oh . . . just take care of number one, huh?" Presley rises to meet her righteous energy: "That's right, doesn't everybody?" he drawls, in the tone of his "Thank you, thankyouverymuch." Stanwyck is overtaken by a kind of moral unrest: "No," she says, making the word land. "No," she repeats, making her protest sink in. "You learn that and you might start coming alive from the waist up."

Stanwyck seems actually to reach Elvis in this scene; he looks shaken when she leaves it. The gritty representative of the Depression 1930s rebukes the irresponsible, narcissistic neo-Boomer, and the exchange has a weight that embarrasses the purgatorial movie itself. I'm not sure how she achieves this effect, but it partly has to do with the measured rhythm of her delivery and also the need to make a large statement to her audience, an audience that she's begun to lose. Though *Roustabout* is a waste of her time and ours (in the last number, she gets lost in the crowd), in that one scene Stanwyck is as galvanizing as she ever was.

Stanwyck wasn't equipped for idleness (few people are, of course, but especially those who have always put work first). Surely she felt lonely and unappreciated at times during this period. As always, though, she looked at her situation and made the best of it. "I live very simply," she told John Kobal. "I have a nice home and a few friends. I don't go to many big parties or premieres or anything like that, mainly because I don't care for them. And I have a few good friends, and I enjoy them as I hope they enjoy me. And apart from my housekeeper, I live alone. Well, of course, I'm a bachelor woman!" she insisted, giving it a name and making it sound sensible and fancy-free. "But so many people take it out of context," she continued, "then they dramatize it and it's like, 'Here's Madame X walking down the street, poor old soul.' Well, that's not true at all. Hundreds of thousands of people live alone . . ."

And some of them learn to like it. I won't dramatize her personal life at this point, since she obviously didn't herself. Self-pity, Stanwyck felt, will kill you. But a lack of self-pity can sometimes edge into overall bitterness about life, so that sometimes, in her interviews, only a small bit of bleak humor stands between Stanwyck's straight-shooting view of herself and the abyss that swallowed up Lily Powers. "Romance can't be forced, dreamed up, arranged," she said, when asked about her romantic life in the late 1960s. She spoke from experience, for the Hollywood publicity machine had actually tricked her into caring about her own arranged marriage, and she knew too well how "make believe" in life can murder your pride.

In 1965, Stanwyck finally got herself the western series she had long hoped for, *The Big Valley*, which ran for four seasons and lived on, so to speak, in syndication. For some Baby Boomers, *The Big Valley* is the credit that Stanwyck is remembered for, and the show still has its fans. *The Big Valley* has a kind of tranquilizing effect. Where Stanwyck's movies urge you to sit up and take notice of them, *The Big Valley* invites you to put up your feet and relax. Everything about this show is small, and it even manages to miniaturize Stanwyck. Her high-falutin' billing reads, "And Starring Miss Barbara Stanwyck," and though I suppose she's earned such a designation, it does her no favors.

As Victoria Barkley, the matriarch of the big valley of the title, Stanwyck is asked to play mom to three actors so square-jawed, manly, and personality-free that it's hard to tell them apart (Lee Majors, who plays the illegitimate Barkley heir, has blond hair, and the other two have dark hair, but that's about all that distinguishes them). Linda Evans, who plays Victoria's daughter, is usually dressed in such tight pants that she's basically there to walk up and down the family staircase so we can enjoy the view.

In most of the episodes, the Barkleys are menaced by a bad seed, or a group of bad seeds, or a malcontent of some sort, and by the end of the hour the bad guys have been vanquished—but not before these bad guys have admitted What Makes Me So Bad, while the Barkley's nod and smile at them understandingly. There's a "learning lessons" smugness here that's deeply dispiriting. Like many American TV shows, *The Big Valley* fetishizes the family as a source of strength, and Stanwyck goes along with this complacency in a way that feels detached and almost medicated sometimes, or at least terribly tired. She rarely seems like a mother to her children, but it's tough to do anything with these particular children.

So often on *The Big Valley*, Stanwyck is asked to just listen . . . to nothing. To react . . . to nothing. Or nothing much. Eventually, even her moments of inspiration, usually having to do with the handling of props, or self-contained monologues about Victoria's hard past, get lost in the shuffle in the overall torpor of this interminable television serial, which has so very little on its mind beyond cranking out another hour of TV fodder. When a director like Joseph H. Lewis is at the helm, suddenly there are actual camera movements and careful compositions, but nothing can pierce the formula scripts.

Stanwyck looks stylishly thin on the show (almost too thin, sometimes), and the costumers keep putting her into absurdly incongruous pastel purple or blue dresses, suffocating, girly clothes that don't suit her grit. Every once in a while, there will be an episode that allows Victoria to get her hands dirty, and Stanwyck relishes the few chances the show gives her to be tough. She's especially fine in "Earthquake," where she's trapped underground with a whining Charles Bronson, playing a lazy drunk that Victoria has to whip into shape. "Stop feeling sorry for yourself, you're alive!" she says to Bronson at one point. That attitude is what got her through this unrewarding work.

"Make the best of things," had always been Stanwyck's basic survival tactic, and there are treasurable little moments on *The Big Valley* when she revives her Sugarpuss O'Shea sexuality, just to prove that it's still operational, the knowing look followed by a slow turn. But in an awful episode like "Teacher of Outlaws," where Victoria has to teach a thug how to read, the sentimentality is of such a low nature that it's hard to watch Stanwyck having to endure it. She won a second Emmy for the show, and it kept her busy, but that's all it did. (Once, as I passed a sex shop in Greenwich Village, I saw a life-size cardboard cut out of Stanwyck's Victoria Barkley in the window with a balloon caption that read, "Come in and explore my big valley!" I hope it might have made Stanwyck laugh.)

After *The Big Valley* was cancelled, the remainder of Stanwyck's acting career, with the exception of *The Thorn Birds*, was dependent, regrettably enough, on offers from schlock TV producer Aaron Spelling, who promised her a Nolan Miller wardrobe and a chance to work, in that order. She made three ABC movies of the week for Spelling, and the most that can be said for the first, a haunted house effort called *The House That Would Not Die* (1971), is that it's not one of the better TV films of its sort from this period and not one of the worst. Stanwyck looks stylish in her black and white Miller wardrobe. She still knows how to run down a staircase and enter a room like a star, and she thoroughly enjoys the scenes that call for her to roughhouse and get thrown around the set by her possessed co-stars. The second, *A Taste of Evil* (1971), was another chiller of the "thunderstorm and billowing curtain" school, directed, like *House*, by John Llewellyn Moxey. In the first half, Stanwyck plays a rather distracted, concerned mother of a daughter (Barbara Parkins) who had been raped as a girl. Parkins, who was on TV's *Peyton Place*, is such a non-actress that she kills any interest in her scenes with Stanwyck, and the film is directed incompetently (in one scene near a pool, a boom mic is visible in the frame for quite a while).

Once Parkins is led away to recuperate, Stanwyck picks up the slack, revealing that her character is trying to drive her daughter mad for money. This evil mother is only slightly more interesting than the good mother of the first scenes, but Stanwyck gets a lot of mileage out of a speech where she spews out her unnatural hatred of her daughter and even admits that she was glad when the handyman (Arthur O'Connell) raped the girl. In the last third, Stanwyck runs around in the rain with a gun at some length, and at a certain point her hair gets all wet so that the sculptured white helmet hair she's been hiding under collapses; in several shots, Stanwyck looks very much like her younger self, the child/woman of *Forbidden*. The extreme white hairdo she favored in this period probably limited her opportunities, locking her too firmly into advanced age visually, when she could have pulled off middle age easily with a dark wig.

She was set to play in a TV film called *Fitzgerald and Pride*, but three days into shooting she became ill and had to be hospitalized for removal of a kidney. She was replaced by another Brooklyn native, Susan Hayward. After her hospital stay, Stanwyck claimed that she had crossed over from life into death: "For two days I was on the other side," she said. "It's very cold there and it's very dark." Out of the hospital, in her third Spelling TV movie, a soapy effort called *The Letters* (1973, she played a rich woman who dominates her sister (Dina Merrill) and then marries the sister's lover (Leslie Nielsen). Three key scenes were cut from her performance due to time considerations (it was a story done in three parts).

At this point, several years passed without any work at all. I'm afraid that in 1980 Spelling tempted Stanwyck to do an episode of *Charlie's Angels* called "Toni's Boys," which was supposed to lead to a series of her own where she would operate with three hunky male Angels. As a kid, I saw this episode re-run and couldn't understand why the actress I knew from *Double Indemnity* and *The Lady Eve* was appearing on such a low-class show. The plot is a blur, but I vividly remember her saying at one point, "It seemed like a good idea at the time!" as if she were semi-apologizing to us. No need.

On October 27, 1981, at one in the morning, Stanwyck was awakened by a flashlight shining into her face. She heard a man's voice asking her where he could find her purse and her jewelry. She turned on her bedside lamp and saw that the man was wearing a ski mask. The thief ordered her to turn out the light and not to look at him. "I want your jewelry or I'll kill you," he said. Stanwyck told him that her jewelry was in a top drawer in her dressing room, but the robber couldn't find it, and when she turned on her light again, he pistol-whipped her. "I told you not to look," he yelled. He finally found some jewels, then grabbed Stanwyck and threw her in her bedroom closet; he didn't lock the door, but he warned her that if she came out, he would kill her. She stayed in the closet for a long while with blood running down her face, until she thought that the coast was clear. Then she crawled out and called the police. She was treated for her injuries at Cedars-Sinai Medical Center. They never caught the thief.

If Stanwyck had been isolated before, now she became almost totally secluded. Her few friends noticed a change in her, and a decline. "The shock was tremendous to her," said her costumer friend Nolan Miller. "I don't think she ever got over it." Stanwyck had always prided herself on being tough, but there's not much you can do to combat an experience like this, especially when you're old and ill and frail, as she was at this point. She had left Brooklyn so many years ago and had found what she felt was a paradise in California. Now, it was as if that was spoiled, too, as if crime and bad luck had followed her.

In 1982, Stanwyck was presented with a special Academy Award, and she accepted it gratefully, remembering William Holden—who had recently died—in her speech. At the 1978 Oscars, Holden had departed from the prepared script and paid tribute to this woman that he loved. "Oh, Bill," she said to him, quickly averting her face from the camera, not wanting us to see how moved she was. It was the protective instinct of someone who has been so deeply hurt that she tries not to lay herself open in any way; she reserved that openness only for her work.

The year after she won her Oscar, Stanwyck had her last real chance as an actress, a television miniseries adaptation of Colleen McCullough's 1977 Australian romance novel, *The Thorn Birds*. The book is wordy, page-turning trash that makes *Gone with the Wind* look like *The Idiot*. A popular novel of the twenties like *Stella Dallas* has at least pretensions to literary quality and sometimes seems better than it actually is, but McCullough's book is grindingly obvious and not at all well written. When the mega-rich Irish bitch Mary Carson stares at her beloved Father Ralph de Bricassart in the nude, McCullough writes: "She eyed his flaccid penis, snorting with laughter." That's a fair enough example of this material.

McCullough's Mary is sixty-five, has "a shock of red hair" and just a few wrinkles on her somewhat blotchy skin. She gets fat as she ages, and she exits this life cursing Father Ralph's impotence in labored, unpleasant language. Stanwyck was excited when she won the part (Bette Davis had wanted it), and she knew that the miniseries was going to be an event, so she went to bat for her character when she felt the script she was sent had softened her (Mary's rougher edges were reinstated). Sensing that this would probably be her last major appearance, Stanwyck seems to have entirely worked out her performance beforehand. In his memoir, her Father Ralph, Richard Chamberlain, wrote that at the first read-through she told the cameraman not to miss the various facial nuances she had planned, "don't miss *that* look," and so on. This is not the way the young or middle-aged Stanwyck worked when she was making her feature films, but she may have felt that she'd be pretty much on her own in TV-land, as she had been all those years on *The Big Valley*, and so she decided to safeguard what would be her final statement as an actress. There would be nothing left to chance.

The Thorn Birds certainly looks better than the rest of her TV work. It has handsome, textured visuals, both in the interiors of Mary Carson's home (where a lot of smoky light is used) and in the landscape spectacle photography of the Australian outback (actually filmed in Simi Valley in California), with herds of sheep and stray shots of kangaroos used as tourist filler. We first see Stanwyck's Mary when she's looking at Chamberlain's Ralph as he says Mass. Her first close-up features a highly ambiguous expression, very open, questioning and vulnerable. She seems to be wondering just why she's in love with Ralph, but when he slips her the communion wafer, she lowers her chin and eyes and then looks up and shoots him a sizzling sort of "take it or leave it" look (the kind of look that Stanwyck didn't want the cameraman to miss). Stanwyck does her best work in these early scenes with her face, which has barely aged. There isn't much she can do with some of her dialogue but speed through it and coast on her own natural charisma, signaling to us, "Alright, some of this might be silly, but *I'm* not, so pay attention."

At her best in this miniseries, Stanwyck makes Mary Carson predatory in a way that we can enjoy; she plays the manipulativeness of this woman with all the heady, distracted style that she patented fifty years before. But there's a delicacy about her, too, and it has to do partly with age. There are times when she has trouble with some of her *s* sounds because of her dentures, and that chorus girl stride has been decimated. Only her hands are as they were before, and so she uses these expressive hands more than ever, as Mary keeps everyone around her under her control. Stanwyck lightens this self-important epic soap with her vitality, so that sometimes she seems to be "performing" instead of acting. It's so hard to make Mary Carson human.

When Ralph comes in from the rain and strips to dry himself off, Mary approaches him stealthily, telling him about his beauty, then putting her hands on his back, then moving them down his chest slowly, sensuously, like Jean playing with Hopsie's hair in *The Lady Eve*, like Phyllis pawing Walter at the end of *Double Indemnity*. It's difficult to think of another elderly actress who could have played this scene of sexual hunger without giving rise to embarrassment or laughter. Somehow, even after all the time that has passed, Stanwyck can still turn it on, that sexuality of hers that seemed to have a life of its own, and it hasn't been reduced by age. The resurgence of this Stanwyck sexuality, so important in her performing arsenal, threw her for a loop momentarily on the set; when she first started to stroke Chamberlain's chest, she screwed up her lines, then admitted, "What the hell, it's the first time in twenty years I've had a naked man in my arms." A laugh for the crew, and a measure of her own personal loneliness in these last decades.

Chamberlain's Father Ralph keeps telling Mary about their relationship during their scenes together. This is the basic problem with the writing, which goes back to the book. It's almost all telling and no showing, so that Stanwyck really has little to play except for the "malice" that's been called for in dialogue. But Mary's last scene with Ralph and its accompanying monologue give Stanwyck an opportunity and an opening that she seizes with the desperation of an actress making one last stand, and she doesn't play it safe. It's an aria, something Stanwyck had been excelling at since at least 1930 (though it sounds like she was also doing it on stage in *The Noose*), and it can proudly take its place beside her earlier large outbursts of feeling. Since this outburst is her last—and since that is the subject of the speech itself—Stanwyck's aria tears at us precisely because it's bigger than life, bigger than the TV miniseries that houses it. Once more, Stanwyck presses that emotional button inside of herself, and what explodes out of her is the bitterness of a neglected old woman, the confusion of a young woman being extinguished—and all sorts of other messy things.

Mary is climbing the stairs with Ralph after her seventy-fifth birthday party. She says she's tired of living, and Stanwyck emphasizes Mary's feeble, drooping body that can barely hold her head up straight. Duke frames Chamberlain and Stanwyck in a two shot as Mary asks for a kiss goodnight, and Ralph starts to give her a kiss on her hand. "No!" she shouts, abruptly, throwing his hand down. "On my mouth! Kiss me on my mouth as if we were lovers!" We cut to Ralph putting her off, and then we see Mary in the first of her raging close-ups. He says that he can't kiss her because he's a priest, and she shouts that he's "some impotent, useless thing that doesn't know how to be either!" (This line is post-dubbed so badly that it threatens the scene that Stanwyck is building, but not for long.)

Ralph says that she doesn't really love him; he's just a reminder of what she can no longer be. At this, we cut back to a close-up of Stanwyck, nodding her head toughly. Then she begins her aria. "Let me tell you something, Cardinal de Bricassart," she says, leaning back and winding up for the punches, "about *old age* and about that God of yours," she continues, her husky voice drizzling gravelly contempt all over her words. "That vengeful God who ruins our bodies and leaves us with only enough wit . . . for regret!" She raises her voice on this line and gives it a ringing, upward inflection, socking "for regret," so that her voice breaks.

Her small blue eyes have widened, and they're such young eyes; the hurt in them is young hurt. "Inside this stupid body I am still young!" she declares, shaking her head, as if she can't believe she's been stranded like this, let down and humiliated by age. "I still feel," she says, "I still want," and then, "I still *dream*!" so that "dream" is filled with all the tears in the world. "And I still love you, oh God how much!" she cries, throwing her head back with total abandon.

And then she just stands there in close-up, completely naked and exposed, her eyes scanning the distance and seeing only emptiness and death. She slowly raises herself up and chokes back the tears that have started, leaning sideways and twisting her mouth to make a harrowingly specific sound that squashes all her feelings back down. She's stopped this eruption, somehow, but a tear glitters near her left eye anyway, like some diamond that will not dare to slide down her cheek. Exhausted, she looks at this man she loves and can never have, and the bitterness comes back into her face, a look of "you'll get yours," accompanied by a barely perceptible nod. Then she closes the doors to her bedroom.

When we next see Mary, she's a corpse in bed, and Stanwyck makes herself look like a corpse, even if her eyes flutter slightly when

Chamberlain closes them and puts pennies on her lids. After two hours running time, Mary is dead, and there are a lot more hours of *The Thorn Birds* to go, of course, which really just boils down to waiting for Meggie (Rachel Ward) to sleep with the priest that she has loved since childhood, and waiting through all those commercials repeating Henry Mancini's score with teaser tidbits of sex on the beach. Watchable as the rest of it is, Stanwyck's aria shames the project as a whole, and the image it leaves of white hair, white dress, and glistening, "Why, God?" blue eyes is not to be forgotten.

In its familiar rawness and its go-for-broke honesty, Stanwyck's last aria lets us see that she still had it in her to give another major performance, but her age, her ill health, and the era she went out in kept her from that possibility. I'm grateful at least that she got to deliver that speech, in close-up, with the camera respectfully registering the depth of her accumulated experience and the miraculously pristine and still protesting lost innocence that first revealed itself in *Ladies of Leisure*. Stanwyck won her third and last Emmy for Mary Carson; she graciously spent most of her speech praising fellow nominee Ann-Margret.

On June 22, 1985, she was dealt another blow when her house caught on fire. Bizarrely, this was the third major house fire Stanwyck had suffered; there had been two in the thirties which had cost her many photos and mementoes. During this third fire, her best friend, Frank's first wife Nancy Sinatra, tried to shield Stanwyck from reporters, but several of them saw her try to rush into the house to save a few things she loved. When the firemen stopped her, she said, "Please," and she had to fight back her tears. It's enough to make you wonder why some people are plagued by such bad luck, and enough to make you marvel at the stoicism that people like Stanwyck develop to get through things like this.

She must have wondered about lousy luck, too; I mean really, *three* house fires? But she even managed to turn this tragedy into a dark-humored story for a reporter. "I dialed 911," she recalled, "and about the time I got out on the street, the engines and the crews had arrived, and I said, 'OK, fellas, you're on.'" (As if this third fire were a vaudeville routine!) "They rushed in and right away they started bringing out my paintings. Only in Beverly Hills!" she joked. I'd love to think Stanwyck actually said, "OK, fellas, you're on," to the firemen, but it's enough that she chose to re-write it this way after the fact. Though she liked to present herself as a salty bulwark against cultural pretension, Stanwyck had a modest appreciation for visual art, especially the landscapes of French painter Maurice de Vlaminck.

The work she was offered in the wake of this fire was unfortunate. I think we can all agree to forget that her last official credit is for the abortive *Dynasty* spin-off, *The Colbys*, decadent 1980s late-night soap trash in which she was given little to do. She didn't fit in with the campy fighting and overblown clothes, and she made her displeasure with the series public and quit the show early. "I always say Aaron Spelling burned down my house to shanghai me back into television," she said, mordantly. It's not a happy last glimpse of her; she's pretty crotchety by this point and has to hang onto tables and chairs during confrontation scenes, an aged Mexicali Rose still trying to unlock that door to get away from the sub-Joan Collins thesping of Stephanie Beachum.

Still, in the midst of the most depleted circumstances, with everyone around her doing the most remorseless, straight-ahead soap TV acting, a colorfully dressed Stanwyck, in spite of her diminished physicality and scorched-earth voice, is sometimes able to create detailed, beat-by-beat character work even with rock-bottom material. At this late stage, fighting against every type of limitation, she's trying new things, gussying up her "ageless," too-nice character Constance Colby Patterson by opening her small eyes wider than she usually does so that we can see the least little flicker of emotion in them (she had had cataracts removed right before the series was shot). Constance has a cowboy lover (Joseph Campanella) she gets to smooch. Campanella said that Stanwyck continued their love scenes after "cut" had been called. "Oh, God, hold me," she told him. "Nobody has said that to me in years." One last grasp at the world of romantic make-believe on screen.

Constance has her mental competency challenged, and she gets hit by a car. She dies off-screen, and most of her part consists of rote, "the old gal's still got it!" condescension. "Acting is as important to me as eating and sleeping," Stanwyck once said. Then, gleefully predicting her own end, she continued: "I'll retire when they take me off the set in a wheelchair—and then I hope I'll give a good show, creaking joints, garbled speech, falling wig and all." If Stanwyck had to participate in a venture like this, it would have been far more edifying to see her play a wicked old woman in a wheelchair bent on some kind of revenge, à la Friedrich Dürrenmaat's *The Visit*.

In 1987, Stanwyck became the fifteenth recipient of the American Film Institute's Life Achievement Award; she was the third woman so honored (the first two were Bette Davis and Lillian Gish). The AFI had waited a bit too long to honor Stanwyck. Many of her best co-stars had died, and of her major collaborators, only Fred MacMurray and Billy Wilder were on hand to pay tribute to her. Linda Evans told a touching story about being on the set of *The Big Valley* after her own mother had died; Stanwyck looked at Evans for a long moment and said, "Well, I guess I'll just have to be your Mom from now on," her maternal side reserved for a professional context, but no less real for that. Jane Fonda hosted, sensitively, as she had for Bette Davis's tribute in 1977, yet the evening seemed rather half-hearted, or as if something were missing.

That missing element, of course, was Frank Capra, who had been awarded his own AFI a few years before and was still alive; he was not in attendance here. Stanwyck had thrown out her bad back before the ceremony (and of course Capra gave her that bad back on *Forbidden*), so she spent most of it watching from backstage on a couch. Used to tributes like this and weary of their phoniness, Stanwyck began her acceptance speech by saying, "And honest to God, I can't walk on water," deflecting all the adulation with a firm "cut the bullshit" vibe that would have stunned Davis or Gish or Katharine Hepburn, who lapped up tributes like this as their due.

She dwelled on Capra: "He taught me what film could do for me, and what I could do for film," she said, forthrightly. "That's why I'm here tonight, Mr. Frank Capra." Chevy Chase and Sylvester Stallone stared up at her vacantly as she finished her speech with the words from an old Irish prayer: "May the good Lord keep his arms around all of you, always." In one telling reaction shot, Catherine Deneuve looked up at Stanwyck with proper reverence as one film goddess to another, but it was all rather less than heartwarming, mainly because an event like this is a part of show business that Stanwyck wasn't built for, and God bless her for that.

Emphysema and other serious health issues kept Stanwyck bedridden up to her death in 1990. In these last few inactive years, she experienced periods of depression. She was afraid that she had been forgotten, and so her faithful press agent, Larry Kleno, and her business manager, Morgan Maree, made a concerted effort to get her some more fan mail. They talked discreetly to the press about her condition and put Maree's address out there so that people could send Stanwyck postcards and letters. These letters were read to her, but they didn't seem to make much of a dent in her mood. "How could this happen to me?" she asked her friend Nolan Miller, from her sickbed. "I never expected to become an invalid. I always expected to be trampled by a wild stallion or run down by a stagecoach. But never this."

Given a scrapbook on her career, she soon lost interest and stared out her window, waiting patiently for death, as most of us do at a certain point in old age. During her last stay in the hospital in early 1990, she refused food, and after eleven days of this she went into a coma and then finally died. There was no funeral. Kleno said that she had seen too many Hollywood burials and didn't want show biz to intrude on her own passing. Following her instructions, Kleno rented a helicopter and scattered her ashes over Lone Pine desert in California, a location where she had made some of her westerns.

Of her peers, Bette Davis had died the previous year, and Katharine Hepburn would go on and on some more, but her sharp mind went long before her body did in 2003. These two women were much starrier than Stanwyck, who actually wrote both of them fan letters on occasion but never got a response from them. They had always generated the most colorful publicity; they both wrote mythmaking autobiographies, whereas Stanwyck shied away from writing her own book. Davis and Hepburn made their lives into a narrative for us, whereas Stanwyck was unwilling or unable to do so. Because of this difference, Davis and Hepburn have lasted longer in the popular imagination than Stanwyck has, but their late indulgences on TV, in putative movies but mainly in declamatory interviews, left behind a trail of "look at me" elderly embarrassments that Stanwyck's admirers don't have to deal with.

Stanwyck didn't do talk shows, and she didn't make a series of horror movies, as Davis did, or appear in ramshackle TV vehicles that exploited her perceived off-screen life, as Hepburn did. Mighty as they were and continue to be, Davis and Hepburn were actors who sometimes indicated emotions, or ran roughshod over them. Stanwyck only did that once, in *Sorry, Wrong Number*, her last Oscar bid. If the silent-era Lillian Gish is the true progenitor of American screen actresses, Stanwyck, Davis and Hepburn are the holy trinity for the classic studio era; no one else had careers of such size. Of the three, Stanwyck worked with the best directors and is the one whose style is the least dated and the most natural. She blazed a new trail, and she still shows the way for all actors.

Today, Meryl Streep has staked her claim as the fifth American actress who simply cannot be ignored, and of course she has never been acclaimed for being natural. Like Davis, she often puts the idea of acting up front, using different voices and gaits and movements for each of her characters. In Streep's 1980s prime, if you were to look at *Silkwood* (1983) and then *A Cry in the Dark* (1988), you'd see two women who are different not only physically, but also emotionally and even mentally. These two Streep performances display the kind of tough-minded, detailed character work that Davis always championed. And Davis was a Streep fan; she even wrote Streep a fan letter. In recent years, Streep has garnered the kind of love and publicity that Hepburn started to reap in the late 1960s, becoming a kind of exception that proves the rule that women are discarded or marginalized on screen when they age.

There are many links between Streep and her forebears, Davis and Hepburn, but there are few if any links to Stanwyck, who begins to seem like an anomalous and rather lonely example of quieter and deeper emotional expressivity and filmic questing. Put it this way: Davis and Hepburn and Streep all returned to the stage every now and then as they got older, and their acting style didn't need much amplification of scale for the theater. But Stanwyck's style is almost entirely based on the smallest movements of her eyes and shifts of her facial expression to convey her feelings; her best line readings aren't directed out at us, but rather draw us in and seduce us into her multi-leveled, maze-like consciousness.

Jennifer Jason Leigh possesses probably the closest modern equivalent to Stanwyck's rugged integrity. She hasn't been able to make a career as large and coherent as Stanwyck's, but her self-immolating work in *Georgia* (1995) is certainly the equal of Stanwyck's *Stella Dallas*, and in *Mrs. Parker and the Vicious Circle* (1994), Jason Leigh offered a performance that took the most idiosyncratic behavioral choices of a Davis or a Streep and melded them with Stanwyck's sense of stubborn verisimilitude. Stanwyck herself might have been impressed by Jessica Lange's hungry sexuality in *The Postman Always Rings Twice* (1981) or her call-the-cops arias of anger in *Frances* (1982). Like Jason Leigh, Lange hasn't been able to sustain her career in the ostentatious, publicity-driven way of Davis or Hepburn or Streep, but she has carried on Stanwyck's tradition. These two actresses and a few others have worked in the Stanwyck style in fits and starts, but none of them has had Stanwyck's force or her stamina.

Conversely, I would think that Stanwyck would have been repelled by the neuroticism of Actors Studio women like Kim Stanley, Geraldine Page, Julie Harris, and Sandy Dennis. That kind of pushy fifties thesping has largely died out; it was a necessary spasm in American acting, maybe, an explosion of often unfocused emotional jags later taken up by Ellen Burstyn and Gena Rowlands, who as they aged became grande dames of the private moment twitch. Looking outside America, the closest correlative to Stanwyck is probably Anna Magnani, with her large but controlled emotional outbursts and her way of clarifying so many thoughts and feelings all at once. The self-loving exhibitionism of Jeanne Moreau feels as far from Stanwyck's achievement as the goddessy radiance of Vanessa Redgrave. Both Moreau and Redgrave are actresses of equal size and stature and both are far too tricky and attention-seeking to have much in common with the chorus girl who was asked to take off her make up by Frank Capra.

After the premiere of *Sunset Boulevard* (1950), Stanwyck was so moved that she actually knelt and kissed the hem of Gloria Swanson's dress. Though Swanson's performance as forgotten silent movie star Norma Desmond is a landmark, its fussy hugeness couldn't be farther from Stanwyck's direct naturalism. Yet Stanwyck recognized the personal honesty of Swanson's work, and she also recognized how hard it is to give everything you have and everything you are to a camera. Stanwyck loved the movies, even at their most extreme and artificial, yet she was the actress who most often reminded the movies of reality. Crying alone in your room. Making love with someone you're scared of. Lashing out and hurting other people. Reminding other people of their responsibilities, as she did in movies with Elvis and Marilyn Monroe. Stanwyck had the kind of wary Depression fatalism best expressed by the moment in *Stage Door* (1937) when Ginger Rogers tells Katharine Hepburn, "We started off on the wrong foot, let's stay that way."

What a life, as Jean Harrington sighed to Hopsie. Real real life is not something Stanwyck wanted to go through again, but her real movie life might have tempted her, as it continues to tempt us. Praising her idol Pearl White, Stanwyck said, "Her memory still inspires me. In my humble opinion, this explains the *why* of motion pictures." She might have been talking about her own career, which seems increasingly pure and dedicated as we move farther away from it. Stanwyck's very lack of "star" eccentricity has kept her more obscure than Davis or Hepburn or Streep, but it has also had the effect of making her work seem less cluttered, more truly exposed, more questioning—and more deeply revealing of both her own actorly nature and human nature itself.

FILMOGRAPHY

1927

Broadway Nights, First National
Director: Joseph C. Boyle
Producer: Robert T. Cane
Cast: Lois Wilson, Sam Hardy, Louis John Bartels, Philip Strange, Barbara Stanwyck

1929

The Locked Door, United Artists
Director: George Fitzmaurice
Producer: George Fitzmaurice
Cast: Rod La Rocque, Barbara Stanwyck, William "Stage" Boyd, Betty Bronson, Mack Swain, ZaSu Pitts

Mexicali Rose, Columbia
Director: Erle C. Kenton
Producer: Harry Cohn
Cast: Barbara Stanwyck, Sam Hardy, William Janney, Louis Natheaux, Arthur Rankin

1930

Ladies of Leisure, Columbia
Director: Frank Capra
Producer: Harry Cohn
Cast: Barbara Stanwyck, Ralph Graves, Lowell Sherman, Marie Prevost, Nance O'Neil

1931

Illicit, Warner Bros.
Director: Archie Mayo
Producer: Darryl F. Zanuck
Cast: Barbara Stanwyck, James Rennie, Ricardo Cortez, Charles Butterworth, Joan Blondell

The Miracle Woman, Columbia
Director: Frank Capra
Producer: Harry Cohn
Cast: Barbara Stanwyck, Sam Hardy, David Manners, Beryl Mercer, Russell Hopton

Night Nurse, Warner Bros.
Director: William Wellman
Producer: Darryl F. Zanuck
Cast: Barbara Stanwyck, Ben Lyon, Joan Blondell, Clark Gable, Charlotte Merriam, Charles Winninger

Ten Cents a Dance, Columbia
Director: Lionel Barrymore
Producer: Harry Cohn
Cast: Barbara Stanwyck, Ricardo Cortez, Monroe Owsley, Sally Blane, Blanche Friderici

1932

Forbidden, Columbia
Director: Frank Capra
Producer: Harry Cohn
Cast: Barbara Stanwyck, Adolphe Menjou, Ralph Bellamy, Dorothy Peterson, Thomas Jefferson

The Purchase Price, Warner Bros.
Director: William Wellman
Producer: Jack Warner
Cast: Barbara Stanwyck, George Brent, Lyle Talbot, Leila Bennett, Murray Kinnell

Shopworn, Columbia
Director: Nicolas Grinde
Producer: Harry Cohn
Cast: Barbara Stanwyck, Regis Toomey, ZaSu Pitts, Lucien Littlefield, Clara Blandick

So Big!, Warner Bros.
Director: William Wellman
Producer: Jack Warner
Cast: Barbara Stanwyck, George Brent, Dickie Moore, Bette Davis, Guy Kibbee

1933

Baby Face, Warners Bros.
Director: Alfred E. Green
Producer: Darryl F. Zanuck, William LeBaron
Cast: Barbara Stanwyck, George Brent, Donald Cook, Arthur Hohl, John Wayne, Henry Kolker

The Bitter Tea of General Yen, Columbia
Director: Frank Capra
Producer: Walter Wanger
Cast: Barbara Stanwyck, Nils Asther, Walter Connelly, Gavin Gordon, Clara Blandick, Toshia Mori

Ever in My Heart, Warner Bros.
Director: Archie Mayo
Producer: Hal Wallis
Cast: Barbara Stanwyck, Otto Kruger, Ralph Bellamy, Ruth Donnelly, Laura Hope Crews, Frank Albertson

Ladies They Talk About, Warner Bros.
Director: Howard Bretherton and William Keighley
Producer: Raymond Griffith
Cast: Barbara Stanwyck, Preston Foster, Lyle Talbot, Lillian Roth, Maude Eburne, Ruth Donnelly

1934

Gambling Lady, Warner Bros.
Director: Archie Mayo
Producer: Robert Presnell
Cast: Barbara Stanwyck, Joel McCrea, Pat O'Brien, C. Aubrey Smith, Claire Dodd

A Lost Lady, Warner Bros.
Director: Alfred E. Green
Producer: None credited
Cast: Barbara Stanwyck, Frank Morgan, Ricardo Cortez, Lyle Talbot, Rafaela Ottiano

The Secret Bride, Warner Bros.
Director: William Dieterle
Producer: Henry Blanke
Cast: Barbara Stanwyck, Warren William, Glenda Farrell, Grant Mitchell, Arthur Byron

1935

Annie Oakley, RKO
Director: George Stevens
Producer: Cliff Reid
Cast: Barbara Stanwyck, Preston Foster, Melvyn Douglas, Moroni Olsen, Pert Kelton

Red Salute, United Artists
Director: Sidney Lanfield
Producer: Edward Small
Cast: Barbara Stanwyck, Robert Young, Hardie Albright, Cliff Edwards, Ruth Donnelly

The Woman in Red, Warner Bros.
Director: Robert Florey
Producer: Harry Joe Brown
Cast: Barbara Stanwyck, Gene Raymond, Genevieve Tobin, John Eldredge, Dorothy Tree

1936

Banjo on My Knee, 20th Century Fox
Director: John Cromwell
Producer: Darryl F. Zanuck
Cast: Barbara Stanwyck, Joel McCrea, Helen Westley, Buddy Ebsen, Walter Brennan

The Bride Walks Out, RKO
Director: Leigh Jason
Producer: Edward Small
Cast: Barbara Stanwyck, Gene Raymond, Robert Young, Ned Sparks, Helen Broderick

His Brother's Wife, Metro-Goldwyn-Mayer
Director: W.S. Van Dyke
Producer: Lawrence Weingarten
Cast: Barbara Stanwyck, Robert Taylor, Jean Hersholt, Joseph Calleia, John Eldredge

A Message to Garcia, 20th Century Fox
Director: George Marshall
Producer: Darryl F. Zanuck
Cast: Wallace Beery, Barbara Stanwyck, John Boles, Herbert Mundin, Alan Hale

The Plough and the Stars, RKO
Director: John Ford
Producer: Cliff Reid
Cast: Barbara Stanwyck, Preston Foster, Barry Fitzgerald, Denis O'Dea, Una O'Connor

1937

Breakfast for Two, RKO
Director: Alfred Santell
Producer: Edward Kaufman
Cast: Barbara Stanwyck, Herbert Marshall, Glenda Farrell, Eric Blore, Donald Meek

Internes Can't Take Money, Paramount
Director: Alfred Santell
Producer: Benjamin Glazer
Cast: Barbara Stanwyck, Joel McCrea, Lloyd Nolan, Stanley Ridges, Lee Bowman

Stella Dallas, United Artists
Director: King Vidor
Producer: Samuel Goldwyn
Cast: Barbara Stanwyck, John Boles, Anne Shirley, Barbara O'Neil, Alan Hale

This Is My Affair, 20th Century Fox
Director: William Seiter
Producer: Darryl F. Zanuck
Cast: Robert Taylor, Barbara Stanwyck, Victor McLaglen, Brian Donlevy, Sidney Blackmer

1938

Always Goodbye, 20th Century Fox
Director: Sidney Lanfield
Producer: Darryl F. Zanuck
Cast: Barbara Stanwyck, Herbert Marshall, Cesar Romero, Ian Hunter, Lynn Bari

The Mad Miss Manton, RKO
Director: Leigh Jason
Producer: Pandro S. Berman
Cast: Barbara Stanwyck, Henry Fonda, Sam Levene, Frances Mercer, Stanley Ridges, Whitney Bourne

1939

Union Pacific, Paramount
Director: Cecil B. DeMille
Producer: William LeBaron
Cast: Barbara Stanwyck, Joel McCrea, Akim Tamiroff, Robert Preston, Brian Donlevy

1940

Golden Boy, Columbia
Director: Rouben Mamoulian
Producer: William Perlberg
Cast: Barbara Stanwyck, Adolphe Menjou, William Holden, Lee J. Cobb,
Joseph Calleia

Remember the Night, Paramount
Director: Mitchell Leisen
Producer: Mitchell Leisen
Cast: Barbara Stanwyck, Fred MacMurray, Beulah Bondi, Elizabeth Pat-
terson, Willard Robertson

1941

Ball of Fire, RKO
Director: Howard Hawks
Producer: Samuel Goldwyn
Cast: Gary Cooper, Barbara Stanwyck, Oscar Homolka, Tully Marshall,
Dana Andrews, Dan Duryea, Kathleen Howard

The Lady Eve, Paramount
Director: Preston Sturges
Producer: Paul Jones
Cast: Barbara Stanwyck, Henry Fonda, Charles Coburn, Eugene Pallette,
William Demarest

Meet John Doe, Warner Bros.
Director: Frank Capra
Producer: Frank Capra
Cast: Gary Cooper, Barbara Stanwyck, Edward Arnold, Walter Brennan,
James Gleason, Spring Byington

You Belong to Me, Columbia
Director: Wesley Ruggles
Producer: Wesley Ruggles
Cast: Barbara Stanwyck, Henry Fonda, Edgar Buchanan, Roger Clark,
Ruth Donnelly

1942

Flesh and Fantasy, Universal
Director: Julien Duvivier
Producer: Julien Duvivier and Charles Boyer
Cast: Edward G. Robinson, Charles Boyer, Barbara Stanwyck, Betty Field, Robert Cummings

The Gay Sisters, Warner Bros.
Director: Irving Rapper
Producer: Henry Blanke
Cast: Barbara Stanwyck, George Brent, Geraldine Fitzgerald, Nancy Coleman, Gig Young

The Great Man's Lady, Paramount
Director: William Wellman
Producer: William Wellman
Cast: Barbara Stanwyck, Joel McCrea, Brian Donlevy, Katharine Stevens, Thurston Hall

Lady of Burlesque, United Artists
Director: William Wellman
Producer: Hunt Stromberg
Cast: Barbara Stanwyck, Michael O'Shea, J. Edward Bromberg, Iris Adrian, Gloria Dickson

1944

Double Indemnity, Paramount
Director: Billy Wilder
Producer: Buddy DeSylva
Cast: Fred MacMurray, Barbara Stanwyck, Edward G. Robinson, Porter Hall, Jean Heather

1945

Christmas in Connecticut, Warner Bros.
Director: Peter Godfrey
Producer: William Jacobs

Cast: Barbara Stanwyck, Dennis Morgan, Sydney Greenstreet, Reginald
Gardiner, S. Z. Sakall

1946

The Bride Wore Boots, Paramount
Director: Irving Pichel
Producer: Seton I. Miller
Cast: Barbara Stanwyck, Robert Cummings, Diana Lynn, Patric Knowles,
Natalie Wood

California, Paramount
Director: John Farrow
Producer: Seton I. Miller
Cast: Ray Milland, Barbara Stanwyck, Barry Fitzgerald, George Coulouris,
Albert Dekker

My Reputation, Warner Bros.
Director: Curtis Bernhardt
Producer: Henry Blanke
Cast: Barbara Stanwyck, George Brent, Warner Anderson, Lucile Watson,
Eve Arden

The Strange Love of Martha Ivers, Paramount
Director: Lewis Milestone
Producer: Hal Wallis
Cast: Barbara Stanwyck, Van Heflin, Lizabeth Scott, Kirk Douglas, Judith
Anderson

1947

Cry Wolf, Warner Bros.
Director: Peter Godfrey
Producer: Henry Blanke
Cast: Errol Flynn, Barbara Stanwyck, Richard Basehart, Geraldine Brooks,
Jerome Cowan

The Other Love, United Artists
Director: André De Toth
Producer: David Lewis
Cast: Barbara Stanwyck, David Niven, Richard Conte, Gilbert Roland, Joan
Lorring

The Two Mrs. Carrolls, Warner Bros.
Director: Peter Godfrey
Producer: Mark Hellinger
Cast: Humphrey Bogart, Barbara Stanwyck, Alexis Smith, Nigel Bruce,
Isobel Elsom

1948

B. F.'s Daughter, Metro-Goldwyn-Mayer
Director: Robert Z. Leonard
Producer: Edwin H. Knopf
Cast: Barbara Stanwyck, Van Heflin, Charles Coburn, Keenan Wynn,
Margaret Lindsay

Sorry, Wrong Number, Paramount
Director: Anatole Litvak
Producer: Anatole Litvak and Hal Wallis
Cast: Barbara Stanwyck, Burt Lancaster, Ed Begley, Ann Richards, Wen-
dell Corey

1949

East Side, West Side, Metro-Goldwyn-Mayer
Director: Mervyn LeRoy
Producer: Voldemar Vetluguin
Cast: Barbara Stanwyck, James Mason, Van Heflin, Ava Gardner, Cyd
Charisse

The Lady Gambles, Universal
Director: Michael Gordon
Producer: Michel Kraike
Cast: Barbara Stanwyck, Robert Preston, Stephen McNally, Edith Barrett,
John Hoyt

1950

The File on Thelma Jordan, Paramount
Director: Robert Siodmak
Producer: Hal Wallis

Cast: Barbara Stanwyck, Wendell Corey, Paul Kelly, Joan Tetzel, Stanley Ridges

The Furies, Paramount
Director: Anthony Mann
Producer: Hal Wallis
Cast: Barbara Stanwyck, Wendell Corey, Walter Huston, Judith Anderson, Gilbert Roland

No Man of Her Own, Paramount
Director: Mitchell Leisen
Producer: Richard Maibaum
Cast: Barbara Stanwyck, John Lund, Jane Cowl, Phyllis Thaxter, Lyle Bettger

To Please a Lady, Metro-Goldwyn-Mayer
Director: Clarence Brown
Producer: Clarence Brown
Cast: Clark Gable, Barbara Stanwyck, Adolphe Menjou, Will Geer, Roland Winters

1951

The Man with a Cloak, Metro-Goldwyn-Mayer
Director: Fletcher Markle
Producer: Stephen Ames
Cast: Barbara Stanwyck, Joseph Cotton, Leslie Caron, Louis Calhern, Joe DeSantis

1952

Clash by Night, RKO
Director: Fritz Lang
Producer: Jerry Wald, Norman Krasna
Cast: Barbara Stanwyck, Robert Ryan, Paul Douglas, Marilyn Monroe, J. Carrol Naish

1953

All I Desire, Universal

Director: Douglas Sirk
Producer: Ross Hunter
Cast: Barbara Stanwyck, Richard Carlson, Lyle Bettger, Maureen O'Sullivan, Billy Gray

Blowing Wild, Warner Bros.
Director: Hugo Fregonese
Producer: Milton Sperling
Cast: Gary Cooper, Barbara Stanwyck, Ruth Roman, Anthony Quinn, Ward Bond

Jeopardy, Metro-Goldwyn-Mayer
Director: John Sturges
Producer: Sol Baer Fielding
Cast: Barbara Stanwyck, Barry Sullivan, Ralph Meeker, Lee Aaker

The Moonlighter, Warner Bros.
Director: Roy Rowland
Producer: Joseph Bernhard
Cast: Barbara Stanwyck, Fred MacMurray, Ward Bond, William Ching

Titanic, 20th Century Fox
Director: Jean Negulesco
Producer: Charles Brackett
Cast: Clifton Webb, Barbara Stanwyck, Robert Wagner, Thelma Ritter, Brian Aherne

1954

Cattle Queen of Montana, RKO
Director: Allan Dwan
Producer: Benedict Bogeaus
Cast: Barbara Stanwyck, Ronald Reagan, Gene Evans, Lance Fuller

Executive Suite, Metro-Goldwyn-Mayer
Director: Robert Wise
Producer: John Houseman
Cast: William Holden, June Allyson, Barbara Stanwyck, Fredric March, Walter Pidgeon, Shelley Winters, Louis Calhern, Nina Foch

Witness to Murder, United Artists
Director: Roy Rowland
Producer: Chester Erskine
Cast: Barbara Stanwyck, George Sanders, Gary Merrill, Jesse White, Juanita Moore

1955

Escape to Burma, RKO
Director: Allan Dwan
Producer: Benedict Bogeaus
Cast: Barbara Stanwyck, Robert Ryan, David Farrar, Murvyn Vye

The Violent Men, Columbia
Director: Rudolph Maté
Producer: Lewis J. Rachmil
Cast: Glenn Ford, Barbara Stanwyck, Edward G. Robinson, Dianne Foster, Brian Keith

1956

The Maverick Queen, Republic
Director: Joseph Kane
Producer: Herbert J. Yates
Cast: Barbara Stanwyck, Barry Sullivan, Scott Brady, Mary Murphy

There's Always Tomorrow, Universal
Director: Douglas Sirk
Producer: Ross Hunter
Cast: Barbara Stanwyck, Fred MacMurray, Joan Bennett, Pat Crowley, William Reynolds

These Wilder Years, Metro-Goldwyn-Mayer
Director: Roy Rowland
Producer: Jules Schermer
Cast: James Cagney, Barbara Stanwyck, Walter Pidgeon, Betty Lou Keim

1957

Crime of Passion, United Artists

Director: Gerd Oswald
Producer: Bob Goldstein
Cast: Barbara Stanwyck, Sterling Hayden, Raymond Burr, Fay Wray, Royal Dano

Forty Guns, 20th Century Fox
Director: Sam Fuller
Producer: Sam Fuller
Cast: Barbara Stanwyck, Barry Sullivan, Dean Jagger, John Ericson, Gene Barry

Trooper Hook, United Artists
Director: Charles Marquis Warren
Producer: Sol Baer Fielding
Cast: Joel McCrea, Barbara Stanwyck, Earl Holliman, Edward Andrews

1962

A Walk on the Wild Side, Columbia
Director: Edward Dmytryk
Producer: Charles K. Feldman
Cast: Laurence Harvey, Capucine, Jane Fonda, Anne Baxter, Barbara Stanwyck

1964

The Night Walker, Universal
Director: William Castle
Producer: William Castle
Cast: Robert Taylor, Barbara Stanwyck, Judith Meredith, Hayden Rorke

Roustabout, Paramount
Director: John Rich
Producer: Hal Wallis
Cast: Elvis Presley, Barbara Stanwyck, Joan Freeman, Leif Erickson

TV SERIES

The Barbara Stanwyck Show, 1960–61

The Big Valley, 1965–69
The Colbys, 1985–86

TV MOVIES

1971

The House That Would Not Die, ABC
Director: John Llewellyn Moxey
Producer: Aaron Spelling
Cast: Barbara Stanwyck, Richard Egan, Michael Anderson, Jr., Kitty Winn

A Taste of Evil, ABC
Director: John Llewellyn Moxey
Producer: Aaron Spelling
Cast: Barbara Stanwyck, Barbara Parkins, Arthur O'Connell, Roddy McDowall

1973

The Letters, ABC
Director: Gene Nelson and Paul Krasny
Producer: Aaron Spelling
Cast: Barbara Stanwyck, Leslie Nielsen, Dina Merrill

1983

The Thorn Birds, ABC
Director: Daryl Duke
Producer: David L. Wolper and Edward Lewis
Cast: Richard Chamberlain, Rachel Ward, Barbara Stanwyck, Jean Simmons, Piper Laurie

BIBLIOGRAPHY

Alpi, Deborah Lazaroff, *Robert Siodmak*, McFarland, 1998

Basinger, Jeanine, *Anthony Mann*, Wesleyan, 2007

Baxter, Anne, *Intermission: A True Tale*, Putnam, 1976

Busch, Niven, *The Furies*, Popular Library, 1948

Cain, James M., *Double Indemnity*, Vintage, 1989

Cather, Willa, *A Lost Lady*, Vintage, 1972

Capra, Frank, *The Name Above the Title*, Macmillan, 1971

Cagney, James, *Cagney by Cagney*, Doubleday, 1976

Chamberlain, Richard, *Shattered Love: A Memoir*, It Books, 2004

Dicken, Homer, *The Films of Barbara Stanwyck*, Citadel, 1984

DiOrio, Al, *Barbara Stanwyck: A Biography*, Coward McCann, 1984

Douglas, Kirk, *The Ragman's Son*, Simon and Schuster, 1988

Farber, Manny, *Negative Space*, Praeger, 1971

Fonda, Henry (as told to Howard Teichmann), *Fonda: My Life*, Dutton, 1981

Fuller, Samuel (with Christa Lang Fuller and Jerome Henry Rudes), *A Third Face: My Tale of Writing, Fighting and Filmmaking*, Applause Books, 2004

Gallagher, Tag, *John Ford*, University of California Press, 1986

Gardner, Ava, *My Story*, Bantam, 1990

Granger, Farley (with Robert Calhoun), *Include Me Out*, St. Martin's, 2007

Halliday, John, *Sirk on Sirk*, Viking, 1972

Harvey, James, *Romantic Comedy in Hollywood: From Lubitsch to Sturges*, Knopf, 1987

Head, Edith (with Patrick Calistro), *Edith Head's Hollywood*, Dutton, 1983

Kael, Pauline, *5001 Nights at the Movies*, Henry Holt, 1982

Kennedy, Matthew, *Joan Blondell: A Life Between Takes*, University Press of Mississippi, 2007

Kobel, John, *People Will Talk*, Knopf, 1985

Levant, Oscar, *Memoirs of an Amnesiac*, Putnam, 1965

Madsen, Axel, *Stanwyck*, Harper Collins, 1994

Mann, William, *Kate: The Woman Who Was Hepburn*, Henry Holt, 2006

McCarthy, Todd, *Howard Hawks: The Grey Fox of Hollywood*, Grove Press, 2000

McCullough, Colleen, *The Thorn Birds*, Avon A, Reissue Edition, 2010

McBride, Joseph, *Frank Capra: The Catastrophe of Success*, Simon and Schuster, 1992

McGilligan, Patrick, *Fritz Lang: The Nature of the Beast*, St. Martin's, 1997

Odets, Clifford, *Waiting for Lefty and Other Plays*, Grove Press, 1994

Prouty, Olive Higgins, *Stella Dallas*, Triangle Books, Blakistan, 1923

Quirk, Lawrence J., *Fasten Your Seatbelts: The Passionate Life of Bette Davis*, William Morrow, 1990

Sikov, Ed, *On Sunset Boulevard: The Life and Times of Billy Wilder*, Hyperion, 1998

Smith, Ella, *Starring Miss Barbara Stanwyck*, Crown, 1974

Thomson, David, *The New Biographical Dictionary of Film*, Knopf, 2010

Turner, Lana, *Lana*, Random House, 1989

Vidor, King, *A Tree Is a Tree*, Samuel French, 1981

Wagner, Robert (with Scott Eyman), *Pieces of My Heart: A Life*, Harper Entertainment, 2008

Wilkinson, Tichi, and Borie, Marcia, *Hollywood Legends: The Golden Years of The Hollywood Reporter*, Teale Weaver Publishing, 1988

Wood, Robin, *Howard Hawks*, British Film Institute, 1981

PERIODICALS

New York Times, June 21, 1931

Los Angeles Examiner, June 21, 1931

Los Angeles Times, July 25, 1931

Liberty Magazine, September 17, 1932

Photoplay, November 7, 1932

Los Angeles Examiner, December 28, 1932

Photoplay, January 1933

Daily News, July 24, 1937

Photoplay, December 1937

Daily Mirror, March 18, 1938

Motion Picture, May 1938

Daily News, November 11, 1939

New York Times, February 23, 1941

New York Times, March 21, 1943

Hollywood Citizen News, August 17, 1944

Los Angeles Times, July 22, 1945

Liberty Magazine, August 11, 1945

Herald Tribune, July 27, 1947

Los Angeles Daily News, February 22, 1951

American Weekly, May 1951

Hollywood Citizen News, March 28, 1952

Colliers, July 12, 1952

Hollywood Reporter, April 23, 1954

Good Housekeeping, July 1954

Parade, August 7, 1955

New York Journal American, January 8, 1965

Sunday News, August 16, 1965

Pageant, May 1967

TV and Picture Life, November 1967

Movie Mirror, November 1967

Movie Life Yearbook, 1968

Family Weekly, August 4, 1968

American Film, September 1968

TV Radio Mirror, July 1972

Movie, January 1973

American Cinematographer, August 1973

Film Comment, March–April 1981

Daily News, April 13, 1981

Hollywood Studio Magazine, March 1982

People Magazine, November 25, 1985

American Film, July–August 1989

People Magazine, February 5, 1990

INDEX